LASTING EFFECTS OF CHILD SEXUAL ABUSE

SOME OTHER VOLUMES IN THE
SAGE FOCUS EDITIONS

LASTING EFFECTS OF CHILD SEXUAL ABUSE

Edited by
Gail Elizabeth Wyatt
Gloria Johnson Powell

SAGE PUBLICATIONS
The Publishers of Professional Social Science
Newbury Park   Beverly Hills   London   New Delhi

For information address:

SAGE Publications, Inc.
2111 West Hillcrest Drive
Newbury Park, California 91320

SAGE Publications Inc.
275 South Beverly Drive
Beverly Hills
California 90212

SAGE Publications Ltd.
28 Banner Street
London EC1Y 8QE
England

SAGE PUBLICATIONS India Pvt. Ltd.
M-32 Market
Greater Kailash I
New Delhi 110 048 India

Printed in the United States of America

Library of Congress Cataloging-in-Publication Data

Main entry under title:

Lasting effects of child sexual abuse.

 (Sage focus editions ; v. 100)
 Bibliography: p.
 1. Child molesting.   I. Wyatt, Gail Elizabeth.
II. Powell, Gloria J.
RC560.C46L37   1988   616.85′82   88-4366
ISBN 0-8039-3256-1
ISBN 0-8039-3257-X (pbk.)

FIRST PRINTING 1988

Contents

Preface

The idea for this book originated with Gail Wyatt, who has been my friend and colleague for more than twenty years. When Gail received her NIMH Research Scientist Career Development Award, the first Afro-American woman to have achieved such an honor, we would often discuss some of her findings regarding the prevalence and effects of child sexual abuse on Afro-American and White American women. I would also describe some of the complicated cases in the Family Support Program at the Neuropsychiatric Institute at UCLA, which has evaluated and treated sexually abused children and their families since 1976.

As Gail worked diligently on her data analysis, I was constantly in court, supervising trainees, and working toward creating a network of services for victims of child sexual abuse.

In January 1985, Gail told me that she and Stefanie Peters wanted to submit an abstract to the American Psychological Association for a panel presentation of theory and research on the long-term consequences of child sexual abuse. At that time, I had begun my prospective study of 143 sexually abused children and when she invited me to participate, I saw the presentation as an opportunity to share my clinical impressions and research findings with others in the field. We were off and running again, collaborating on yet another project that has taken three years to complete.

The panel was selected for the August 1985 Convention and Gail Wyatt, Stefanie Peters, David Finkelhor, and William Friedrich presented their research to a standing room only audience. I discussed the clinical significance of the findings, and we entertained questions and requests for reprints for sometime thereafter. The responsiveness of those in attendance convinced us that the professional community was in need of research that documented the effects of sexual abuse on children and adult supervisors, as well as discussions of conceptual and theoretical frameworks within which to understand the pervasiveness of these effects. Gail and I came away from that experience, however, wondering if a broader collection on theory, research, treatment, and social policy issues wouldn't better serve the needs of professionals, and we began to explore sources for publication of these and other manuscripts.

Jon Conte offered a great deal of guidance and support, and the editorial board of the *Journal of Interpersonal Violence* devoted a special issue to "The Lasting Effects of Child Sexual Abuse" in December 1987.

My energetic and creative friend did not stop with the special issue. After coediting "The Psycho-Sexual Development of Minority Group Children," I had vowed never to edit another book, but with her perseverance, charm, and power of persuasion, Diana Russell, Jon Conte, Jean Goodwin, John Briere, Lucy Berliner, Judith Becker, Roland Summit, David Corwin, Judy Stein, and others agreed to contribute their work, some to the special issue and all to this book.

Sage Publications agreed to publish the book and another idea became a reality. This volume attempts to take a high-powered microscopic examination of the effects of sexual abuse, its consequences for the individual, the family, and, ultimately, our society. All of the contributors are experienced clinicians and researchers who graciously and enthusiastically supported this effort.

There are many people who helped to get this book to press. We appreciate the indefatigable efforts of Sarah Lowery, who made phone calls, typed correspondence and manuscripts, and all with good humor and encouragement. We are also indebted to our friend and colleague, Barbara Bass, who provided the moral support that we needed. We would, of course, like to acknowledge the support of our families who have always helped us keep a balanced perspective on some of the vicissitudes that we encountered, particularly in finding a publisher who understood the importance of this book. Terry Hendrix, our editor, effectively coordinated the stages of preparation in a supportive and friendly fashion.

Finally, we want to acknowledge the Neuropsychiatric Institute and Hospital and, especially, James Q. Simmons III, M.D., Director of the Division of Mental Retardation/Child Psychiatry, who supported the Family Support Program from its inception. Indeed, this is the first Division of Child Psychiatry in the country that established a specialized treatment and training program in child sexual abuse. For his wisdom, his financial support, and courage, we salute him. We also thank Louis

J. West, M.D., Chair of Psychiatry and Biobehavioral Sciences in the School of Medicine for providing us with a stimulating and supportive environment in which we, as faculty, can think and work.

Gail and I invested much of ourselves in this book and our lives were changed by the effort. During the process, Gail lost her only sister, Sandra, and I became ill for several months. There were times when Gail had to carry on alone, I thank her for her affection and understanding. Such friends are indeed rare.

We dedicate this book to all child advocates. We must ask the right questions, anticipate problems, seek support, demand attention, fight for the rights of even the smallest child, and never stop caring. This is a lot to ask of those committed to the field, and a lot to expect from the unconvinced, but the efforts are worth it. Children are worth it.

—Gloria Johnson Powell,
with help from Gail Elizabeth Wyatt

1

Identifying the Lasting Effects of Child Sexual Abuse

An Overview

GAIL ELIZABETH WYATT
GLORIA JOHNSON POWELL

Child sexual abuse is occurring at a significant rate. According to the most recent incidence figures for a single year (1984), 200,000 new child abuse cases were reported to child protective services in 19 states. However, only 100,000 of these cases were substantiated, 22% involving a male child and 78% involving a female child (American Humane Association, personal communication, Denver, CO, 1984). It is unlikely, however, that the confirmed cases were the only victims of sexual abuse. The fact that 100,000 of these cases were not substantiated demonstrates that a sizable portion of child sexual abuse victims never come to the attention of the child welfare system. In addition, there are increasing numbers of child victims whose abuse is never really counted. Included among this group are those whose abuse is investigated, but does not stand up to the rigors of the court. And, finally, there are unknown numbers of children who remain silent and never tell. Identifying these children necessitates a more careful, sensitive, and consistent approach to the assessment of children's victimization by mental health and health professionals, law enforcement, and social service agencies.

AUTHORS' NOTE: This manuscript was supported by a Research Scientist Career Development Award to the first author (MH269). Correspondence regarding this chapter should be addressed to the first author, UCLA, 760 Westwood Plaza, Los Angeles, CA 90024.

For reasons such as these, it is difficult to assess the prevalence of child sexual abuse and its effects. Children age 12 and under often do not have the cognitive processes to understand the severity of the incidents and often attribute blame for their involvement to themselves (Summit, 1983). Victims below age 18 are often subjected to physical and psychological coercion to ensure their participation and silence in abusive relationships (Finkelhor, 1979). If and when they disclose their abuse, they are often not believed, ignored, punished, and not supported by nonabusing adults and professionals (Russell, 1983; Wyatt & Mickey, 1987). Thus the initial and long-term effects of child victimization are often misinterpreted or undetected by those whose responsibility it.is to protect children.

There are, however, other reasons why child sexual abuse and its effects have presented so many challenges to child advocates. Our society has been resistant to recognizing children's disclosures of these experiences as fact and not fantasy. Some of this resistance stems from theoretical and conceptual frameworks that offer narrow interpretations of sexual acts when reported as having occurred in childhood (Freud, 1962). There are also those who believe that the prevalence and negative effects of child sexual abuse is exaggerated (Coleman, 1986; Green, 1986). Still others consider child molestation to be within the normal range of other voluntary expressions of sexual feelings (DeLora & Warren, 1977), and to have no long-term negative sequelae (Bender & Grugett, 1952).

Usually, when there is inconsistency in identifying the nature and extent of a phenomenon such as abuse, research findings are sought to clarify and enhance our understanding of the epidemiology of the problem and its effects. The research on child sexual abuse, however, has been limited by a variety of factors: the dynamics and consequences of disclosing abuse; the use of theory that misinterprets or overlooks the effects of the experience; and the ambivalence of health care professionals in recognizing their responsibility to protect children from sexual exploitation.

Historically, our society has always had persistent problems regarding sexuality. The inconsistent acknowledgment of and intervention into child sexual abuse represents this resistance. As long as sexuality is denied as being an integral aspect of our personality, developmental processes important to self-actualization will continue to be ignored. If normal sexual experiences are not defined, the nature and effects of abnormal sexual experiences will not be understood.

These limitations notwithstanding, the last 15 years of research have enhanced our knowledge of the nature and extent of child sexual abuse. Current prevalence or lifetime rates for at least one incident having occurred before age 18 range from 6% to 62% for females and from 3% to 31% for males (Peters, Wyatt, & Finkelhor, 1986; Wyatt & Peters, 1986a). There is a substantial range in reported rates, due to methodological variations, especially in data collection, sampling techniques, and to differences in how child sexual abuse is defined (see Peters et al., 1986; Wyatt & Peters, 1986a, 1986b). For example, data have been collected by telephone (Keckley Market Research, 1983; Lewis, 1985; Murphy, 1985), pencil-paper measures (Badgley et al., 1984; Finkelhor, 1979; Fromuth, 1983; Seidner & Calhoun, 1984), and by face-to-face interviews (Bagley & Ramsay, in press; Burnam et al., 1987; Peters, 1984; Russell, 1983; Wyatt, 1985). Bivariate analyses of the circumstances and effects of sexual abuse have been used in research on (1) clinical samples (Herman, 1981; Jehu, Gazan, & Klassen, 1984-1985; Meiselman, 1978; Tsai & Wagner, 1978); (2) probability samples (Badgley et al., 1984; Bagley & Ramsay, in press; Burnam et al., 1987; Finkelhor, 1984; Keckley Market Research, 1983; Kercher & McShane, 1984; Lewis, 1985; Miller, 1976; Murphy, 1985; Russell, 1983; Wyatt, 1985); and (3) nonprobability samples (Briere, 1984; Finkelhor, 1979; Fromuth, 1983; Seidner & Calhoun, 1984). While important in describing the circumstances of abuse, these studies provide little insight into which of the factors related to the experience contribute most to effects of sexual victimization.

Definitions of child sexual abuse are often based upon the following parameters: (1) the age of the child (17 or under); (2) the relationship of the victim to the perpetrator (intrafamilial or extrafamilial); (3) the age difference between the victim and perpetrator; and (4) the type of abuse that occurred (contact with the victim's body versus nonbody contact) (Wyatt & Peters, 1986a). Consequently, information regarding the prevalence and circumstance of the experience (Peters et al., 1986; Wyatt & Peters, 1986a, 1986b) is influenced by these factors.

Females tend to report sexual abuse most often (Finkelhor, 1979; Russell, 1983; Wyatt, 1985), while abuse perpetrated upon males is most often unreported and undisclosed (Finkelhor, 1979; Meiselman, 1978). Recent reports (Condy, Templer, Brown, & Veaco, 1987; Risen & Koss, 1987), however, suggest that male sexual abuse is more prevalent than previously assumed.

The initial and long-term effects of child sexual abuse have recently been reviewed (Browne & Finkelhor, 1986). The initial effects that have been widely noted are fear, anxiety, depression, anger and hostility, aggression, and sexually inappropriate behavior, while the long-term effects most frequently reported are self-destructive behavior, anxiety, feelings of isolation and stigma, poor self-esteem, difficulty in trusting others, a tendency toward revictimization, substance abuse, sexual maladjustment and psychological problems. In summary, it can be concluded that abuse incidents involving (1) fathers, (2) genital contact, and (3) the use of force have been noted to have the most negative consequences for child victims.

While progress has been made, the field of sexual abuse still requires more rigorous empirical work in areas that have yet to be explored. For example, few studies have used control groups or standardized measures in their assessment of the effects of sexual abuse (Browne & Finkelhor, 1986). Although no significant ethnic differences are found when prevalence rates of Blacks (Keckley Market Research, 1983; Kercher & McShane, 1984; Russell, 1986; Wyatt, 1985) or Hispanics (Burnam et al., 1987) are compared to rates for Whites, most studies have not examined the effects of sexual abuse by ethnicity (Peters et al., 1986).[1] And, most important, previous research has included a limited integration of theoretical guidelines with which to understand how abuse affects its victims.

The purpose of this book is to bring together some of the more advanced research, treatment, relevant theory, and current social and policy issues regarding the lasting effects upon child victims, adult survivors, and their families.

This book will differ from most others that are concerned with child sexual abuse in several ways. It presents: (1) a variety of approaches to child abuse research; (2) the samples and measures used in the studies; (3) the various definitions of child sexual abuse; and (4) the theory guiding the research. Attempts have been made to point out similarities and differences in methodologies and theoretical constructs that may prove to be helpful to the reader. We recognize the need to present current theory and research upon which others can cogently build a more complete understanding of the effects of child sexual abuse. It is anticipated that with this open discussion of the strengths and limitations of the subject matter, researchers and professionals will begin to form a consensus of opinion about how research, theory, treatment, and social policy should be conducted or formed within the context of what we know about the many parameters of child sexual abuse.

The initial research in the field of child sexual abuse involved clinical and community samples of adults molested as children. The advantage of using adult survivors was obvious: They could retrospectively report some of the antecedents and consequences of the experience. More recently, research with child victims has been conducted and chapters in this volume will review the strengths and limitations of research with both child and adult samples. Additionally, treatment techniques relevant to children, adolescents, and adults are included.

Specific information regarding the demographic characteristics of samples, such as ethnicity, age, gender, and socioeconomic status are described so the reader can assess the generalizability of the results to other samples or the limitations of the findings due to the sampling techniques used.

The structure of the book is as follows: historical and theoretical treatise, research with adults molested as children, research with child victims, mediating factors to outcomes for children, social policy and new research directions. Each section will include an introduction that will highlight some of the important parameters that are addressed in the chapter.

The contributors are a multidisciplinary group of men and women, who are pioneers in the field of child sexual abuse. Some were the first to attempt to identify and research this problem and others have specialized in the treatment of victims. All of the contributors are activists in enhancing this nation's awareness of the effects of child sexual abuse and in creating social policy that will minimize these effects and prevent the future occurrence of these traumatic experiences that rob children of their childhood.

We hope that those who are in unrelated fields of child sexual abuse will read these chapters along with those who are experienced veterans of research, treatment, and child advocacy. If this volume stimulates thought, discussion, and insight about the lasting effects of child sexual abuse, and an application of the therapeutic strategies suggested, it is likely that more research will be generated to answer questions that will be raised and techniques will be enhanced to advance the field further.

NOTE

1. The terms "Black" and "White" are considered proper nouns by the American Psychological Association. In following the ruling made in November 1986, these terms have been capitalized throughout this book.

REFERENCES

Badgley, R., Allard, H., McCormick, N., Proudfoot, P., Fortin, D., Ogilvie, D., Rae-Grant, Q., Gellinas, P., Pepin, L., & Sutherland, S. (1984). Committee on sexual offenses against children and youth. In *Sexual offenses against children* (Vol. 1). Ottawa: Canadian Government Publishing Centre.

Bagley, C., & Ramsay, R. (in press). Disrupted childhood and vulnerability to sexual assault: Long-term sequels with implications for counseling. *Journal of Social Work and Human Sexuality.*

Bender, L., & Grugett, A. E., Jr. (1952). A follow-up on children who had atypical sexual experiences. *American Journal of Orthopsychiatry, 22,* 825-837.

Briere, J. (1984). *The effects of childhood sexual abuse on later psychological functioning: Defining a "post-sexual-abuse syndrome."* Paper presented at the Third National Conference on Sexual Victimization of Children, Washington, DC.

Briere, J., & Runtz, M. (1985). *Symptomatology associated with prior sexual abuse in a non-clinical sample.* Paper presented at the meeting of the American Psychological Association, Los Angeles, CA.

Briere, J., & Runtz, M. (1987). Post-sexual abuse trauma. *Journal of Interpersonal Violence, 2*(4), 367-379.

Browne, A., & Finkelhor, D. (1986). Impact of child sexual abuse: A review of the research. *Psychological Bulletin, 99,* 66-77.

Burnam, M. A., Stein, J. A., Golding, J. M., Siegel, J. M., Sorenson, S. B., Forsythe, A., & Telles, C. A. (1987). *Sexual assault and incidence of psychiatric disorders in a community population.* Unpublished manuscript.

Coleman, L. (1986, April). Therapists are the real culprits in many child sexual abuse cases. *Tribune,* Oakland, CA.

Condy, S. R., Templer, D. I., Brown, R., & Veaco, L. (1987). Parameters of sexual contact of boys with women. *Archives of Sexual Behavior, 16,* 379-393.

Delora, J., & Warren, C. (1977). *Understanding sexual interactions.* Boston: Houghton Mifflin.

Finkelhor, D. (1979). *Sexually victimized children.* New York: Free Press.

Finkelhor, D. (1984). *Child sexual abuse: New theory and research.* New York: Free Press.

Freud, S. (1962). The etiology of hysteria. In J. Strachley (Ed. and Trans.), *The complete psychological works of Sigmund Freud* (standard ed.). London: Hogarth. (Original work published 1933).

Fromuth, M. E. (1983). *The long term psychological impact of childhood sexual abuse.* Unpublished doctoral dissertation, Auburn University.

Green, A. H. (1986). True and false allegations of sexual abuse in child custody disputes. *Journal of the American Academy of Child Psychiatry, 25,* 449-456.

Herman, J. (1981). *Father-daughter incest.* Cambridge, MA: Harvard University Press.

Jehu, D., & Gazan, M. (1983). Psychosocial adjustment of women who were sexually victimized in childhood or adolescence. *Canadian Journal of Community Mental Health, 2,* 71-81.

Jehu, D., Gazan, M., & Klassen, C. (1984-1985). Common therapeutic targets among women who were sexually abused. *Journal of Social Work and Human Sexuality, 3,* 125-145.

Keckley Market Research. (1983, March). *Sexual abuse in Nashville: A report on incidence and long-term effects.* Nashville, TN: Author.

Kercher, G., & McShane, M. (1984). The prevalence of child sexual abuse victimization in an adult sample of Texas residents. *Child Abuse and Neglect, 8,* 495-502.

Lewis, I. A. (1985). [*Los Angeles Times* Poll #98]. Unpublished raw data.

Meiselman, K. (1978). *Incest: A psychological study of causes and effects with treatment recommendations.* San Francisco: Jossey-Bass.

Miller, P. (1976). Blaming the victim of child molestation: An empirical analysis. Doctoral dissertation, Northwestern University. *Dissertation Abstracts International*. (University Microfilms No. MO 77-10069)

Murphy, J. E. (1985, June). Untitled news release. (Available from St. Cloud State University, St. Cloud, MN 56301).

Peters, S. D. (1984). *The relationship between childhood sexual victimization and adult depression among Afro-American and White women*. Unpublished doctoral dissertation, University of California at Los Angeles. (University Microfilms No. 84-28, 555).

Peters, S. D., Wyatt, G. E., & Finkelhor, D. (1986). Prevalence. In D. Finkelhor (Ed.), *A sourcebook of child sexual abuse*. Beverly Hills, CA: Sage.

Risen, L. I., & Koss, M. P. (1987). The sexual abuse of boys: Prevalence and descriptive characteristics of childhood victimizations. *Journal of Interpersonal Violence, 2*, 309-323.

Russell, D.E.H. (1983). The incidence and prevalence of intrafamilial and extrafamilial sexual abuse of female children. *Child Abuse and Neglect, 7*, 133-146.

Russell, D.E.H. (1986). *The secret trauma: Incest in the lives of girls and women*. New York: Basic Books.

Seidner, A. L., & Calhoun, K. S. (1984, August). *Childhood sexual abuse: Factors related to differential adult adjustment*. Paper presented at the Second National Conference for Family Violence Researchers, Durham, NH.

Summit, R. (1983). The child sexual abuse accommodation syndrome. *Child Abuse and Neglect, 7*, 177-193.

Tsai, M., & Wagner, N. (1978). Therapy groups for women sexually molested as children. *Archives of Sexual Behavior, 7*, 417-429.

Wyatt, G. E. (1985). The sexual abuse of Afro-American and White-American women in childhood. *Child Abuse and Neglect, 9*, 507-519.

Wyatt, G. E., & Mickey, M. R. (1987). Ameliorating effects of child sexual abuse: An exploratory study of support by parents and others. *Journal of Interpersonal Violence, 2*(4), 403-414.

Wyatt, G. E., & Peters, S. D. (1986a). Issues in the definition of child sexual abuse in prevalence research. *Child Abuse and Neglect, 10*, 231-240.

Wyatt, G. E., & Peters, S. D. (1986b). Methodological considerations in research on the prevalence of child sexual abuse. *Child Abuse and Neglect, 10*, 241-251.

PART I

Historical and Theoretical Treatise

This section includes chapters by three outstanding professionals in the field of child sexual abuse, Jean M. Goodwin, Roland C. Summit, and David Finkelhor. These chapters provide a historical perspective as well as theoretical issues regarding the ways in which long-term consequences of child sexual abuse emerge not only for the individual, victim, and the family, but also for social institutions.

Goodwin's chapter conceptualizes the obstacles to rule making regarding incest, the most damaging form of childhood sexual molestation. Folkloric materials such as rhymes, riddles, and fairy tales are used to illustrate the psychological harm caused by incest in many cultures since time immemorial. The anthropological data on the incest taboo provide the reader with not only a historical perspective on attitudes and consequences of incest, but also a transcultural or worldview of this persistent problem. The real substance of the chapter is a five-part analysis of the obstacles to establishing consistent public policy and legal sanctions regarding incest. The axes provide a comprehensive review of the many dichotomies in attitudes and beliefs that create barriers in the development of a viable, effective system for dealing with incest. Indeed, historical attitudes and values result in primarily men as offenders going underpunished and women as victims going undernoted.

Roland C. Summit's chapter elaborates further on the themes developed by Goodwin and provides a comprehensive review of the history of child sexual molestation in psychiatry. He divides his chapter into seven parts, most of which have powerful metaphorical titles. Summit discusses the pervasive paradoxes in societies' perception of child sexual abuse that obscure and belittle observations of victimization. He concludes that it is all of society that protects the secret of child abuse. The present-day case histories provide validation for these observations.

The historical accounts of other psychiatrists who have attempted to deal with child sexual abuse are well researched. It is striking to note the continuing denial of child sexual abuse and the repudiation of those who try to expose it. The clinician who has encountered these situations may experience déjà vu.

The remainder of the chapter focuses on clinical issues such as adult survivors, dissociative states, and the recent data about the increasing incidence of male victims and the discovery of female perpetrators. Society has had difficulty in understanding each of these phenomena. He concludes with the gains that have been made and further gains that must be achieved.

The last chapter in this section by David Finkelhor presents and contrasts two models on the trauma of child sexual abuse. First, he summarizes Finkelhor and Browne's (1985) four traumagenic dynamics, developed from empirical research findings concerning the long-term effects of child sexual abuse. The second model involves the DSM III diagnosis of Post-Traumatic Stress Disorder (PTSD), which characterizes the trauma experienced by the child sexual abuse victim. Finkelhor points out that the PTSD model, created to define the trauma of Vietnam veterans and adults who experience sudden catastrophic events, may not apply to all child sexual abuse victims. It should be noted, however, that the DSM III-R Diagnosis has recently been expanded to include the many traumatic events that children are experiencing—for example, war, witness to murder, and disasters.

Finkelhor's conclusions are salient and insightful in presenting the limitations of adopting a single model that does not encompass the initial and more pervasive effects of child sexual abuse. The three chapters in this section present historical and theoretical information that provide a provocative introduction to the sections on research that follow.

REFERENCE

Finkelhor, D., & Browne, A. (1985). *A model for understanding: Treating the trauma of child sexual abuse.* Paper presented at the meeting of the American Psychological Association, Los Angeles, CA.

2

Obstacles to
Policymaking About Incest

Some Cautionary Folktales

JEAN M. GOODWIN

Folkloric materials—rhymes, jokes, riddles, fairytales—provide the clinical examples and cautionary tales that accompany each culture's version of the universal incest taboo. This chapter will describe these folkloric materials and will review anthropological analyses of the incest taboo. Given the 4% prevalence of father-daughter incest in the general population (Russell, 1984) and the evidence that molestation by a trusted caretaker is one of the most damaging forms of childhood sexual abuse (Briere & Runtz, this volume; Finkelhor, this volume; Peters, this volume), it is remarkable that so little clinical use has been made of these materials. Otto Rank (1912) provided the most recent comprehensive review of the clinical implications of folkloric materials; his book is yet untranslated.

Previously, I used these materials (Goodwin, 1982) to illustrate the psychological harm caused by incest. Today there is some consensus that incest is in fact harmful (Friedrich, 1987; Goodwin, in press). The problem now is how to develop an acceptable system of response that minimizes rather than exacerbates the traumatic effects of this kind of abuse. The disarray in our social and legal response to incest has been well documented elsewhere (Goodwin, in press; Surgeon General's Workshop, 1985). Although legal experts consistently recommend criminal prosecution in these cases (American Bar Association, 1982, 1984), population studies indicate that fewer than 5% of cases result in criminal conviction (Goodwin, 1982; Russell, 1984). The majority of incidents are unreported. The final sections of this chapter propose a five-part analysis, illustrated by clinical, folkloric, and historical examples, of the conceptual obstacles that must be understood if we are to develop an acceptable and workable system.

Obstacles to Policymaking About Incest: Complicating Attitudes and Values

Feminists explain our failure to develop a system to control incest as a result of the excess privilege accruing to men in our society and the inferior status of women; misbehaviors involving primarily men as perpetrators and females as victims tend to remain underreported, underpunished, and underprevented (Brickman, 1984; Herman, 1981; Rush, 1980). There are many data to support this hypothesis including my own experience that, in over 500 cases of alleged parent-child incest, the only one that resulted in criminal conviction of a falsely accused parent was also the only case that alleged mother-son incest.

Other difficulties have been documented, including the multiple practical obstacles to productive involvement of child-victims in our criminal justice system (Goodman, 1985; Rosenfeld & Newberger, 1977; Terr, 1980, 1986; Terr & Watson, 1968). These were illustrated with clarity in the recent Jordan, Minnesota, sex ring cases. Here, the techniques intended to render the child witnesses more competent to testify, isolation from family and friends, repeated questioning, and lengthening preparation time, led to decompensation in the children and confusion in the legal process (Satterfield, 1985).

A review of cross-cultural and historical materials relating to incest suggests that still other aspects of social politics complicate our efforts to design a consistent and effective rule system. When communities, individuals, or families make rules about childhood sexual abuse, they are simultaneously taking positions along at least 5 axes of beliefs and attitudes: (1) the preference for informal controls versus preference for formal legal controls, (2) viewing the child as parental—mainly paternal property versus the view of the child as autonomous individual, (3) the need for inviolate family privacy versus need for community overseeing of child rearing, (4) viewing the child as a sensual expert versus view of the child as a virginal innocent, and (5) viewing sexuality as dangerous and secret versus viewing sexuality as harmless and natural.

This article will use folkloric and cross-cultural materials to contend that, since each pole of each of the five axes contains much that is valuable and true, the center of this conceptual landscape is the most useful place to be. Many of the most heated, fascinating, and unresolvable debates about sexual abuse represent attempts to declare a single extreme position ultimately true and right, while rejecting as illegitimate the interests represented by the opposite pole of that axis. This discussion argues that child victims and their families fare best when they are helped to avoid the hazards of extreme positions and to integrate the positive values along each axis. Informal and formal sanctions, parental and children's rights, family privacy, community overseeing, respect for the child's sexuality, respect for the child's innocence, caution about sexuality, acceptance of sexuality—all are necessary for effective treatment and for effective rule making in this area. Folkloric materials, like detailed unbiased clinical materials, are helpful beacons guiding us to the humanistic center of these debates.

Nature and Value of the Folkloric Archives

Stith Thompson's *Motif Index of Folk Literature* lists more than 20 categories of incest folktales including incest punished; misshapen child from brother-sister incest; child of incest exposed; father, feigning death, returns in disguise and seduces his daughter; flight of a maiden to escape marriage to father; father casts daughter forth when she will not marry him; suicide to prevent brother-sister marriage; God born from incestuous union; new race from incest after world calamity; loss of magic power through incest; incest unwittingly committed; enigmatic statement betrays incest; incest accidentally averted; lecherous father wants to marry daughter; girl got with child by intoxicated father; lustful stepmother; aunt seduces nephew.

Some argue that incest rules do not apply to intrafamilial sexual abuse. Psychoanalysts say the taboo functions only to interdict Oedipal fantasies, and some anthropologists contend that the taboo simply provides a structure for choosing marital partners (Cohen, 1978). However, clinicians treating families entangled in intrafamilial child sexual abuse will find much in these incest motifs that they recognize. Some of us have even written case reports that can be categorized quite precisely into a particular motif (see Goodwin, 1985, on "new race from incest after world calamity").

When anthropologists witness incest, the problems of family isolation and deviance are described in terms remarkably similar to those used by clinician observers (Wilson, 1961). Folktales often incorporate historical data (Blong, 1982), and some famous tales, such as the story of Saint Dymphna, may be the product of centuries of revision and embroidery in the telling of an actual clinical case history (Goodwin, 1982).

The Incest Taboo:
The Need for Prohibition

Every culture has developed a prohibition against incest. Anthropologists explain this universal phenomenon in various ways. Structuralists such as Lévi-Strauss (1949) explain the incest taboo as arising from the human need for allies to assist in times of famine, war, or other catastrophes. Groups are at a survival disadvantage without the kinship and friendship ties forged by the practical exigencies of exogamy—courtship, weddings, the interactions engendered by the existence of two sets of grandparents for each child.

Psychological anthropologists hypothesize that the survival disadvantages of incest relate to the stress, disruption, and confusion caused by the muddling and overlapping of roles within an incest family (Stephens, 1962; Whiting, 1963). They note the havoc that incest inflicts upon even relatively simple structures, such as kinship terminology. For example, a cautionary riddle from the Late Middle Ages describes a chance meeting between a cleric and the woman who long before bore him in incestuous union with her father. The woman, recognizing her son, says "I greet my brother; he is my father's son; he is my father's grandson; his mother is his father's daughter." More complicated versions of this riddle involve a subsequent marriage between the incest progeny and his mother-sister and question how the progeny from that union would address his then mother-aunt-grandmother and his father-brother-uncle (Rank, 1912).

Lindzey (1954) and other anthropologists have asked if there is a genetic basis for the folkloric incest motif, "misshapen child from brother-sister incest." Recent surveys of progeny from first degree mating in humans indicate that only half of pregnancies result in the live birth of a normal child (Adams & Neel, 1967; Goodwin, 1982). Nonspecific mental retardation, double recessive disorders, polygenetic disorders, increased stillbirths, and increased spontaneous miscarriage contribute to the poor outcome. The brother-sister marriages of the pharaohs have been used to illustrate the supposed absence of fundamental genetic contraindications to incest. However, recent reexamination of these lineages indicates that only two of the Ptolemies, one Hawaiian ruler and one Inca, were actual progeny of a brother-sister union (Bixler, 1981, 1982, 1983; Shepher, 1983). It is likely that, as in African kingdoms that survived into the nineteenth century, the brother-sister marriage was a formal entity only; the king's unrelated wives, not the sister-wife, were designated for sexuality and procreation.

Anthropologists interested in these genetic problems link the incest taboo to the Westermarck phenomenon in other animals, also called "stranger preference" (Bateson, 1978; Fox, 1983; Westermarck, 1922). Animals are observed to show decreased sexual preference toward nuclear family members or other conspecifics who have related to the individual since infancy. This phenomenon has been used to explain the rarity of marriages between kibbutz dwellers raised in the same nursery (Spiro, 1965). Insofar as this phenomenon is part of the human apparatus, one might speculate (Finkelhor, 1980, 1986) that children of divorced parents would experience higher rates of incest because they reach sexual maturity among relations who were not in the household during their infancy. Indeed, Diana Russell's (1984) data drawn from a population-based sample of California women, indicate that women with stepfathers had almost an 8-fold increased risk of incest victimization.

In a previous survey (1982), I reviewed clinical and folkloric data that support the concept that the taboo developed because of the interpersonal stresses that surround the incestuous act. Suicidal acts, runaways, and hysterical symptoms are major clinical problems among incest victims. As many as half of the difficult patients we call "borderlines" have been sexually abused (Steele, 1986). Folklore provides numerous illustrations of extreme symptoms in incest victims; one recalls Oedipus gouging out eyes, Hippolytus being trampled by his chariot horses in his panicked flight from his seductive stepmother Phaedra (who later hangs herself), and Cinderella cycle fairytale heroines such as Manekine who lose the function of limbs or lose speech under the stress of a "marriage" offer by father. Those behavioral symptoms that intrude on later parenting abilities—for example, none of the children of Oedipus survived to procreate—may have been observed in other societies and may have contributed to the decision that incestuous behavior, although tempting, is too interpersonally expensive to be condoned. As Freud (1950) said, "Incest is antisocial—civilization consists in this progressive renunciation."

Formal Legal Control
Versus Informal Sanctions

Some incest myths, such as the Navajo Moth-Way Chant, suggest that formal rules against incest are necessary primarily because incest is such a tempting solution to universal conflicts. In this story, the Moth-People are delighted when they realize that if they marry their daughters to their sons, families will never have to part or change and they can be together forever. The Moth-People become so excited at this discovery that they all fly into the flames and perish. How economically this story describes the paranoid intolerance of separation, change, and aging that characterizes some incest families as well as associated tendencies toward immaturity and impulsive self-destructiveness.

The Navajo maintain their very strict prohibition of incest through a series of informal sanctions: Incest participants are said to fall into fires (a common accident in hogans), to have seizures, and to become witches. Even today these sanctions are powerful enough to create serious difficulties for Navajo epileptics, who are automatically assumed to have committed incest and to be at risk for becoming a witch (Goodwin, 1982; Neutra, Levy, & Parker, 1977).

In cultures with formal sanctions against incest, these are severe, with death and exile being the most common (Weinberg, 1955). Under formal rules governing incest, both parties are punished. The extreme severity of these formal rules and their disregard for power differentials between partners is reminiscent of our own legal system. In our system as well as in others, there has been a tendency for informal systems to develop that divert the majority of cases into more workable pathways (Grollig, 1982). For example, in India where the formal punishment for incest is exile, reinforced by folkloric predictions of earthquakes, leprosy, blindness, and sterility; what actually happens is that the accused father "eats his way back" into the community by giving a feast (Elwin, 1939).

Public acknowledgment of incest characterizes many informal religious and tribal sanctions. English Puritans affixed to the offending father a sign describing his sexual misbehavior, a practice similar to the punishment for adultery described in *The Scarlet Letter*. In Africa, such an offense against a female would be reported to the woman's society who would gather at the man's hut and sing loudly all night about the details of his misbehavior. The story of Manekine, the Princess of Hungary (Goodwin, 1982), illustrates the healing potential for the victim of informal sanctions that emphasize public confession and apology by the offender (Trepper, 1986). Here the battered heroine, on overhearing both her father and her husband express remorse for having abused her, regains miraculously both the severed arm and the dead child that their abuse had cost her.

A problem with the informal system is that it requires unified action by a functioning community and it requires an offender capable first of feeling shame or guilt and second of using that feeling to modify aggressive and sexual behaviors. The medieval legends about Judas testify that this is not always the case (Reider, 1960; Tarachow, 1979). Judas is described as another Oedipus abandoned at birth because of prophesies describing his future atrocities. He is taken in and raised by a group of nuns, all 500 of whom he rapes and kills. Judas then takes a job for Pontius Pilate in Jerusalem where he kills a man and is required by Jewish law to make informal restitution by taking the widow as a wife. When she discovers he is her son, she sends Judas to Jesus for more informal sanctions. We all know how this intervention ends. The tale reminds us metaphorically that family violence is not a private affair; someone who rapes a family member may rape others; someone who starts by killing his own father may end by killing everyone's father. Like Judas, the antisocial or paranoid offender and the compulsive pedophile may be poor candidates for informal sanctions.

In current clinical practice, conflict around this polarity occurs most often between professionals attached to the formal criminal justice system and those attached to the more informal therapeutic protective service system. The conflict may be exacerbated if the advocates of the formal approach, emphasizing questions of justice, are males and if females are emphasizing the need for informal agreements about caretaking responsibilities. Carol Gilligan (1982) has provided many examples of males and females failing to understand each other when males focus on issues of justice and females on issues of care.

An increasingly common kind of case that illustrates how both formal and informal sanctions can fail involves inappropriate sexual behaviors by a divorced father during visits with his children. In such a case the care-focused professional usually identifies multiple problems in the family, but may perceive the father's impulsive, paranoid, and/or sociopathic patterns as the most disruptive influence, and may suggest that the mother seek to restrict visitation (Benedek & Schetky, 1985). The worst case occurs if a judge, relatively uninterested in the informal system's attempts to restore adequate caretaking, focuses narrowly on the issue of whether the situation meets formal definitions of rape. If it does not, the judge may be so offended at the mother's "false" accusation and "disregard" for justice that he awards custody to the disturbed father (Armstrong, 1983).

Child as Parental Property
Versus Child as Autonomous Individual

Folktales from the Western Christian tradition acknowledge the difficulty in protecting disenfranchised children from parents who have rights not only as full citizens, but also as owners of the children. Nicholas of Myra, a fourth century Bishop, became the patron saint of children largely because he tried to even this balance of power. When a parishioner announced plans to sell his three daughters into prostitution, Nicholas discretely dropped three golden balls down the family's chimney. The balls landed in the girls' stockings "hung near the chimney to dry" and the world gained a Christmas tradition (Thurston & Attwater, 1981). What the girls gained was the power and autonomy to choose their own mode of sexual expression; they used the gold as their marriage dowries.

Much later, in the fifteenth century, the Baron Gilles de Rais, after serving as one of Joan of Arc's captains, devoted himself to capturing latency age boys, then torturing them; finally sodomizing each boy after hanging him and slitting his throat in a witchcraft ritual. Fragments of the dismembered bodies of some of his estimated 200 victims were found in the Baron's moat. Gilles de Rais is the real-life prototype for the fairytale character "Bluebeard." The fairytale translates into a child's terms the entrapment tactics used by some narcissistic and grandiose offenders. Bluebeard gives his young wife the key to a secret room but orders her not to open it. When curiosity overwhelms her and she finds in the secret room the dismembered bodies of his previous wives, Bluebeard is able to frame his long-planned sadistic attack on her as "punishment" for her curiosity. With family and religious support, the wife in the story copes and survives, but the victims of the actual Baron were so disenfranchised, as peasants as well as children, that they had no defense. The Baron's friends helped him chase down these young human prey on horseback. Only after intervention from another compassionate Bishop and the Inquisition was this macabre hunt halted (Bataille, 1965).

However, children are children and cannot be made equal to adults simply by wishing them so. History tells us that children who escape from inadequate parents often go from the frying pan to the fire, falling into the hands of brothel keepers, gang leaders, cults, or religious groups.

Goldstein, Solnit, and Freud (1980), Rosenfeld and Newberger (1977), Terr (1980, 1981), and Terr and Watson (1968) have discussed at length how a child's legal rights to court protection and removal from parents can lead to years of shifting foster homes and permanent loss of developmental potential. To return to the Saint Nicholas story, our system seems able at times to protect children against being sold into prostitution by parents, but we have much greater difficulty supplying the golden balls—the advocacy and validation—that could guide victimized children into their own chosen futures.

Current controversies that develop out of this polarity include issues of enforcing parental custody or visitation on children who are violently opposed to the interaction. This culminates in the difficulties that surround terminating parental rights. In one case a father, convicted for sexually penetrating his children, almost succeeded in obtaining a court order to require his 2-year-old son to visit him in prison. There had been physical and spousal abuse in the home as well as sexual abuse. The child was to be transported by the paternal grandfather, who had a varied record of felony convictions and inpatient hospitalizations for psychosis. The court's task was to balance the developmental hazards of the proposed visits against the risk that without visits the child might lose forever his tie with his paternal family. Loss of such a tie, even in the face of massive disturbance in a family, is viewed by courts as terribly serious. In another case, police were called because of a 4-year-old girl's screams when left off for a visit with her father. She had complained to relatives and therapists that she was afraid of the father's physical and sexual abuse, but the judge in the custody case saw the mother's manipulativeness as the major problem. Visitation was court ordered, so police were forced to leave the child screaming in the hands of the father.

Such inexorable tightening of the abuser's control despite reasonable complaints, is a recurring theme in folklore, as illustrated in the legend of Saint Dymphna. Dymphna is a princess whose father asks her to marry him after the mother's death. The young princess seeks help from her confessor, the monk Gerebernus, who finds a boat. Despite the monk's inability either to steer or navigate, they somehow manage to land in Belgium. (I have often thought that the disoriented but willing Gerebernus should be the patron saint of therapists working with incest victims.) However, the father, meanwhile, has organized an army of searchers who track them down to their forest refuge. Bystanders actually help lead the abusive father to the refugee victim, because they disbelieve her tale of incest; they appreciate the credibility of the victim too late, after witnessing the father behead her and Gerebernus (Goodwin, 1982).

The Family's Need for Privacy Versus the Community's Need to Oversee Child Rearing

Odd things happen in even the most functional of families. Western civilization has evolved in the direction of giving families as much privacy and latitude as possible. A Renaissance story illustrates this laissez faire attitude. The painter Vasari was decorating the bedroom ceilings in the Medici Palace. One morning when Vasari climbed up to his scaffolding to paint, he saw the young princess Isabella, still asleep in her bed. A few hours later he saw her father, Cosimo de Medici, enter the room. Vasari could not see either the bed or the two Medicis from his post, but he could hear the unmistakable sounds of intercourse. He waited very quietly until both had left the room, then he, too, crept away. He told friends that he didn't feel like painting any more that day (McCarthy, 1963). Some have questioned the authenticity of this story. What is well documented is that Isabella ended her life as a victim of family violence; she was strangled to death by her husband (Micheletti, 1979).

Our excessive embarrassment and caution about interfering in family matters stands in contrast to the attitude of the Kalahari Bushmen of southern Africa. These desert dwellers live in small groups. They are expert hunters and trackers who sleep within view of each other in circumstances that make sexual secrets impossible. Group members who break the incest taboo do so under the intense scrutiny and teasing of the community and are swiftly dissuaded by these informal sanctions (Draper, 1978).

In our culture, groups such as VOCAL (Victims of Child Abuse Legislation) argue that community overseeing does more harm than good. Such groups point to the high rate of unsubstantiated reports of child abuse and neglect, saying that even a negative investigation stigmatizes innocent parents. However, overreporting is necessary in order to net a high enough proportion of actual cases to reduce morbidity and mortality (Goodwin, 1982). Perhaps someday it will be possible for our culture to provide community support for parents that is not stigmatizing. The Bushmen have a single expletive that translates as "Take this child off my hands." Parents use this expletive many times each day without fear of guilt or stigma, and children are always in the arms of an attentive, caring adult.

Currently, the medical model responds to incest from the privacy pole of this axis, while the criminal justice model emphasizes the need for community overseeing of family behaviors. A recent study (James & Womack, 1978) indicates that physicians actually report to protective services only 42% of the incest cases they confirm. Other surveys indicate that this is not because of ignorance of what the law requires (Attias & Goodwin, 1985) but because of mistrust of the protective service system and because of a tendency to underestimate the seriousness of sexual abuse, including the likelihood of physical damage and of involvement of other children. A preventive medicine model, analogous to that used in infectious disease, has been proposed to help physicians balance their duty to protect a patient's privacy with the duty to protect the family and the community (Surgeon General's Workshop, 1985). The development of specific protocols, such as in reporting venereal disease, has been helpful in allowing physicians to integrate the need for investigation as part of their medical role as diagnosticians and public health advocates, so they do not feel so much like prying police when they collect a complete family violence history.

Child as Virgin Innocent Versus Child as Sensuality Expert

Therapeutic wisdom in the past decade recommends telling child incest victims they have done nothing wrong and that there was nothing they could have done to prevent the adult's misbehavior (Sgroi, 1981). This position is stated more completely and poetically in a Polynesian myth. After a terrible catastrophe, a brother and sister find themselves the only survivors. For weeks they take turns searching their island for another human being. Months pass. At last they decide they must mate to try to repopulate their world. A malformed child is born. More months pass. A large party of survivors led by an old man discovers the sibling pair. The brother and sister are overcome by guilt and remorse. However, the old man, after listening carefully to their story, tells them, "There was nothing else you could do" (Dixon, 1916). This therapeutic model is apt for sibling incest survivors seen clinically. These victims often blame each other bitterly, failing to take into account the magnitude of the family catastrophe with which they were coping.

However, other folkloric materials portray the child not as an innocent, but an expert in sensuality and evil. A medieval English mystery play describes a girl who seduces her father, kills her mother, kills her baby born of the incestuous union, kills her father, and then repents and is forgiven (Wells, 1916). This tale mirrors the picture of the victim often painted by the incestuous father. "What man could have resisted her?" complained one stepfather who had begun fondling his child when she was a preschooler. However, some victims, too, adopt this seductress self-representation, rejecting the suggestion that their role was passive. I recall one adult incest survivor who had successfully resisted years of therapeutic attempts to tell her she had done nothing wrong. She finally revealed her secret. Years after her father had stopped initiating intercourse with her, the patient, then a young woman, had sought him out, and successfully seized sexual control. Shortly after they had intercourse "for the last time," her father died of a stroke; she had always blamed herself. Like many victims she had learned to identify with the aggressor, and had also learned, long before puberty, to seek the pleasures of coital orgasm. Even though in this case the perpetrator was dead at the time treatment began, he still had to be dealt with as an introjected part of the patient's identity. As long as she was protecting her therapists from this part of her experience, treatment made no impact on her patterns of guilt, self-punishment, and low self-esteem.

Therapists working in this area repeatedly argue about whether the focus should rest on the interpersonal situation or on the victim's inner life. Extreme situationalists may err in tending to view the incest victim as a tabula rasa shaped only by external events. They may forget that more than a third of normal children have learned to masturbate by age one year (Kestenberg, 1968; Rutter, 1971) and that the sexual aspects of incest, while important, are only one factor in its traumatogenesis (Finkelhor, 1987). Extreme inner-world proponents may err, as Freud has been accused of erring, in losing touch with the character of the perpetrator and the needs of other family members (Erikson, 1962; Masson, 1984; Ross, 1982). In real life, of course, the two approaches cannot be separated. If the therapist will listen, the more the survivor can recall and explain about the situation, the more he or she reveals about inner experience and conflicts and vice versa.

Sexuality as Dangerous and Secret Versus Sexuality as Harmless and Natural

Even the most sexually knowledgeable and tolerant societies design and enforce an incest taboo of some kind. The ideal of the Rene Guyon Society

(1974)—relatively indiscriminate sexual partnering between children and adults—seems not to exist in nature. However, cross-culturally, parent-child nudity, communal sleeping arrangements, and tolerance for masturbation and peer sex play in children coexist with stringent incest taboos. The incest taboo regulates not child sexuality itself so much as the impingement of uncontrolled sexual impulses on parenting roles and on the child's own future role performance. Sexual behaviors performed openly according to community sanctions seem not to be experienced as abusive. For example, mothers in many cultures use genital manipulation to soothe and pleasure infants. Some cultures prescribe the deflowering of pubertal girls by an adult male or by the father. This is not experienced as incest, although incest can occur in these cultures, as in one case where the father continued having intercourse with his daughter secretly after the public ritual. There may be as yet unstudied sequelae even of sanctioned sexual practices with children older than age 4 to 6. In most cultures this is an age at which children move toward more personal and sexual privacy.

While sexually permissive cultures may overload children with sexual experiences, the sexually puritanical cultures have different kinds of difficulties maintaining the incest taboo. Here secrecy and fears about sexuality can create a climate in which incest fathers can easily seduce their naive prey while normative inhibitions about sexuality conceal and perpetuate the abuse. Many incest fathers justify their activities as "sex education." The father's own sex education is sometimes so terribly limited as to preclude the possibility of finding an adult sexual partner outside the family. An Indian folktale expands this concept. In this story the first father, on the occasion of his son's wedding, wants to tell the young man and his bride about sex. However, the father's own knowledge is so tenuous and incomplete that he cannot convey in words what must be done, so the father ends by deflowering the bride himself (Elwin, 1931). Once such an event occurs, the victim's own lack of sexual knowledge and terminology can render her unable to complain. Those who find extreme the current educational emphasis on the sexual self-protection of children should remember that this effort is filling an enormous vacuum. Before "Thousand-furs" was reinstated in collections of Grimm's fairytales in the late 1970s, after years of suppression, children in our culture had perhaps the most restricted opportunity to hear and discuss explicit incest tales that has ever existed in a human culture. As one African folktale grimly reminds us, "If parents don't teach their children about sex, life will teach them."

Conclusion

Previous discussions of our current problems in enforcing the incest taboo have focused on our culture's tendency to overvalue male needs and ignore female needs and on our judicial system's tendency either to treat child witnesses as adults or to exclude them from the legal process. The present discussion lists five additional sets of problems: (1) insistence on exclusive use of either formal or informal sanctions, (2) refusal to acknowledge either the child's rights as an individual or his or her natural dependency, (3) excessive exaggeration or minimization of the importance of family privacy, (4) refusal to acknowledge either the child's innocence or his or her sensuality, and (5) excessive exaggeration or minimization of the dangers of sexuality. In a 1979 article on the pitfalls of investigating sexual abuse allegations, we suggested that professionals examine their own biases before engaging in such evaluations (Goodwin, Sahd, & Rada, 1979). The present discussion provides a beginning listing of those problematic biases. Forensic evaluators are particularly at risk for losing perspective, because our adversary legal system tends to split apart truths, forcing each side toward whichever extreme yet partial position favors one particular side of the argument. Disturbed victims also gravitate toward extreme positions, sometimes taking the therapist with them. For example, victims who dissociate into multiple personalities may produce alters who advocate opposing extremes; one alter may be a virgin while another is hypersexual; one alter may be pursuing criminal charges against the father while another keeps the secret faithfully. Folklore provides an antidote to this fragmentation, telling us stories in which opposing polarities can be integrated. In stories, as well as in reality, the needs of both females and males in the family make empathic sense; victims wish to protect as well as punish family members, and children are simultaneously as sensual as they are innocent. Folklore also provides cautionary examples of the problems that arise when extreme positions prevail, and its cross-cultural origins tend to free us from culture-bound perspectives.

Social history tells us that making the incest taboo work is an inevitable human chore. Folklore tells us that it may be possible to carry out this chore with some measure of creativity, good humor, and even wisdom.

REFERENCES

Adams, M. S., & Neels, J. V. (1967). Children of incest. *Pediatrics, 40,* 55-62.

American Bar Association National Legal Resource Center for Child Advocacy and Protection. (1982). *Innovations in the prosecution of child sexual abu·se cases.* Washington, DC: American Bar Association.

American Bar Association National Legal Resource Center for Child Advocacy and Protection. (1984). *Child sexual abuse and the law.* Washington, DC: American Bar Association.

Armstrong, L. (1983). Incest—In the age of No-Fault Abuse. *Workshops in Non-Violence, 19,* 11-13.

Attias, R., & Goodwin, J. (1985). Knowledge and management strategies in incest cases. *Child Abuse and Neglect, 9,* 527-533.

Bataille, G. (1965). *Le proces de gilles de Rais: Les documents.* Paris: G. de Laval.

Bateson, P. (1978). Sexual imprinting and optimal outbreeding. *Nature, 273,* 659-660.

Benedek, E. P., & Schetky, D. H. (1985). Allegations of sexual abuse in child custody and visitation disputes. In D. H. Schetky & E. P. Benedek (Eds.), *Emerging issues in psychiatry and the law.* New York: Brunner/Mazel.

Bixler, R. H. (1981a). Incest avoidance as a function of environment and heredity. *Current Anthropology, 22,* 639-643, 649-654.

Bixler, R. H. (1981b). The incest controversy. *Psychological Reports, 49,* 267-283.

Bixler, R. H. (1982). Comment on the incidence and purpose of royal sibling incest. *American Ethnologist, 9,* 580-582.

Blong, R. J. (1982). *The times of darkness. Local legends and volcanic reality in Papua, New Guinea.* Seattle: University of Washington Press.

Brickman, J. (1984). Feminist, nonsexist, and traditional models of therapy: Implications for working with incest. *Women and Therapy, 3,* 49-67.

Cohen, Y. (1978). The disappearance of the incest taboo. *Human Nature,* pp. 72-78.

Dixon, R. B. (1916). *Oceanic mythology* (Vol. 9). Boston: Marshall Jones.

Draper, P. (1978). !Kung women: Contrasts in sexual egalitarianism in foraging and secondary contexts. In R. Reiter (Ed.), *Toward an anthropology of women.* New York: Monthly Review Press.

Elwin, V. (1931). *Myths of Middle India.* Oxford: Oxford University Press.

Elwin, V. (1939). *The Baiga.* New York: AMS.

Erikson, E. H. (1962). Reality and actuality: An address. *Journal of the American Psychoanalytic Association, 10,* 451-474.

Finkelhor, D. (1982). Sexual abuse: A sociological perspective. *Child Abuse and Neglect, 6,* 95-102.

Finkelhor, D. (1986). *A sourcebook on child sexual abuse.* Beverly Hills, CA: Sage.

Fox, R. (1983). *The red lamp of incest: An enquiry into the origins of mind and society.* Notre Dame, IN: University of Notre Dame Press.

Freud, S. (1950). Extracts from the Fliess papers. *Standard Edition, 1,* 257.

Friedrich, W. N. (1987). Behavior problems in sexually abused young children: An adaptational perspective. In G. Wyatt & G. Powell (Eds.), *The lasting effects of child sexual abuse.* Newbury Park: Sage.

Gilligan, C. (1982). *In a different voice. Psychological theory and women's development.* Cambridge, MA: Harvard University Press.

Goldstein, J., Freud, A., & Solnit, A. (1980). *Beyond the best interest of the child.* New York: Free Press.

Goodman, G. (1985). Children's testimony in historical perspective. *Journal of Social Issues, 40,* 9-31.

Goodwin, J. (1982). *Sexual abuse: Incest victims and their families.* Boston: Wright/PSG.

Goodwin, J. (1985). Persecution and grandiosity in incest fathers. In P. Pichot, R. W. Berner, & K. Thaw (Eds.), *Psychiatry: The state of the art* (Vol. 6). New York: Plenum.

Goodwin, J. (1987). Developmental impacts of incest. In J. Noshpitz, I. Berlin, J. Call, R. Cohen, S. Harrison, & L. Stone (Eds.), *Handbook of child psychiatry* (Vol. 5, pp. 103-110). New York: Basic Books.

Goodwin, J. (in press). Obstacles to rulemaking about incest: Social and historic contexts. In *Sexual abuse: Incest victims and their families.* Boston: Wright/PSG.

Goodwin, J., Sahd, D., & Rada, R. (1979). Incest hoax: False accusations, false denials. *Bulletin of the American Academy of Psychiatry and the Law, 6,* 269-276.

Grollig, F. X. (1982). Anthropological perspective on incest. In D. Renshaw (Ed.), *Incest: Understanding and treatment.* Boston: Little, Brown.

Guyon, R. (1974; orig. 1941). *The ethics of sexual acts.* New York: Octagon.

Herman, J. (1981). *Father-daughter incest.* Cambridge, MA: Harvard University Press.

James, J., & Womack, W. (1978). Physician reporting of sexual abuse of children. *Journal of American Medical Association, 240,* 1145-1146.

Kestenberg, J. (1968). Outside and inside, male and female. *Journal of the American Psychoanalytic Association, 16,* 456-520.

Levi-Strauss, C. (1949). *Les structures elementaires de la parente.* Paris: Presses universitaries de France.

Lindzey, G. (1954). *Handbook of social psychology.* Boston: Addison-Wesley.

Masson, J. M. (1984). *The assault on truth.* New York: Farrar, Strauss & Giroux.

McCarthy, M. (1963). *The stones of Florence.* New York: Harcourt, Brace, Jovanovich.

Micheletti, E. (1979). *I Medici a Firenze.* Firenze: Becocci Editore.

Neutra, R., Levy, J., & Parker, D. (1977). Cultural expectations versus reality in Navajo. Seizure patterns and sick roles. *Culture, Medicine and Psychiatry, 1*(2), 255-275.

Rank, O. (1912). *Das inzest-motif in dichtung und sage.* Leipzig: Franz Deuticke.

Reider, N. (1960). Medieval Oedipal legends about Judas. *Psychoanalytic Quarterly, 29,* 515-527.

Rosenfeld, A. A., & Newberger, E. H. (1977). Compassion vs. control: Conceptual and practical pitfalls in the broadened definition of child abuse. *Journal of the American Medical Association, 237,* 2086-2088.

Ross, J. M. (1982). Oedipus revisited; Laius and the "Laius complex." *Psychoanalytic Study of the Child, 37,* 169-200.

Rush, F. (1980). *The best kept secret: Sexual abuse of children.* Englewood Cliffs, NJ: Prentice-Hall.

Russell, D. (1984). *Sexual exploitation.* Beverly Hills, CA: Sage.

Rutter, M. (1971). Normal psychosexual development. *Journal of Child Psychology and Psychiatry, 11*(4), 25-283.

Satterfield, S. (1985). *The legal child abuse in the Jordan, Minnesota, sex ring case.* Presented at the annual meeting of the American Academy of Psychiatry and the Law, Albuquerque, NM.

Sgroi, S. M. (1981). *Handbook of clinical interventions in child sexual abuse.* Lexington, MA: Lexington Books.

Shepher, J. (1983). *Incest: A biopsychosocial view*. New York: Academic Press.

Spiro, M. E. (1965). *Children of the kibbutz*. New York: Schocken.

Steele, B. (1986). Notes on the lasting effects of early child abuse throughout the life cycle. *Child Abuse & Neglect, 10*, 283-291.

Stephens, W. N. (1962). *The Oedipus complex: Cross-cultural evidence*. Glencoe, IL: Free Press.

Surgeon General's Workshop on Violence and Public Health. (1985). *Report*. Washington, DC: Health Resources and Services Administration.

Tarachow, S. (1979). Judas, The beloved executioner. In J. T. Coltrera (Ed.), *Lives, events and other players: Directions in psychobiography* (pp. 77-99). New York: Jason Aronson.

Terr, L. (1980). The child as witness. In D. Schetky & E. Benedek (Eds.), *Child psychiatry and the law*. New York: Brunner/Mazel.

Terr, L. C. (1981). The child psychiatrist and the child witness: Traveling companions by necessity if not by design. *Journal of the American Academy of Child Psychiatry, 25*, 462-472.

Terr, L. C., & Watson, A. S. (1968). The battered child rebrutalized: Ten cases of medical-legal confusion. *American Journal of Psychiatry, 124*, 1432-1439.

Thompson, S. (1955-1958). *Motif index of folk literature* (6 Vols.). Bloomington: Indiana University Press.

Thurston, H. J., & Attwater, D. (1981). *Butler's lives of the saints* (Vol. IV). Maryland: Christian Classics.

Trepper, T. S. (1986). The apology session. In T. S. Trepper & M. J. Barrett (Eds.), *Treating incest: A multimodal systems perspective*. New York: Haworth.

Weinberg, S. (1955). *Incest behavior*. New York: Citadel.

Wells, J. E. (1916). *A manual of writings in Middle English, 1050-1400*. New Haven, CT: Yale University Press.

Westermarck, E. (1922). *The history of human marriage* (Vol. II). New York: Allerton.

Whiting, B. B. (1963). *Six cultures: Studies of childrearing*. New York: John Wiley.

Wilson, P. J. (1961). Incest: A case study. *Social and Economic Studies, 12*, 200-209.

3

Hidden Victims, Hidden Pain

Societal Avoidance
of Child Sexual Abuse

ROLAND C. SUMMIT

Apparitions in the Fog

Sexual abuse of children is a serious problem that has been long neglected and sorely misunderstood. The effects of undetected abuse far outweigh the immediate trauma observed in child victims, and the recognized victims are such a small proportion of those actually victimized that we have only begun to appreciate the impact of sexual abuse on society as a whole. A noncomplaining, apparently normai child may be suffering grotesquely perverse sexual assault in the company of a caretaker who is conspicuously trustworthy and who seems incapable of malice or perversion. Adult survivors may be impaired in self-esteem, basic trust, intimacy, sexual function, and mental health, and may on occasion pose a threat to personal and public safety, yet the root cause of these problems is likely to be overlooked by the individuals themselves and by the professionals mandated to address those problems. In order to discover and ameliorate the pervasive impact of sexual abuse there is a need for research, training, specialized response systems, and an aggressive outreach to encourage prevention, discovery, disclosure, intervention, treatment, and prosecution.

AUTHOR'S NOTE: Correspondence regarding this chapter should be addressed to Roland C. Summit, M.D., Department of Psychiatry, Harbor—UCLA Medical Center, 1000 W. Carson, Torrance, CA 90509.

Sexual abuse of children is a limited problem that is being built out of proportion in a hysterical climate of overconcern. Most allegations are without foundation. Large numbers of noncustodial parents and responsible professionals face a lifetime of disgrace because overzealous specialists urge children to voice complaints that common sense should define as preposterous. A child actually victimized will tell someone, and anyone who is so deviant as to molest a child will be an obvious misfit among normal adults. Those victims or victimizers who somehow elude ordinary notice would certainly show up in psychological testing and in clinical evaluations. Most sexual abuse is nonviolent, nonpenetrating, and harmless. If there is harm, it results more from societal horror and criminalization than from the sexual experience itself. It is obvious that the worst thing we could do is to frighten children with warnings or interrogations when it is only exceptional individuals who are at risk. If there is a problem for children or for adults molested as children, it should be addressed within traditional resources, shielded from the misguided enthusiasm of expert "child abuse finders." Specialized focus on child sexual abuse is the *cause* of the false epidemic of the 1980s. To control the problem we need to control the experts.

The two paragraphs above are mutually antagonistic, yet each represents a composite of values, a position, held by large numbers of reasonable people (Hechler, 1988). Of the two, the second position is the more time-honored and resourceful. It is a baseline of knowledge, authority, and common sense against which the more alarming, radical claims of the occasional advocates, the "believers" in child sexual abuse, have always been measured.

The first position, that of the believers, is the upsetting one. It is bound to be suspect, since it derives from observations and beliefs that are both irrelevant and unconvincing to most of adult society. Yet those are the beliefs to be examined in this volume and that is the position that will be defended in this chapter. It is my thesis that child sexual abuse exists in society as a phenomenon that is most conspicuous for its presumed absence. One of the clues to how important it is may be the effort we devote to keeping it out of sight.

This chapter will illustrate the nature of a *shared negative hallucination* (Goodwin, 1985) obscuring every aspect of child sexual abuse. While blindness to abuse has been described as a male sexist phenomenon (Armstrong, 1978; Rush, 1980), a style of dysfunctional families (Lustig, Dresser, Spellman, & Murray, 1966), and as a reflection of psychiatric avoidance (Masson, 1984; Peters, 1976), a broader view is needed to understand the pervasive paradoxes in societal perception.

Drawing on observations of current controversies, historical precedents, and the experiences of present-day adult survivors of sexual abuse, it will be illustrated that it is all of society, not just those immediately affected, that protects the secret of child sexual abuse. We have overlooked or outrageously trivialized this subject, not because it is peripheral to major social interests, but because it is so central that we have not yet dared to conceptualize its scope. Much as the individual victim is compelled into silence, self-punishment, dissociation, and identification with the aggressor, we as a society move thoughtlessly to deny sexual abuse and to conceal vast aggregates of pain and rage. Telltale outcroppings are resolutely covered over, fragmented, or mislabeled to protect our faith in a false concept of the status quo.

Paradox and impassioned prejudgments obscure any rational evaluation of child sexual abuse. Public and professional beliefs and counterbeliefs about this subject still resemble superstition more than science. Sexual abuse, which has gained such spectacular exposure in the past ten years, may be still so enshrouded in myth that we are able to catch only fleeting glimpses of the reality. Each brief clearing of the fog brings out believers who claim fantastic insights, only to be scorned and forced to recant by those who insist that the believers have been bedazzled by an apparition, something false and dangerous.

What are the factors that might obscure observation and belittle recognition? Victim secrecy and ambivalence contribute, of course (Summit, 1983). But it is adult skepticism that blinds us to all but the most blatant sexual assaults. We may find some commonsense empathy with the need of an incest victim to hide the abuse in order to protect the family, but we insist that children of normal families would tell, and that parents and community would believe if exposed to an out-of-family predator. Adult society also tends to assume that threats to child safety will be defined by prosecutors and that assaults on mental health will be of interest to clinicians. One also assumes that the greater the number of children involved, and the more intimate the observed contact with the suspect, the more obvious the abuse would be. None of those assumptions proved true in the following case.

"Johnny," a 9-year-old from Los Angeles, complained of a bellyache on the dawn of his second day of school in Big Pine, a very small mountain resort in the eastern Sierras. His mother urged him not to be afraid of his new school. He became more adamant in his refusals and more desperate in his excuses, until he blurted out an unbelievable story. He said he had been invited by an older boy to join a noontime club and taken to a classroom blindfolded for an initiation by a teacher that included being stripped, orally raped, and both threatened into silence and invited into continuing participation. Johnny's mother called a relative who was a deputy sheriff in another community. A covert investigation implicated Mr. "Friendly," who was one of the most trusted and indispensable teachers in the district. He was loved for his remarkable devotion to children, which extended to volunteer coaching and spending weekends taking groups of fifth and sixth grade boys on fishing excursions in his camper.

Mr. Friendly quietly accepted arrest after a search of his classroom cabinets yielded sexual devices, cameras, and large quantities of both still and motion pictures depicting Friendly in oral and anal group sex with students. These films apparently were shot in his classroom, camper, and outdoor campsites. Investigation revealed that Mr. Friendly had initiated into his "club" almost every fifth grade boy in town over the past four years, a suspected total of over a hundred children. He used confidential school files to reinforce silence through guilt and fear: "I know your mother has been in a mental hospital. If she found out what you're doing it would put her right back into the booby hatch."

Even though everyone knew everybody's business in this isolated community, and despite glaring clues, there was universal avoidance of suspecting Mr. Friendly as a menace. One father remembered finding his son partially undressed in bed with the man when he had come to pick him up after a birthday party. It was not the least unusual for Mr. Friendly to help out at any gathering of boys, and the father had been embarrassed at his initial alarm. He was vastly relieved when Mr. Friendly explained that he had rescued the boy from a fight and was soothing him in the darkened room with massage.

After Friendly's arrest, the cover-up became deliberate and victim-punitive. Police officers sequestered their own sons from questioning. Teachers signed letters of support for Friendly when a defense attorney planted the story that a disgruntled clique of girls had falsely accused the teacher of sexual touching. Three mental health specialists provided independent evaluations to the court. All recommended outpatient counseling and diversion from imprisonment so Friendly could resume his contributions to school and community. One promised a cure through sexual therapy for his wife, who was described as frigid and frustrating. All agreed that the boys were willing participants, and that Friendly was not an active danger to children. Overruling the experts, the judge found Friendly to be a mentally disordered sex offender and sentenced him to a closed treatment facility.

The community sealed over without a trace of its scandal. A Mental Health Department project to provide confidential counseling for the boys died without a single referral. A new high school teacher arriving five years later asked his colleagues about the unusual behavior of his eleventh and twelfth grade students. They reminded him of little boys giggling over bathroom humor and avoiding close relationships with girls. None of his fellow teachers endorsed his concern. No one even hinted at the legacy of Mr. Friendly.

The above story is not unusual. Thousands of such complaints are voiced every year against trusted authorities (Abel, 1987): teachers, coaches, bus drivers, physicians, therapists, ministers, lawyers—even judges. Neither should it be surprising that parents and colleagues alike seized on reassuring alternatives to the unthinkable premise that a whole town full of boys would collude in secret orgies with a distinguished educator. Nor is it strange that none of the families came forth for treatment, or that designated experts were more protective of the suspect than the victims. We should understand by now that most people will overlook clues, blame victims, and stigmatize victim families as sick rather than consider that trusted friends could be sexual predators.

What *is* unusual in the Big Pine phenomenon is that someone believed the child, that the authorities acted on the complaint, that the material evidence was not lost, and that a trusted caretaker was actually brought to trial and convicted.

Such an outcome has little apparent impact on the immediate community, let alone on extended public policy. Mr. Friendly was convicted on the testimony of three children, on just enough charges to ensure substantial penalty. There was no review or repudiation of the misleading role of the clinical evaluations, no censure for the attorney who knowingly promulgated a deceptive smokescreen, and no public health effort to measure long-term effects upon children and community. In fact, the active efforts of the public were directed toward containment, avoidance, and erasure. A protective folk wisdom emerges to trivialize even the most ominous discoveries: Three boys, one of them a meddlesome outsider, had sex with a teacher some years back. Nothing to get too excited about.

The menace of the perpetrator is typically effaced by focusing morbid attention on the silence and implied complicity of young participants. When allegations surface involving children too young to dissemble and suspects so obviously innocent as to be immune from suspicion, then suspicion falls on those who choose to believe that such a conspiracy could exist. The more outrageous the allegations the greater is the de facto immunity for the accused and the more punitive is the burden of proof imposed on the victim and their believers.

The following case, from the Country Walk residential community near Miami (see Hollingsworth, 1986), is alone among an epidemic of very similar cases to be validated both by conviction of those charged and the corroborating testimony of a participant adult.

Symptoms and clues were rationalized away for six months while some 25 infants and toddlers of both genders were sexually exploited with assaultive games and bloody rituals in a babysitting service operated by a neighbor, Frank, and his young wife, Iliana. Two mothers heeded their toddlers' complaints and withdrew their children. But they agreed to keep the reason secret to avoid alarming other parents. A doctor advised against chemical screening for a self-battering, apparently drugged 3-year-old. A social worker discounted an anonymous complaint, relying only on the reassurances of the attractive proprietor. When another anonymous tip finally reached the police months later, the investigation was blasted by defense attorneys as a witch hunt. So were the "brainwashing" diagnostic interviews of the children videotaped by an "unqualified" couple with doctorates in child development. The motives, methods, and lifestyle of these specialists were ridiculed in the media for the year preceding trial. The innocence of 17-year-old Iliana seemed indisputable; she sailed through two polygraphs without a hitch. Yet she later testified to participating in the same bizarre atrocities uncovered in the children's interviews.

The convictions in the Country Walk case did nothing to offset the triumphant skepticism emerging from similar mass allegations in some 45 investigations throughout the United States. The stories of all these children, such as those in Miami, were considered incredible and unreliable. They had been pried from uncomplaining children by self-styled specialists in sexual abuse. Defense attorneys invented a theory that blames the interviewer for creating false allegations: The hapless defendants are the victims of an unhealthy alliance of prosecutors, therapists, and hysterical parents whose leading questions have subliminally cued naive children into believing they were abused.

That argument is echoed by VOCAL (Victims of Child Abuse Laws) across the nation. Expert opinions can be hired to dignify the same argument for the defense of any accused adult. In courtrooms, talk shows, and printed exposés dedicated disbelievers label as dangerous to society any professional or parent who expresses belief in a child's disclosures. The prosecutor of the massive allegations of ritual abuse in Jordan, Minnesota, was stripped of immunity and nearly impeached from public office. She was held to answer to millions of dollars of civil suits until exonerated by a federal court of appeals. The psychologists who accepted police referrals to evaluate children in a suspect California preschool and a mother who warned other mothers of her concerns were hit with similar suits.

Is it possible that the two mothers in Country Walk who hid their suspicions made the socially expected choice? Was Johnny's mom pathologically suspicious for reporting Mr. Friendly? Is it really dangerous to talk about abuse as real or to ask children questions if abuse is suspected? Is it wrong to try to illumine the apparitions lurking in the fogbanks of uncertainty?

In Big Pine and Country Walk, just as in any incestuous family, in any family sexually assaulted from outside, in any courtroom, and within every forum of society, there is certain pain in discovery and humiliation in full disclosure. Anyone who tries to encourage unwanted awareness becomes a target for censure (Sgroi, 1978). Unlike ordinary frontiers of discovery, sexual abuse provokes an authoritarian insistence for obscurity over enlightenment. Adult society denies sexual abuse, not in spite of previous suspicions but because of them. So many phantoms have merged back into the mists and so many expeditions have been dismissed as folly that new discoveries are doomed to prejudice.

Lessons from Previous Expeditions

It is clear that historical explorers of the subject suffered pain and humiliation. When Josephine Butler crusaded in 1870 for the abolition of child prostitution and railed against men in high station who exploited children, she was reviled and treated obscenely by London police and brothel keepers alike. When William Stead, editor of the *Pall Mall Gazette*, supported her cause, he spent 3 months in prison (Rush, 1980).

Ambroise Tardieu (cited by Masson, 1984, pp. 14-54), the dean of forensic medicine in France, published in 1860 a startling exposé entitled "a Medico-Legal Study of Cruelty and Brutal Treatment Inflicted on Children." He had discovered and described in detail what was to be acknowledged a hundred years later as the Battered Child Syndrome (Kempe, Silverman, Steele, Droegemueller, & Silver, 1962). His carefully documented, potentially sensational observations were totally ignored by his peers.

Tardieu uncovered thousands of cases of child sexual abuse in his book on rape. Reviewing an eleven-year period from 1858-1869 he cited 11,576 people accused of completed or attempted rape in France. Of these, almost 80% (9,125) involved child victims, mostly girls aged 4-12 (Masson, 1984, p. 23). Tardieu's work engendered a rich, if transient, school of victimology within French legal medicine, including the publication of a new journal, *Archives of Criminal Anthropology and the Penal Sciences,* which solicited studies of child sexual abuse.

Tardieu generated an oasis of concern for children in a generally indifferent, adult-preoccupied society. Challenging the tradition that children typically lied about sexual assault, a few clinicians dared to argue for the truth and reality of those complaints. Such trust in children invited adult retaliation. Despite Tardieu's enormous influence on other aspects of forensic medicine, his belief in sexual abuse was rejected by his successors.

Within a year of Tardieu's death, Alfred Fournier took the platform of the Academy of Medicine on October 26, 1880, to proclaim that children were faking sexual abuse. In a widely quoted address entitled "Simulation of Sexual Attacks on Young Children" he warned that respectable men were targets of extortion from perfidious children and their lower-class parents (Masson, 1984).

Paul Brouardel, Tardieu's student and heir to the chair of legal medicine at the University of Paris, teamed with Fournier in disavowing Tardieu and attacking the treachery of children: "Girls accuse their fathers of imaginary assaults on them or on other children in order to obtain their freedom to give themselves over to debauchery" (quoted in Masson, 1984, p. 44). Brouardel asserted that 60% to 80% of children's complaints were unfounded. His 1909 comments about misguided believers are a perfect harbinger of arguments used today to silence complaints in custody cases and preschools:

> It can happen that the parents act in good faith, but that in their ignorance of infantile pathology they take simple inflammations of the vulva to be the result of criminal sexual assaults on their child. Panicked by findings that seem to her very grave and significant, the mother presses the child with questions and reaches, unconsciously, it must be added, the point where she suggests to the child an account that will serve as the basis for the future accusations. Indeed if the mother's ignorance is one of the elements of the slander, the other is the extreme suggestibility of the child. (Masson, 1984, p. 45)

Brouardel coined an attractive argument for victim blame. His explanation in the definitive address of the 1880s, "The Causes of Error in Expert

Opinion with Respect to Sexual Assaults" (1883), is echoed unchanged in the forensic arguments of the 1980s:

> The child comforts herself by telling herself fantasies that she knows are false on every point. . . . This child, to whom one ordinarily paid only the most minor attention, finds an audience that is willing to listen to her with a certain solemnity and to take cognizance of the creations of her imagination. She grows in her own esteem, she herself becomes a personage, and nothing will ever get her to admit that she deceived her family and the first people who questioned her. (Masson, 1984, pp. 44-45)

Those who took up the cause of the children were quickly forgotten. Those who blamed the complainers (the children, their parents, and anyone else who believed the children) could be assured of adult approval and power. In 1882, Dr. Claude Bourdin passed on the challenge in "Children Who Lie": "It is up to the educators and particularly medical doctors to destroy the myth of the infallible sincerity of the child" (Masson, 1984, p. 48).

Sigmund Freud was one medical doctor who, for a time, attempted to refute that challenge. Had he prevailed in his early assertion that child sexual assault was commonplace and that it caused emotional illness in many of its victims, he might have shifted the balance of victimization in future generations and changed the course of history. Instead, by reversing his seduction theory Freud gave the world a powerful, scientific "endorsement of incredulity" (Goodwin, 1985, p. 5), which has been counter-therapeutic and repressive to anyone appealing for help with actual abuse. Speculation about how it might have been is irrelevant, however, because if the young scientist had stuck to his first position he would have forfeited his right to influence anyone. He would have been overpowered and invalidated, his name relegated along with Tardieu to a footnote in the arcane history of premature explorers of child trauma. Until it was time for society to believe in the more basic concept of child abuse, Freud's uncovering of sexual abuse could have no more potential to influence social policy and to protect children than Tardieu's discoveries 35 years earlier.

Fortunately for Freud, if not for society, the young researcher bowed to the scorn and abuse he received from his mentors. The dramatic story of his brief advocacy and subsequent recantation of his seduction theory is already well documented (Goodwin, 1985; Herman, 1981; Masson, 1984; Peters, 1976; Rush, 1980) and it will not be repeated in detail here. Freud hoped to make history with his presentation of "The Aetiology of Hysteria" before the Vienna Society for Psychiatry and Neurology on April 21, 1896.

He believed he had found the fountainhead of mental illness in connecting hysteria to early childhood sexual assault. Within two weeks he was feeling the pain of the inevitable alienation. "I am as isolated as you could wish me to be: the word has been given out to abandon me, and a void is forming around me" (Masson, 1984, p. 10).

Freud found acceptance and power with the assertion of a new theory, a universal conflict presumably underlying all mental illness. The Oedipus Complex, which was to become the irreducible foundation of psychoanalysis, was a perfect reversal of the seduction theory. Now children were traumatized not by actual sexual assault but by projections of their own wishful masturbatory fantasies. Complaints against adult caretakers reflected false images erupting from a child's grandiose demand for possessive control over the parent. Out of the hopeless gap between insatiable child and unreachable adult flowed a river of toxic frustration and vengeance, the true fountainhead of neurosis.

When Freud chose to believe in what he heard from his patients he identified with children and discovered a lost world of hidden pain. In order to join the ranks of his elders he had to renounce that brief sighting and try another route through the mist. Freud pondered whether accusations of sexual abuse were real or fantastic and found there was only one answer for ascension into the fellowship of the elite. By diverting his prodigious awareness into more acceptable channels, Freud took his place as the charismatic center of a distinguished group of physicians who became known as the psychoanalytic circle. Psychoanalysis was to become a dominant force in Western concepts of psychology and social science for the next half century.

One member of the psychoanalytic circle failed to respect the death of the seduction theory. Sandor Ferenczi was, of all the group, most intimately affiliated with the master. Freud spoke of him as a son and his children cherished Ferenczi's merry visits to the household. Ferenczi was the founder of the International Psycho-Analytic Association and a guiding force in psychoanalytic thought. But Freud and the others disowned him in the last year of his life when he insisted on reexploring sexual assault.

Ferenczi was tantalized by the glimpses of sexual trauma that glimmered out of his analysands' most murky and hesitant recollections. He discovered that an authoritarian manner and analytic aloofness were too imposing to allow patients to risk retrieving humiliating secrets. He experimented with a radically different style of "mutual analysis," in which by becoming less authoritarian he could create a reassuring contrast between himself and the overbearing antagonist in previous molestations. *"It is this confidence that establishes the contrast between the present and the unbearable traumatogenic past,* the contrast that is absolutely necessary for the patient in order to enable him to re-experience the past no longer as hallucinatory reproduction but as an objective memory" (Ferenczi, 1932, p. 160). He found that the most traumatic events were isolated from conscious recollection but could be retrieved in trancelike states, during which patients seemed to be living through all their experiences and feelings as if they were actually a child again. They could reach and sustain this state only if the analyst avoided expressing any prejudgment or interpretations: "The patient gone off into his trance is *a child indeed* who no longer reacts to intellectual explanations, only perhaps to maternal friendliness; without it he feels lonely and abandoned in his greatest need" (p. 160). During these frightening sessions Ferenczi actually took the role of a mother, cradling the patient on his lap and offering reassuring kisses and caresses.

Ferenczi's radical experiments were alarming on several counts. From the available record it is hard to know which was more objectionable to Freud, the departure from accepted analytic technique, the apparent erotization of the analysis, or Ferenczi's insistent voyages into the off-limit fogbanks of sexual trauma. The psychoanalytic ring was bound to close against the threat. Like Freud 36 years before, Ferenczi hoped to change entrenched beliefs by presenting outrageous discoveries. And like his mentor before him, Ferenczi was banished from kinship. Unlike his teacher, Ferenczi did not recant his beliefs, so he remains an awkward footnote in the chronicle of scientific thought.

Sandor Ferenczi presented his climactic paper "Confusion of Tongues Between Adults and the Child" to the International Psycho-Analytic Congress in Wiesbaden in September 1932. Eight months later (May 24, 1933), he was dead. His final work was taken as reason enough for Freud to prove that Ferenczi's terminal illness had left him crazy (Masson, 1984, p. 182), especially since it was such a tenacious perseveration of the naive beliefs that Freud himself had already disowned.

Discarded Lessons

What Ferenczi learned from his patients and presented at Wiesbadden sounds not crazy but brilliant in the light of present concerns. Like Tardieu and Freud, Ferenczi established that childhood sexual trauma was common in the best of families, and that it was devastating to emotional development. Anticipating the incredulity that still discredits normal victim behavior, he explained the silence and the paradoxical compliance of the abused children:

> The overpowering force and authority of the adult makes them dumb [mute] and can rob them of their senses. *The same anxiety, however, if it reaches a certain maximum, compels them to subordinate themselves like automata to the will of the aggressor, to divine each one of his desires and to gratify these; completely oblivious of themselves they identify themselves with the aggressor.* (Ferenczi, 1932, p. 162)

He knew that children will be trapped into silent maladjustments if they are not believed by their parents:

> Usually the relation to a second adult—in the case quoted above, the mother—is not intimate enough for the child to find help there; timid attempts towards this end are refused by her as nonsensical. The misused child changes into a mechanical, obedient automation or becomes defiant, but is unable to account for the reasons of his defiance. His sexual life remains undeveloped or assumes perverted forms. (p. 163)

And he anticipated the connection between sexual assault and dissociative states, including a remarkable prescience for what would be rediscovered 50 years later as multiple-personality disorder:

> When the child recovers from such an attack, he feels enormously confused, in fact, split—innocent and culpable at the same time—and his confidence in the testimony of his own senses is broken. (p. 162)

> If the shocks increase in number during the development of the child, the number and the various kinds of splits in the personality increase too, and soon it becomes extremely difficult to maintain contact without confusion with all the fragments, each of which behaves as a separate personality yet does not know of even the existence of the others. (p. 165)

"Confusion of Tongues Between Adults and the Child" is a humble appeal to an all-knowing, adult-centered world to revisit the tenderness of children. Ferenczi's central message is not only that child sexual abuse is dreadfully important, but that authoritarian pretense deafens adults and ties the tongues of victims against meaningful dialogue and discovery. He tried to tell us that unless we can look behind our intellectual reassurances and learn from those we have learned to belittle, we will never discover the origins of our most hidden pain.

A Societal Blind Spot

In every eye there is a spot that is incapable of sight. The optic disc exists as a black hole right next to the central point of clearest vision. Yet anyone who has not learned the trick of finding it would swear there is no such void.

Throughout history there have been human beliefs and group phenomena that exhibit the perceptual equivalent of a blind spot. A people will develop a cherished view and defend it against revision, despite the presence of a glaring central defect. It took 18 centuries to give up the sacred notion that the world was the center of the universe, for example, despite an irrefutable accumulation of evidence to the contrary.

Something of the same dilemma confronts the potential believer in child sexual abuse. Anyone proclaiming it as vitally important imposes a dismal flaw in our hope for a just and fair society. All of our systems of justice, reason, and power have been adjusted to ignore the possibility of such a fatal flaw. Our very sense of enlightenment insists that anything *that* important could not escape our attention. Where could it hide? Parents would find it out. Doctors would see it. The courts would spot it. Victims would tell their psychiatrists. It would be obvious in psychological tests. Our best minds would know it. It is more reasonable to argue that young upstarts are making trouble. You can't trust kids. Untrained experts are creating a wave of hysteria. They ask leading questions. No family is safe from the invasion of the childsavers. It's time to get back to common sense. We are an enlightened society.

We were not so enlightened that we rewarded Galileo for unwanted truth in 1633 nor Ferenczi in 1933. We were even more strident in impeaching the child believers in 1986 than we were in silencing Freud in 1896. It took a hundred years to acknowledge Tardieu's discovery of battered children and we are again trying to discredit his documentation of the sexually abused.

What if we *are* protecting a massive societal blind spot? What if judges have been trained not to hear, doctors schooled not to see, and psychiatrists encouraged not to believe? What if the instruments of social scientists have been calibrated to filter out an insistent static of posttraumatic pain that is central to the origins of violence and emotional disturbance? What if our charts are still embellished with monsters to prevent explorers from going over the brink? Who will sail beyond allowable frontiers and where would such a voyage end?

In a rational world there should be rational avenues to enlightenment. Thousands of people have survived the trip in the hidden world of sexual abuse. Why not ask them what it was like?

Adult Survivors:
Pilots into the Fog

Unlike other social issues that can be defined and verified by the observations of the people involved, sexual abuse depends largely on unstated inference. Our view depends on that tiny fraction of reports that are voiced and recorded, and then only on those which we choose to believe. We miss the vast prevalence of victims who remain silent. Another dimension of abuse is lost even to those who have experienced it: Those who develop the merciful gift of dissociation will have no memory of intolerable abuse (Putnam, 1985).

We have avoided confronting child sexual abuse not only through protective disbelief among the outsiders but through dedicated hiding by the insiders. Much as child victims steer through the hazards of adult disbelief with the self-discrediting behaviors of the sexual abuse accommodation syndrome (Summit, 1983), adults hide from exposure and try to avoid connections with their past. Adult survivors do not usually present their shameful credentials for inspection. They pass as ordinary citizens, as eccentrics, as mental patients and suicides. A tiny fraction become child molesters, rapists, even serial killers. Whatever the outcome, we will all take pains to ignore any linkage to childhood trauma.

Survivors can lead us, one by one, into the oblivion of their past, but only if we are willing to follow, like Ferenczi, without protest, steering the hulk of our presumptive wisdom through uncharted waters. We have to consider that even the distorted recollections of someone who has survived the journey might be more reliable than the beautiful engravings of landlocked geographers. Like Columbus, we have to take the chance that the mapmakers were wrong. And like Ferenczi, we must risk losing our father if we are to discover our child.

Sarah, at 32 knew she had a problem with her father. She overachieved to qualify for his approval and cut her skin to punish herself for continuing failures. She was dreadfully afraid of relationships and used obesity and contemptuous sarcasm to keep people at bay. She had been suicidal, depressed, and obsessed with anxiety for the past 6 years, dependent on tranquilizers and a psychoanalyst for survival. Her extremes in avoidance and dependency and her flamboyant reversals of affect were classic for borderline character, as was her little-girl naivete and tendency to posture and talk like a baby when stressed.

Sarah experienced idetic images of sexual contact with her father during a transference crisis in therapy, eventually evolving memories of anal and vaginal rape as well as other times when she playfully and expertly drew her father into sexual interaction. Initially she was sure these were monstrous fantasies unearthed from her crazy, evil core. She hated herself for entertaining such thoughts about her beloved father even as she hated herself for the possibility that she might have actually done these things with him.

Stephanie was in continuous psychiatric care for 25 years, including 3 years in closed wards following a psychotic break and suicide attempt at age 16. She kept trying to appease the devil, who shouted inside her head to voice judgment and demand punishment for her stupidity. Massive amounts of medication barely muted the command hallucinations, and she continued to hope that death would appease the affront that her miserable presence imposed on the world.

For Stephanie, images of sexual abuse emerged first as drawings made by a child interspersed among other scenes drawn for recreation by the recovering adult. Although Stephanie had learned earlier, at tremendous mutual effort, to trust her therapist and to communicate her forbidden thoughts, and although they had eventually discussed grotesque excesses of physical and emotional abuse, memories of sexual abuse were last to emerge and were accompanied by unprecedented depths of self-punishment and pain.

Both these survivors required painful effort to remember and to accept that they had been sexually abused. They also relied on therapists who came to believe, but not to insist, that the memories were real. Ferenczi and Freud both based their discoveries on patients who required extraordinary guidance to penetrate the amnesia that protected their childhood idealism. Freud argued persuasively in 1896 that it was the painful elusiveness that proved that the memories were neither invented nor coached (Masson, 1984, p. 91).

When Freud renounced the seduction theory he apologized for his impetuous, wishful logic, concluding instead that he had influenced those 18 patients to invent substantiation of his own designs. No wonder survivors who attempt to validate forbidden glimpses of their past have typically encountered disbelief and rejection in therapy. And no wonder the expert witnesses who discredit children rely on Freud's secondary, adult-protective rationalizations to discredit his rash, initial belief in the empiric evidence that children's disclosures were real. Even though over half of the psychiatric inpatient population may be victims of abuse (Carmen, Rieber, & Mills, 1984) such information is rarely considered in diagnostic or treatment formulations. Judith Herman discovered the clinical importance of incest during her psychiatric training, not only from the pain she found in the many patients who acknowledged abuse, but from the backlash she experienced in presenting such cases to her mentors. "They convinced us that any secret so long and vigorously suppressed must be worth pursuing" (1981, p. vii).

Dissociative States

Disbelief of childhood victimization by psychiatrists is not the cause of societal avoidance as much as an authoritarian reflection of it. Underlying all the mutually complementary temptations to avoid the pain of discovery is a fundamental challenge to logic: Something worth believing must be something worth remembering. If something is *real* it is available to consciousness. Anything unthinkable tends to be unspeakable and unknowable. Guardians of logic will reject assertions of the unknown.

The core confusion and the perennial objection to validation resides in a characteristic of the abuse cycle that we have repeatedly refused to acknowledge: dissociation. The more dreadful the abuse the more likely it will be shielded from consciousness. If we define abuse according to what survivors choose to remember, we systematically ignore those most telling assaults that must be forgotten.

Freud alleged that the abuse was real precisely because it was actively forgotten, only to disavow it later on for the same reason. Janet described the mechanisms of posttraumatic dissociation and symptom formation rather perfectly in 1889, only to be overshadowed by the Freudian revisions favoring Oedipal, intrapsychic trauma. Ferenczi's success in loosening the tongues of his mute, dissociated patients fell on traumatically deafened ears. Stephanie and Sarah built their tattered lives around silent, damaged children that they hid from their therapists and even from themselves. Modern researchers who search out the custodian of secret childhood trauma hiding within multiple personalities are accused by more orthodox psychiatrists of creating an hysterical illusion. Those who discover the hidden pain are condemned for manipulating patients into imaginary illness to suit the therapists' grandiose and impertinent beliefs (Goodwin, 1985).

Herman and Schatcow (1986) found that fully 62% of the adults in an incest survivors' group had earlier "forgotten" all or most of their childhood abuse. Country Walk children, theoretically too young to be capable of operational thought, managed for almost a year to protect their homes from any crossover to the ravages of their other world. Their tormentor, Iliana, herself a teenaged victim of her husband's sexual tyranny, presented to the outer world an alibi of physiologically perfect composure. Even when she later described her participation in the unthinkable, it was as an automation, somehow detached from conscience and ordinary consciousness: "*I* didn't do those things. I couldn't do those things. Frank *made* me do them" (I. Fuster, personal communication, September 27, 1985). What she described, in addition to unimaginable adult depravity, was the picture of toddlers able to concentrate their attention on playing with a toy as if oblivious to the concurrent invasion of their rectums and vaginas (Hollingsworth, 1986).

What these survivors are telling us, if we could only bear to synthesize the essence of such disparate and paradoxical reports, is that much of the hidden world of child sexual abuse is very nearly unbearable. Sexual touching, so often trivialized by words such as fondling or molestation (annoyance), is only the physical expression of a climate of invasion, isolation, and abandonment. Sexual abuse is so developmentally toxic that it must be walled off and enshrouded in a kind of psychological cocoon, set aside from the mainstream of consciousness to remain dormant or to grow as it will, emerging unpredictably in some alien metamorphosis.

What we might see in these apparitions, if we were not so afraid of recognizing their origins, is the challenge to apply preventive and therapeutic alternatives to psychic avoidance. Abuse is terrible enough, but ignoring abuse makes the experience intolerable. Institutionalizing ignorance denies every human being the advantages of enlightenment. Discovery may seem to be overburdened by pain, but confrontation, acceptance, and specialized, countertraumatic therapies can provide unprecedented growth and inspiring recovery. Sarah is now a successful executive who is learning to keep her "child" safe and growing at home. Stephanie earned a master's degree in psychology with highest honors. She is equally impressive in counseling handicapped children and in shepherding the growth of her own hidden children. She has been free of medication for nearly ten years and has sustained and overcome several bouts of life-threatening physical illness. She is self-endorsing and enthusiastically alive.

Dissociation is not a weakness or a pathological trait, any more than being sexually victimized is a confirmation of badness or unworthiness. Children will be victimized as long as adults allow it, and healthy, normal children will find a better refuge in their minds if we will not provide it in reality. The perpetrators and the victims understand what must be done to protect the secret, and together we as a society of unresponsive adults insist that survival is better served by dissociation than by disclosure.

Dissociation offers the appeal to children to buy time in their own generation, in hopes of finding healing acceptance and caring in the next. Unlike the great cryogenic fiasco this is a real and reasonable dream. The frozen remnants of a hopeless child *can* be revived and restored, if we will only use without prejudice and fear the techniques already available.

Considering the numbers in need and the potential benefits of specific services, it is a grotesque reflection of our societal blind spot that there is no standard of recognition, evaluation, diagnosis, referral, or treatment for survivors of sexual abuse. Each individual is at risk of being ignored, misdiagnosed, mistreated, or overtreated in a random search for professional understanding.

Unrecognized Challenges

Even as society moves haltingly toward recognition and healing of some of the childhood victims, it is repelled and in danger of rejecting all victims in the face of newer, still more threatening discoveries. We are willing to concede that girls may be at risk of sexualization by their fathers but we fight back at claims that diffuse into more sacred domains. These forbidden sanctuaries include victimization of boys, women who are victimizers, and the unholy chimera of everything forbidden and impossible: Sexual abuse of boys and girls by men and women as part of bizarre, cultic rituals.

There are numbing implications that occult groups preying on children do exist, possibly in substantial numbers. Therapists find ritual abuse in the childhood of about a fifth of their adult patients with multiple-personality disorder (Braun, 1986). Children in many of the current multiple-victim cases describe sacrifice, bloodshed, and murder. These allegations are so outrageous that reasonable people refuse to discuss them and believers are quashed into silence. Considering the lessons from legendary witch hunts, it seems obvious to many that these, too, are dangerous little voices coached by overzealous inquisitors.

Yet that reassuring argument is insubstantial and dismally familiar. We seem to welcome the "reasonable explanation" that grotesque perversions don't really exist. A hundred years ago an influential doctor proclaimed, "the enormity of the accusation destroys its probability" in dismissing the claims of a diagnosed hysteric that she and her brother had been sexualized by their father and mother (Masson, 1984, p. 49). Freud found several female perpetrators in his original research. Of the 18 victims he described, 6 were males. Two of his disciples in the psychoanalytic circle, Jung and Rank, were themselves male victims of child sexual victimization (Goldwert, 1986). The study of pedophiles establishes an overwhelming, often exclusive preference of boys, leading Gene Abel (1987) to believe that hidden boy victims must outnumber victimized girls. How many are blind to victimization issues because they have never come to grips with their own assaults in childhood?

Country Walk should assure us that the smallest children can hide the biggest secrets, and that the best parents can be the last to know. Big Pine should prove that no conspiracy is too pervasive to hide. It should be self-evident that boys can be appealing victims, that female caretakers are not immune from subversion, and that perversion thrives on perversity. We have no right to believe in only the most normal of the abnormal. We should be wary of profiles and precedents that prejudge what is incredible about a victim's account. There is no objective point of reference for the recent warning from the official voice of child psychiatry that "the field of child sexual abuse is rapidly changing as we move from underreporting to the problem of hypervigilence and frequent overreporting" (Shetky, 1986, p. 490). Again and again we close ranks against discomfort, not because we have explored its outer limits but because the earliest discoveries are already too much to bear.

On a Clear Day

There is a sad, self-preserving irony about a world that cannot see its own cruelty filled with victims who can't give voice to their pain. After 125 years of discarded enlightenment, we still act as if victims are freaks and as if it is a virtue to be ignorant of sexual victimization. We pretend nobody is involved, even though the veterans may outnumber the recruits. Projections of any of the prevalence surveys to include elective and dissociative denials would insist that childhood sexual assault is a normative experience, yet we ignore the implications of a society populated with the walking wounded.

Any gathering of our associates and friends contains people who were molested as children. Every extended family, every neighborhood, every church congregation, every medical society, every class in law school, and most every football team, legislative caucus, and jury conceals people who are hiding unspeakable memories of "unusual" childhood sexual experiences. Those experiences may have been agonizing or ecstatic or a confusing mixture of both, but the fact that they can't be shared says something about our collective fear of finding out.

We are all players in a strange charade in which everyone assumes the role of the untouched. Perpetrators circulate in unknown numbers, making policy and influencing opinion while a horde of survivors shrinks from one another as if each were the enemy. Some of those who assume they are untouched by sexual abuse are aggressively indifferent to the problem, protective of adults and judgmental of victims in order to distance themselves from their own hurt child imprisoned within. In the absence of someone to call roll, and in the preservation of agonizing shame, each survivor exists as an alien hiding among an army of peers. If we could find the courage to face our superstitions head on, we would see that the apparitions veiled in the fog aren't really monsters at all. They are our children. They are us.

The world of denial is not quite what it was in 1860 or in 1895 or in 1930. In this latest cycle of discovery we believed in the Battered Child Syndrome and by 1965 enacted laws to require professional awareness. Scientific interest has grown for the last 20 years to produce an impressive foundation of data (Finkelhor et al., 1986). Specialized treatment programs, including recovery groups for survivors, are growing in numbers and in stature. A total of 1,600 professionals attended the Fourth National Conference on the Sexual Victimization of Children (Children's Hospital, 1986). And there are leaders who are extending the roll call among the invisible army. Christina Crawford's *Survivor's Network* (1986) has a mailing list of 3,000. There is a growing national constituency among feminist advocacy groups and other community awareness programs. There may be hope for a survivors' revolt that will finally open our ears to children and open our eyes to the societal flaws we have chosen to overlook.

If we are wise enough to learn from our children and strong enough to resist the aggressive objections of our adult insecurity, we will allow a growing recognition of our hidden pain. Clinicians, researchers, social scientists, and the army of survivors emerging within the professions as well as throughout the general public will endorse the wisdom of mutual recognition and the power of massive disclosure.

On that clear day we can turn the pressures for dissociation into agendas for correction. We will be ready to explore the potential of human development freed from fundamental betrayal and abandonment. It is not grandiose to suggest that such a shift in caring might strengthen women, sensitize men, and actually eliminate substantial amounts of heartbreak, alienation, mental disorder, and mayhem. If we can accomplish that level of rational clarity we will have redeemed the discarded promise of Sandor Ferenczi (1932b, p. 294):

It would please me if you would take the trouble to examine, in practice and in theory, what I have communicated here, and especially if you would follow my advice to pay closer attention than you have in the past to the strange, much veiled, yet critical manner of thinking and speaking of your children, patients and students, and, so to speak, loosen their tongues. You will hear much that is instructive.

REFERENCES

Abel, G. E., with Harlow, N. (1987, August). The child abuser. *Redbook,* pp. 98-100, 138-139.

Armstrong, L. (1978). *Kiss daddy goodnight.* New York: Hawthorn.

Braun, B. G. (1986, September 19-21). Comments as chair of the plenary discussion forum at the third annual meeting of the International Society for the Study of Multiple Personality and Dissociation, Chicago.

Carmen, E. H., Rieber, P. P., & Mills, T. (1984). Victims of violence and psychiatric illness. *American Journal of Psychiatry, 141,* 378-383.

Children's Hospital National Medical Center, Washington, DC. (1986, May 14-17). The fourth national conference on the sexual victimization of children, New Orleans.

Crawford, C. (Ed.). (1986). *Survivor's network,* 18653 Ventura Blvd. #143, Tarzana, CA 91356. Vol. 2, no. 2.

Ferenczi, S. (1932a). Confusion of tongues between adults and the child: The language of tenderness and of passion. In M. Balint (Ed.) & E. Mosbacher (Trans.), *Final contributions to the problems and methods of psychoanalysis.* (1955). New York: Basic Books. (The reference date refers to Ferenczi's presentation to the International Congress. The paper was first published in German in 1933 [*Zeitschrift für Psychoanalyse*]. First publication in English was in the *International Journal of Psychoanalysis* [1949], *30,* 225-230.)

Ferenczi, S. (1932b). Confusion of tongues between adults and the child (The language of tenderness and the language of [sexual] passion). (A new translation by J. M. Masson & M. Loring). In J. Masson (1984), *The assault on truth* (Appendix C, pp. 283-295). New York: Farrar, Straus & Giroux. (Note: This translation was selected for the final paragraph to correct an apparent error in the 1955 Balint version, in which "speaking *of*" is represented as "speaking *to* your children.")

Finkelhor, D., Araji, S., Baron, L., Browne, A., Peters, S. D., & Wyatt, G. E. (1986). *A sourcebook on child sexual abuse.* Beverly Hills, CA: Sage.

Goldwert, M. (1986). Childhood seduction and the spiritualization of psychology: The case of Jung and Rank. *Child Abuse and Neglect, 10,* 555-557.

Goodwin, J. (1985). Credibility problems in multiple personality disorder patients and abused children. In R. P. Kluft (Ed.), *Childhood antecedents of multiple personality* (pp. 2-19). Washington: American Psychiatric Press.

Hechler, D. (1988). *The battle and the backlash: The child sexual abuse war.* Lexington, MA: Lexington Books.

Herman, J. L. (1981). *Father-daughter incest.* Cambridge, MA: Harvard University Press.

Herman, J. L., & Schatcow, E. (1986, May). *Verification of memories of childhood sexual trauma.* Paper presented at the annual meeting of the American Psychiatric Association, Washington, DC.

Hollingsworth, J. (1986). *Unspeakable acts.* Chicago: Contemporary Books.

Janet, P. (1889). *L'automatisme psychologique.* Paris: J. B. Bailliere.

Kempe, C. H., Silverman, F. N., Steele, B. F., Droegemueller, W., & Silver, H. (1962). The battered child syndrome. *Journal of the American Medical Association, 181,* 17-24.

Lustig, N., Dresser, J. W., Spellman, S. W., & Murray, T. B. (1966). Incest: A family group survival pattern. *Archives of General Psychiatry, 14,* 31-40.

Masson, J. M. (1984). *The assault on truth: Freud's suppression of the seduction theory.* New York: Farrar, Straus & Giroux.

Peters, J. (1976). Children who are victims of sexual assault and the psychology of offenders. *American Journal of Psychotherapy, 30,* 398-432.

Putnam, F. W. (1985). Dissociation as a response to extreme trauma. In R. P. Kluft (Ed.), *Childhood antecedents of multiple personality* (pp. 66-97). Washington: American Psychiatric Press.

Rush, F. (1980). *The best kept secret: Sexual abuse of children.* Englewood Cliffs, NJ: Prentice-Hall.

Sgroi, S. M. (1978). Introduction: A national needs assessment for protecting child victims of sexual assault. In A. W. Burgess, A. N. Groth, L. L. Holmstrom, & S. M. Sgroi (Eds.), *Sexual assault of children and adolescents* (pp. iv-xxii). Lexington, MA: Lexington Books.

Shetky, D. H. (1986). Editorial: Emerging issues in child sexual abuse. *Journal of the American Academy of Child Psychiatry, 25,* 490.

Summit, R. C. (1983). The child sexual abuse accommodation syndrome. *Child Abuse & Neglect, 7,* 177-193.

4

The Trauma of Child Sexual Abuse

Two Models

DAVID FINKELHOR

Research into the impact of sexual abuse on children has passed through two phases, and is entering a third. In what might be called the initial or "catalogue" phase, clinicians recorded the wide range of symptoms and problems that they observed in children and adults who had been sexually abused. Next came the "documentation" phase, in which researchers began to measure the impact using recognized indices of psychopathology, comparison groups, and statistical procedures to try to partial out the specific contribution of the abuse.

Some of the articles in this volume reflect the best of the documentation phase. These and other work (reviewed in Browne & Finkelhor, 1986) portray the following general picture. Groups of individuals who have been sexually abused as children have impaired mental health as shown in both clinical samples and in samples of the general population. For children in the immediate aftermath of the abuse, where most of the work has been done with clinical cases, the most commonly documented symptoms are

AUTHOR'S NOTE: I would like to thank Donna Wilson for help in preparing this manuscript. I also would like to acknowledge the very helpful comments and criticisms of Lucy Berliner, John Briere, David Corwin, Jean Goodwin, Stefanie Peters, Dan Saunders, and Gail Wyatt. The completion of this work has been supported by grants from the National Center on Child Abuse and Neglect, the National Institute of Mental Health, and the Eden Hall Farm Foundation. Correspondence concerning this article should be addressed to David Finkelhor, Family Research Laboratory, University of New Hampshire, Durham, NH 03824.

fears, aggressiveness, and inappropriate sexual behavior. Problems have also been confirmed in the areas of self-esteem, guilt, somatic complaints, concentration, isolation, and an overly intense need to please. For adults, the studies show that 20% to 50% of abused women in the general population have identifiable mental health impairments. The effects most clearly documented are anxiety, depression, dissociation, sexual problems, and drug and alcohol abuse. Sexually abused women have also been shown by several studies to be at higher risk of later victimization. A number of other problems have also been confirmed: poor self-esteem, hostility toward parents, men, or others, feelings of isolation, sleep disturbances, and eating disorders.

Although the important work of documenting the effects of abuse is still far from complete, the field is already moving on into yet a third phase. In this phase, which might be called the "modeling" phase, researchers and clinicians are beginning to propose models to explain why these particular effects occur. These models connect what is known about the phenomenon of sexual abuse with what is observed in the attitudes, feelings, and behavior of victims of sexual abuse, using more general theories about the process of traumatization. This third phase is a crucial one for deepening our understanding of sexual abuse and enlarging our ability to intervene to prevent some of the serious negative consequences of abuse.

Sexual Abuse and
Post-Traumatic Stress

Among the models being proposed to explain the trauma of sexual abuse, the one most frequently mentioned is the *Post-Traumatic Stress Disorder* (PTSD) model. A number of papers have appeared in the literature since 1984 suggesting that the impact of child sexual abuse is best understood by thinking of it and treating it within the framework of PTSD (Courtois, 1986; Donaldson & Gardner, 1985; Eth & Pynoos, 1985; Frederick, 1986; Goodwin, 1985; Lindberg & Distad, 1985). PTSD is an increasingly widely and well-recognized concept, which has been defined by the DSM III (American Psychiatric Association, 1980) as including the following components:

(1) The existence of recognizable stressor that would evoke significant symptoms of distress in almost anyone.

(2) The reexperiencing of the trauma either through (a) recurrent intrusive recollections, (b) dreams, or (c) sudden feelings.

(3) A numbing of responsiveness or reduced involvement in the external world indicated by diminished interest in activities, feelings of estrangement from others, and constricted affect.

(4) In addition, at least two of the following set of symptoms need also be present: hyperalertness, sleep problems, survival guilt, problems with memory or concentration, avoidance of activities or the intensification of symptoms when exposed to stimuli related to the traumatic event.

At its inception, the PTSD concept was formulated exclusively in application to adults, particularly around the trauma of war (Trimble, 1985). Increasingly, however, clinicians have seen its applicability to children as well (Benedek, 1985; Pynoos & Eth, 1985a). PTSD has been applied to the situation of children who have been caught in natural disasters (Frederick, 1985), who have been victims of violent crime (Terr, 1985), who have witnessed the violent death of a loved person (Pynoos & Eth, 1985b), and now to sexual abuse.

Putting sexual abuse into the framework of PTSD has had a number of important salutary effects on the field. First it has provided a clear label and description of a phenomenon that many victims of sexual abuse are suffering from. All the symptoms indicated in the DSM III criteria have been noted singly and in combination in victims of sexual abuse.

Second, the PTSD formulation has suggested that the effects of sexual abuse need to be looked at in a structured way. What may be involved is a syndrome with core etiology, rather than just a catalogue of symptoms.

Third, the notion of PTSD has put sexual abuse into a broader context and erected bridges to other types of trauma. Sexual abuse is no longer seen as totally unique but sharing dynamics with other trauma, the study of which may shed light on sexual abuse.

Fourth, it has brought new interest in sexual abuse. Researchers who have been studying other traumas have seen in sexual abuse an opportunity to study another manifestation of their subject matter.

Fifth, it has increased the salience of the problem of sexual abuse by adding it to the list of well-recognized psychological stressors.

Finally, considering sexual abuse as a form of PTSD may act to reduce some of the lingering stigma that clings to victims. In some quarters there is a prejudice that a person is traumatized by sexual abuse only if she has a hysterical predisposition or an unnecessary preoccupation with sexual puritanism. Such a presumption may be heard in Kinsey, Pomeroy, Martin, and Gebhard's (1953) remark that "it is difficult to understand why a child, except for cultural conditioning should be disturbed at having its genitalia touched." However, talking about sexual abuse as a PTSD-type stressor clearly places sexually abused children in the company of the victims of devastating and uncontrollable disasters, such as wars and earthquakes, and thus challenges the idea that the trauma is self-inflicted.

Problems with PTSD Formulation

All these important contributions are not enough, however. Conceptual marriages can have elegant implications but be fundamentally flawed. The key question is does sexual abuse really fit into PTSD? Before we celebrate that we have found the model that explains the traumatic impact of sexual abuse, we have to acknowledge that the PTSD formulation has some serious limitations. First, it does not adequately account for all the symptoms. Second, it accurately applies only to some of the victims. Finally, and most seriously, it does not truly present a theory that explains how the dynamics of sexual abuse lead to the symptoms noted. These are serious limitations that deserve extended discussion and further study.

Differences in Emphases

First, when critically examined, the fit between PTSD and the symptoms of sexual abuse is somewhat forced. It is true that sexual abuse victims do have PTSD symptoms, and that almost all the symptoms of sexual abuse can be tied to the PTSD framework. But the emphases are different. PTSD puts its central focus on the intrusive imagery, the nightmares, and the numbing and deadness in affect and social relations. Although these symptoms can be present in the aftermath of sexual abuse, they do not include some of the symptoms that have been most stressed by clinicians and researchers. Sexual abuse researchers have tended to emphasize the fear, the depression, the self-blame, and the sexual problems, above others. Although fear and depression fit fairly well (they are not completely the same as the intrusive imagery and numbing described in PTSD), the self-blame and sexual problems reflect a different emphasis. Moreover, Briere and Runtz (1988) cite the commonly observed symptoms of suicidality, substance abuse, and revictimization as also falling outside of the usual PTSD boundaries. These differences are more than a problem of symptom labeling. They reflect a trauma that may share elements with PTSD, but is qualitatively different.

One sign of this difference is the area of the person where researchers see the trauma as located. PTSD locates almost all of the trauma in the affective realm—the explosion of affect or the constriction of affect or the defense against affect. By contrast, with sexual abuse, observers have located the symptoms in the cognitive as well as the affective realm. These cognitive disturbances include distorted beliefs about the self and others, self-blame, sexual misinformation, and sexual confusions. Jehu et al. (1985/1986) state that "women who were sexually abused in childhood often hold distorted beliefs arising from this experience that appear to contribute to mood disturbances such as guilt, low self-esteem and sadness." Corwin (1985), in defining the "sexually abused child's disorder," notes the importance of "age inappropriate awareness" about sexuality, knowledge and interests that have been inculcated prematurely in the child. The self-blame and negative attitudes toward the self seem to be acquired by learning via the reactions that others have toward the child. Looking at sexual abuse in the PTSD framework may tend to obscure and give lesser importance to these cognitive, and possibly other, traumas that are not emphasized in the PTSD formulation.

Victims Without PTSD

The fact that symptoms in sexual abuse may go beyond the affective realm does not necessarily mean PTSD is absent. However, the second problem with the PTSD formulation is that, for many victims of sexual abuse, the PTSD symptoms *are* absent. Kilpatrick and colleagues (1986), for example, specifically evaluated PTSD symptomatology in a sample of 126 adult women sexually abused as children and found it *currently* present in only 10% and *ever present* in only 36%. Some of these victims seemed to manifest other symptoms common to sexual abuse, such as depression, substance abuse, and sexual problems, without the signs of PTSD.

Thus when Frederick (1986) says, "All victims of child molestation usually develop Post-Traumatic Stress Disorder," or Goodwin (1985) says, "Most incest victims who request treatment meet criteria for Post-Traumatic Disorder," this is an exaggeration. Moreover, it is an exaggeration with some possibly dangerous effects. Clinicians could easily subsume sexual abuse into PTSD and come to rely on PTSD symptomatology for diagnosing a history of sexual abuse. Expert witnesses may soon testify in court cases that alleged victims probably were not abused because they do not manifest PTSD. Not only would they be missing many real victims, but it might lead to the presumption that a sexual abuse victim without PTSD was necessarily less traumatized. These are unwarranted inferences based on current research and are reasons to urge that the notion of sexual abuse trauma be kept distinct from PTSD.

Theoretical Problems

Ultimately, however, the best way to check the fit of a model is to look at its explanatory underpinnings and see if they apply. Does the theory of PTSD make sense in regard to sexual abuse? Does sexual abuse fit its dynamics? Unfortunately, PTSD does not have a clearly formulated theory. As a model, it is mostly a syndrome defined by a group of symptoms, rather than an explanation of how these symptoms develop. There is no consensus on theory. Different people have tried to explain the general PTSD syndrome in different ways. Unfortunately, no explanation fits the problem of sexual abuse very well.

For example, in one generalized formulation of PTSD, Pynoos and Eth (1985b, p. 38) say that the PTSD symptoms result from "an overwhelming event resulting in helplessness in the face of intolerable danger, anxiety and instinctual arousal." Although not a detailed explanation, it is clear how this is derived from the experiences around which the PTSD formulation was built—war combat, natural disaster, stranger rape. The fit is less clear with sexual abuse. Although some sexual abuse, that which is most like stranger rape, conforms to this model ("overwhelming event," "helplessness," "intolerable danger"), much does not. Much sexual abuse does not occur under conditions of danger, threat, and violence. Many abusers, misusing their authority or manipulating moral standards, act with the child's trust (Armstrong, 1978; Finkelhor, 1979). Sometimes the fact of having been abused is recognized only in retrospect as children learn more about appropriate sexual conduct. The trauma of sexual abuse can result from the meaning of the act ("I am being exploited") as much as from the physical danger. Moreover, sexual abuse may be less of an "event" than a "relationship" or a "situation." It often goes on for a period, and may change in meaning over time. The trauma may come from the betrayal in the relationship or from being trapped in a situation, rather than from an overwhelming event. The fact that it often goes on over a period of time and derives its trauma from meanings as much as from physical threat makes it quite different from the model invoked in Pynoos and Eth's (1985b), and others, view of PTSD.

Another commonly cited explanation of PTSD is based on Horowitz's (1976) work. Horowitz posited a completion tendency in human beings that is triggered by the traumatic event. The mind tries to integrate the experience of the event into existing "schemata," to which it is foreign; until this integration is complete, the memories of the event remain active and have a tendency to interrupt other functioning. This explains the repetitions and the nightmares. The numbing seen in PTSD patients is accounted for as a defense people use against the breakthrough of these intrusive images (Green, Wilson, & Lindy, 1985).

Here again, although the theory seems well suited to traumas such as war shock and rape, it seems a very superficial account of the trauma of sexual abuse. The notion of a completion tendency may explain why sexual abuse victims have nightmares and flashbacks, and why children may reenact abuse situations with their playmates. But it does not explain the anger that victims feel, the worthlessness, and the self-blame. Moreover, the problem for some sexual abuse victims is not failure to integrate the sexual abuse experience, but what might be called an "overintegration" of the experience, that is, they take the behavior learned in the abusive situation and apply it indiscriminately to other situations where it is inappropriate.

Another intriguing explanation of the PTSD phenomenon comes from Janoff-Bulman (1985). She traces the symptoms to the fact that a traumatic event shatters the assumptions that victims have held about the operation of the world, assumptions such as "I am safe," "I am good," and "The world is just and bad things do not happen to good people." She writes, "The state of disequilibrium that results [from the shattering of assumptions] is marked by intense stress and anxiety, and characteristic symptoms are often those described by post-traumatic stress disorder" (p. 22). This theory, like the others, describes some of what happens to many sexual abuse victims, and it also, interestingly, is able to encompass some of the cognitive influences mentioned earlier ("I must be bad because a bad thing happened to me"). But here again some portions of the characteristic sexual abuse symptoms do not fit. Sexualized behavior seems better accounted for by learning or conditioning than by the shattering of assumptions. Moreover, Janoff-Bulman's explanation more than others raises the question of whether PTSD theory can be easily transferred from adults to children. Certainly there are great differences in the assumptions children make about the world compared to adults.

In summary then, the PTSD model leaves something to be desired in its application to sexual abuse. It clearly describes a portion of the problem—some symptoms and some victims—but it is less than complete. To encompass sexual abuse fully, the notion of PTSD could be broadened, as some have tried to do, both in relation to sexual abuse and in relation to other stresses, such as illness (Nir, 1985) or divorce (Wilson, Smith, & Johnson, 1985). But as the notion of PTSD is broadened, it loses meaning, becoming little more than a list of all the symptoms of mental health impairment, which are, almost by definition, signs of stress. At that point, the PTSD concept loses much of its usefulness and violates the spirit of psychiatric diagnosis itself.[i]

Understanding the problem of sexual abuse will not benefit from being subsumed within a diluted and atheoretical notion of PTSD. Because of some of the unique characteristics of responses to sexual abuse, particularly some of the sexual trauma, it seems preferable to delineate a separate syndrome relating to it. This syndrome could use some of the concepts and dynamics described in PTSD, but remain specific to sexual abuse in its particulars. Such has been the recommendation of other researchers and clinicians as well, such as Briere and Runtz (1988), Corwin (1985), and Summit (1983).

Four Traumagenic
Dynamics of Sexual Abuse

An alternative to the PTSD formulation is a model we have developed and called the Traumagenic Dynamics Model of Child Sexual Abuse (Finkelhor & Browne, 1985). It is an eclectic, but comprehensive model that suggests a variety of different dynamics to account for the variety of different types of symptoms. It incorporates some elements of the PTSD model, but is also broad enough to explain sexual abuse of the non-PTSD variety.

The model proposes four traumagenic dynamics to account for the impact of sexual abuse: traumatic sexualization, betrayal, stigmatization, and powerlessness. A traumagenic dynamic is an experience that alters a child's cognitive or emotional orientation to the world and causes trauma by distorting the child's self-concept, worldview, or affective capacities. For example, the dynamic of stigmatization distorts the child's sense of his or her own value or worth. The dynamic of powerlessness distorts the child's sense of his or her ability to control his or her own life. When a person tries to cope with the world through these distortions, what we see are the psychological and behavioral problems that are characteristic of sexually abused children and adults.

There are some important aspects of this model that are important to note in light of the earlier discussion of PTSD. First, PTSD is incorporated into the model; it is one distortion among others, particularly a distortion of affective capacities. Second, the model includes both affective and cognitive distortions; so it may be children's ideas about the world that are affected as well as their emotional responses. Third, the trauma is not described as "shattering" of assumptions as in Janoff-Bulman (1985), but as a distortion of assumptions. Since children are impressionable, they may be traumatized when they are taught or inducted into incorrect, misleading, or dysfunctional assumptions. Finally, the distortions are not seen as a failure to incorporate the new experience into previous schemata, as in Horowitz's (1976) notion of PTSD. The assumptions and coping mechanisms the child develops may be adaptive and well integrated to the experience of the abuse and its aftermath, but may be dysfunctional in coping with a world where abuse is not the norm.

At this point, each of the traumagenic dynamics will be described to show what it includes and the impact it makes.

Traumatic Sexualization

Traumatic sexualization, the first dynamic, refers to the conditions in sexual abuse under which a child's sexuality is shaped in developmentally inappropriate and interpersonally dysfunctional ways. Several distinct processes combine to contribute to traumatic sexualization.

(1) Sexually abused children are often rewarded, by offenders, for sexual behavior that is inappropriate to their level of development.

(2) Because of the rewards, sexually abused children learn to use sexual behavior, appropriate or inappropriate, as a strategy for manipulating others to get their needs met.

(3) Because of the attention they receive, certain parts of sexually abused children's anatomy becomes fetishized and given distorted importance and meaning.

(4) Children become confused and acquire outright misconceptions about sexual behavior and sexual morality as a result of things that offenders tell them or ways that offenders behave.

(5) Finally, a child's sexuality can become traumatized when frightening and unpleasant memories become associated in the child's mind with sexual activity.

These are among the most important of the dynamics that traumatize a child's sexual capacities. They are among the dynamics unique to sexual abuse since they do not occur in other traumas of childhood such as parental divorce or physical abuse.

Betrayal

In the second dynamic, betrayal, children discover that someone on whom they were vitally dependent has caused them or wishes to cause them harm. Present to some degree in most abuse situations, betrayal can operate in several ways. Sometimes the betrayal occurs at the time of the first abuse, as children realize that a person they trusted is treating them with callous disregard for their wishes or well-being. In other cases of abuse, children experience the betrayal belatedly, in the realization that they were tricked into doing something bad through the use of lies or misrepresentations.

It is often assumed that the main component of betrayal lies in the closeness of the relationship between the offender and the child. But another, just-as-important element may be how taken-in the child feels by the offender regardless of who the offender is. Thus a child who was suspicious from the outset of father's activities may feel less betrayed in this sense than the child who initially experienced the contact as loving and nurturing and then was shocked by the revelation of what had happened.

The dynamic of betrayal in sexual abuse encompasses not only the child's experience with the offender but also with nonoffending family members. Many sexually abused children experience their greatest sense of betrayal when they find that their mothers (or other important people) are unable or unwilling to believe and protect them (Herman, 1981). Some sense of betrayal may be inevitable even when parents behave completely protectively, because most children of a young age tend to believe that their parents are omnipotent and capable of warding off harm. The limitations of their own parents' power may be experienced as betrayal, in addition to the more malevolent activities of perpetrators.

Stigmatization

Stigmatization, the third dynamic, refers to the negative messages about the self—evilness, worthlessness, shamefulness, guilt—that are communicated to the child around the experience. These messages are communicated in several ways. Abusers say it directly when they blame the victim ("you seduced me") or denigrate the victim ("you bitch"). They also say it indirectly through their furtiveness and pressures for secrecy. But much of the stigmatization comes from the attitudes the victims hear or the moral judgments they infer from those around them. Victims are likely to know, or discover at some point, that sexual abuse and incest are regarded as deviant. These inferences are often reinforced by the specific comments they may hear in the wake of disclosure; for example, that they, or other abuse victims, are "seductresses," "spoiled goods," or unfit companions for other children in the case of girls; or "queer" in the case of boys. Even when a child is not blamed or labeled, simply the fact of having been a victim, of having his or her assumptive world shattered (to use Janoff-Bulman's, 1985, formulation) is likely to impel the child to search for self-attributions to explain "why it happened to me," "why I was chosen." Because so many negative attributions exist concerning molested children, it is hard for sexually abused children to escape the dynamic of stigma.

The degree of stigma and type of stigma may differ for different children. One of the assumptions made about sexual abuse virtually from the beginning by most clinicians and researchers is that the forms of stigma vary for males and females. For example, males may be more stigmatized by the homosexual connotations of their abuse, while girls suffer from the "spoiled goods" attribution (Rogers & Terry, 1984). Interestingly, this points to another of the problems with using the PTSD framework in regard to sexual abuse. Applying to the experience of both Vietnam vets and rape victims, the PTSD notion nonetheless appears to have made little room for distinctions based on gender, a need that is very great in regard to sexual abuse.

Powerlessness

There are two main components to the traumagenic dynamic of powerlessness: (1) a child's will, wishes, and sense of efficacy are repeatedly overruled and frustrated, and (2) a child experiences the threat of injury or annihilation. (The term *disempowerment* might be a more exact description of the dynamic, but this term is cumbersome.) Many aspects of the sexual abuse experience can contribute to powerlessness, but certain of them are particularly significant and particularly common. Perhaps the most basic form of powerlessness, and one central to sexual abuse itself, is the experience of having one's body space repeatedly invaded against one's wishes, whether this occurs through force or deceit. This is a unique element to the sexual abuse trauma, shared perhaps in physical abuse and in experiences of overintrusive parenting.

A second core form of powerlessness is the experience of violence, coercion, and threat to life and body that occur in some types of sexual abuse. This is a traumatic dynamic present in many catastrophic events and is the key dynamic ("overwhelming event," "intolerable danger") in the

PTSD conceptualization. Both these forms of powerlessness—invasion and life threat—are exacerbated when children resist by fighting back, running away, or trying to outsmart the abuser and are frustrated in their efforts to end the abuse. Ongoing vulnerability, entrapment, and the associated emotions of fear and anxiety also contribute to the dynamic. Finally, children often experience an enormous, unexpected, and devastating increase in powerlessness in the aftermath of abuse, when they find themselves unable to control the decisions of the adult world that may visit upon them many unwanted events—separation from family, prosecutions, police investigations—in addition to the termination of abuse.

Effects Associated with Each Dynamic

This traumagenic dynamics model of sexual abuse is obviously very eclectic and complex in its account of the traumas of sexual abuse. However, one virtue of this model is that it allows a full accounting for the range of symptomatic behavior found in victims. Most of the effects that have been noted in the literature can be conveniently categorized and explained by one or two of the dynamics (see Table 4.1). The fit is not perfect; some effects seem associated with several dynamics. But on the whole, the model gives a plausible framework for the variety and diversity of impacts that have been noted. What follows are some illustrations.

Traumatic Sexualization

The impact of traumatic sexualization is already observed in the symptomatic behavior of many young children. Clinicians note sexual preoccupations, compulsive masturbation and sex play, and sexual knowledge and behaviors that are inappropriate to their age group (Adams-Tucker, 1981; Corwin, 1985; Friedrich, Urquiza, & Beilke, 1986; Gomes-Schwartz, Horowitz, & Sauzier, 1985). Some children, especially boys, become sexually aggressive themselves and begin to victimize peers or younger children. Others become sexually promiscuous (Browning & Boatman, 1977; Weiss et al., 1955).

Among adults there are other symptoms that are readily connected to the dynamic of traumatic sexualization. Sexual problems—including aversion to sex, flashbacks during sex, difficulty with arousal and orgasm—are frequently reported in the literature (Briere, 1984; Courtois,

TABLE 4.1
Traumagenic Dynamics in the Impact of Child Sexual Abuse

I. Traumatic Sexualization

Dynamics

Child rewarded for sexual behavior inappropriate to developmental level.

Offender exchanges attention and affection for sex.

Sexual parts of child fetishized.

Offender transmits misconception about sexual behavior and sexual morality.

Conditioning of sexual activity with negative emotion and memories.

Psychological Impact

Increased salience of sexual issues.

Confusion about sexual identity.

Confusion about sexual norms.

Confusion of sex with love and care-getting and arousal sensations.

Aversion to sex-intimacy.

Behavioral Manifestations

Sexual preoccupations and compulsive sexual behaviors.

Precocious sexual activity.

Aggressive sexual behaviors.

Promiscuity.

Prostitution.

Sexual dysfunctions: flashbacks, difficulty in arousal, orgasm.

Avoidance of or phobic reactions to sexual intimacy.

II. Stigmatization

Dynamics

Offender blames, denigrates victim.

Offender and others pressure child for secrecy.

Child infers attitudes of shame about activities.

Others have shocked reaction to disclosure.

Others blame child for events.

Victim is stereotyped as damaged goods.

Physchological Impact

Guilt, Shame.

Lowered self-esteem.

Sense of differentness from others.

Behavioral Mainfestations

Isolation.

Drug or alcohol abuse.

Criminal involvement.

Self-mutilation.

Suicide.

III. Betrayal

Dynamics

Trust and vulnerability manipulated.

Violation of expectation that others will provide care and protection.

(continued)

TABLE 4.1 (continued)

Child's well-being disregarded.
Lack of support and protection from parent(s).
Psychological Impact
    Grief, depression.
    Extreme dependency.
    Impaired ability to judge trustworthiness of others.
    Mistrust; particularly of men.
    Anger, hostility.
Behavioral Manifestations
    Clinging.
    Vulnerability to subsequent abuse and exploitation.
    Allowing own children to be victimized.
    Isolation.
    Discomfort in intimate relationships.
    Marital problems.
    Aggressive behavior.
    Delinquency.
IV. Powerlessness
Dynamics
    Body territory invaded against the child's wishes.
    Vulnerability to invasion continues over time.
    Offender uses force or trickery to involve child.
    Child feels unable to protect self and halt abuse.
    Repeated experience of fear.
    Child is unable to make others believe.
Psychological Impact
    Anxiety, fear.
    Lowered sense of efficacy.
    Perception of self as victim.
    Need to control.
    Identification with the aggressor.
Behavioral Manifestations
    Nightmares.
    Phobias.
    Somatic complaints; eating and sleeping disorders.
    Depression.
    Disassociation.
    Running away.
    School problems, truancy.
    Employment problems.
    Vulnerability to subsequent victimization.
    Aggressive behavior, bullying.
    Delinquency.
    Becoming an abuser.

1979; Langmade, 1983; Tsai & Wagner, 1978). Also connected here is the observation that some victims, because of their own inappropriate sexual socialization, find themselves inappropriately sexualizing their children in ways that lead to sexual or physical abuse (Gelinas, 1983; Herman & Hirschman, 1977; Justice & Justice, 1979; Steele & Alexander, 1981; Summit & Kryso, 1978).

Betrayal

A number of the effects commonly noted in victims of sexual abuse seem reasonably to be connected with the experience of betrayal that they have suffered. The depression, noted in many studies, is plausibly seen as a result of the disenchantment, disillusion, and loss of a trusted figure (Adams-Tucker, 1981; Benward & Densen-Gerber, 1975; Browning & Boatman, 1977; Herman, 1981; Peters, 1988). Another symptom related here is the extreme dependency and clinging behavior seen especially in young victims (Jones & Bentovim, n.d.; Lustig et al., 1966). This same need may show up in adulthood in the form of a desperate search for a redeeming relationship (Steele & Alexander, 1981; Summit, 1983) or in impaired judgment about the trustworthiness of other people (Briere, 1984; Courtois, 1979; Gelinas, 1983; Tsai & Wagner, 1978). When studies show the vulnerability of former victims to later physical, psychological, and sexual abuse (Briere, 1984; DeYoung, 1982; Fromuth, 1986; Herman, 1981; Miller et al., 1978; Russell, 1983), and their difficulty in recognizing a partner who may become sexually abusive to their children, the underlying factor may be both overdependency and impaired judgment.

There is an opposite cluster of symptoms that is also related to the dynamic of betrayal. Abuse victims are often observed to be hostile and angry (Briere, 1984; Courtois, 1979; Peters, 1976), to distrust men or intimate relationships in general, to have a history of failed relationships or marriages (Courtois, 1979; DeYoung, 1982; Herman, 1981; Meiselman, 1978). The anger and hostility may be a primitive way victims try to protect themselves from future betrayals. The distrust and difficulty in intimacy is another form of protection. And the antisocial behavior may be a form of retaliation for betrayal.

Stigmatization

Other effects of sexual abuse are naturally grouped in relation to the dynamic we have called stigmatization. Reports indicate that victims often feel isolated and gravitate to stigmatized levels of society—for example, among drug abusers, into criminal subcultures, or into prostitution (Benward & Densen-Gerber, 1975; Briere, 1984; Silbert & Pines, 1981). When it reaches its extreme forms, stigmatization appears in the form of self-destructive behavior and suicide attempts (Bagley & Ramsay, 1986; Briere, 1984; DeYoung, 1982; Herman, 1981). Victims of sexual abuse often score as having low-self esteem on psychological tests (Bagley & Ramsay, 1986). Accounts from victims often stress the degree to which they believe they are the only person who has had this experience and that others will reject them if they discover this secret (Benward & Densen-Gerber, 1975; Courtois, 1979; Herman & Hirschman, 1977).

Powerlessness

The powerlessness dynamic in sexual abuse seems connected to three somewhat distinct clusters of effects. The first cluster includes fear and anxiety, which reflect the experience of having been unable to control a noxious event, and the PTSD symptoms: nightmares, phobias, hyper-vigilance, dissociation, somatic complaints, sleep problems, deadness of affect. These symptoms are noted in both young children and adults (Adams-Tucker, 1981; Anderson, Bach, & Griffith, 1981; Briere, 1984; Browning & Boatman, 1977; Burgess & Holmstrom, 1978; DeFrancis, 1969; Gelinas, 1983; Goodwin, 1982; Justice & Justice, 1979; Kaufman, Peck, & Tagiuri, 1954; Peters, 1976; Sloan & Karpinski, 1942; Summit, 1983; Tuft's New England Medical Center, 1984). The second cluster is the impairment to a person's coping skills. Having been frustrated in the attempt to protect oneself, the victim has a low sense of efficacy. This translates into learning problems, school difficulties, employment diffi-culties, running away, and more generalized despair and depression (Adams-Tucker, 1981; Anderson, Bach, & Griffith, 1981; Browning & Boatman, 1977; Herman, 1981; Kaufman et al., 1954; Meiselman, 1978; Peters, 1976). The often demonstrated fact that sexual abuse victims are at higher risk for later sexual assault is a plausible effect of the powerlessness as victims are seen by potentially predatory men as being incapable of effective resistance (DeYoung, 1982; Fromuth, 1986; Herman, 1981; Russell, 1983). Finally, powerlessness may produce a compensatory reaction, an unusual need to control or dominate, seen particularly in male victims (Groth, 1979; Rogers & Terry, 1984). In this cluster of effects we group aggressive and delinquent behavior, or becoming an abuser or molester, all stemming from the desire to be powerful and even fearsome to compensate for past powerlessness.

The preceding should give a sense of how the model goes about explaining the trauma of sexual abuse, first dividing the trauma into four areas and then showing in each area how the dynamics of the abuse experience connect to effects seen in victims. Some clarifications are warranted. First, the model presumes that each of the dynamics are present to different degrees in different abuse experiences. Some experiences are very traumatically sexualizing (for example, when the child's own sexual responses are evoked) and some are not (when the child is simply a passive object). Some involve massive amounts of powerlessness (when a great deal of violence and harm are present) and some much less. There are even abuse experiences where some of the traumatizing dynamics are entirely absent. For example, if a child is able to take action effectively to bring a halt to the abuse at the very beginning, the experience may not be at all disempowering; in fact it may be empowering. The model presumes that the extent of the impact in each area will be related to the degree to which the traumagenic dynamic is present, and that in some cases there is no dynamic and no effect. This should be possible to verify empirically.

A second clarification concerns the "overdetermination" of effects. It should be clear, psychological dynamics being what they are, that it is rarely possible to say that an effect has a single cause. Some of the effects commonly seen in sexual abuse victims have been categorized with two or more of the traumagenic dynamics described here. Some may in fact require the conjunction of two or more dynamics, for example, powerlessness and stigmatization, in order to be present. However, an intriguing hypothesis suggested by the model is that similar effects may have somewhat different manifestations depending on the dynamic with which they are associated. Thus stigma-related depression may have different manifestations compared to powerlessness-related depression.

Sexual Abuse as Situation and Process

One virtue of the traumagenic dynamics model is that it allows sexual abuse to be conceptualized as a situation or a process rather than simply as an event. In the discussion of PTSD, it was mentioned that one characteristic of sexual abuse that distinguished it from PTSD type of events (such as earthquakes) was the fact that it was often an extended process of traumatization. Different parts of the process contribute different traumagenic dynamics. Thus clinicians have often observed that the harm of some sexual abuse experiences lies less in the actual sexual contact than in the process of disclosure or even in the process of intervention.

The traumagenic dynamics described here are not limited to one part of the process. They operate before, during, and after the sexual contact. They apply as much to the disclosure and intervention as to the abuse itself. Thus much of the stigmatization involved in sexual abuse may occur after the experience itself, as the child encounters reactions among family, friends, and acquaintances. A child who is relatively unstigmatized by the molestation itself may experience massive stigmatization if blamed by family. Similarly, a large part of the powerlessness dynamic may be inflicted in the course of intervention. If many agencies become involved in investigation, if the child is handled roughly by investigators, if the child is separated against his or her will from family and neighborhood, the child's sense of powerlessness may be vastly increased.

The dynamics, it should be noted, also can be applied to the child's life prior to the abuse. The four dynamics are ongoing processes, and the impact that the sexual abuse has always needs to be understood in relation to the child's life beforehand. For example, a child may have experienced a substantial amount of betrayal from other sources prior to the abuse. The child may come from an unstable family, where the loyalty of significant others was continually in doubt. The betrayal of the sexual abuse may be all the more serious because it is a compounding of a dynamic that already existed. By contrast, a child may come from a situation prior to the abuse that makes the dynamics in the abuse much easier to handle. An eldest child with important responsibilities, living in a healthy family environment, may have acquired a well-developed sense of personal efficacy and powerfulness. The impact of the powerlessness dynamic within the sexual abuse may be less on this sort of child. These examples illustrate how the four traumagenic dynamics can be used to analyze sexual abuse as a process, rather than simply as an event.

Conclusion

This chapter has discussed two models for conceptualizing the traumatic impact of child sexual abuse, the Post-Traumatic Stress Disorder model and the Four Traumagenic Dynamics model. The PTSD model was criticized for failing to fit and explain fully the trauma of sexual abuse as it has been described by clinicians and researchers. The Traumagenic

Dynamics model was described in some detail as an approach to the unique combinations of impacts seen in child sexual abuse victims.

The most important point is that the understanding of the trauma of child sexual abuse is still in its early stage. Only since 1984 has anyone been proposing models to understand the trauma. It would be premature for the field to adopt uncritically one particular framework at such an early point. There is a need for open-mindedness and exploration while new ideas are developed. There is a need for skepticism and criticism while any models are subjected to empirical testing. Only in this way will we develop the conceptual tools that are crucially important to understanding the problem of sexual abuse and mitigating its effects on victims.

NOTE

1. One of the main intents of DSM III was to create distinct conditions that could be defined by clear criteria and differentiated from other conditions. One of the conditions from which PTSD must be differentiated is an adjustment disorder, and to do so, according to the DSM III training guide (DiClemente, 1981), the distinguishing feature needed for PTSD is the presence of a stressor that is "outside the range of usual human experiences." Given the large number of children who experience sexual abuse in one form or another (Peters, Wyatt, & Finkelhor, 1986; Russell, 1983), one might well question whether it truly qualifies as outside this range of usual human experience. Although sexual abuse is unusual in the sense of our images of normal childhood, it is not statistically unusual at all. (I am indebted to Stefanie Peters for bringing this point to my attention.)

REFERENCES

Adams-Tucker, C. (1981). A sociological overview of 28 abused children. *Child Abuse & Neglect, 5*, 361-367.

American Psychiatric Association. (1980). *Diagnostic and statistical manual of mental disorders* (3rd ed.). Washington, DC: American Psychiatric Association.

Anderson, S., Bach, C., & Griffith, S. (1981). *Psychosocial sequelae in intrafamilial victims of sexual assault and abuse*. Paper presented at the Third International Conference on Child Abuse and Neglect, Amsterdam.

Armstrong, L. (1978). *Kiss daddy goodnight*. New York: Hawthorn.

Bagley, C., & Ramsay, R. (1986). Disrupted childhood and vulnerability to sexual assault: Long-term sequels with implications for counseling. *Social Work and Human Sexuality, 4*, 33-48.

Benedek, E. P. (1985). Children and psychic trauma: A brief review of contemporary thinking. In S. Eth & R. S. Pynoos (Eds.), *Post-traumatic stress disorder in children* (pp. 3-16). Los Angeles, CA: American Psychiatric Association.

Benward, J., & Densen-Gerber, J. (1975). *Incest as a causative factor in anti-social behavior: An exploratory study.* Paper presented to the American Academy of Forensic Science, Chicago.

Briere, J. (1984). *The effects of childhood sexual abuse on later psychological functioning: Defining a "post-sexual-abuse syndrome."* Paper presented to the Third National Conference on Sexual Victimization of Children, Washington, DC.

Briere, J., & Runtz, M. (1988). Post-sexual abuse trauma. In G. Wyatt & G. Powell (Eds.), *The lasting effects of child sexual abuse.* Newbury Park: Sage.

Browne, A., & Finkelhor, D. (1986). Impact of child sexual abuse: A review of the research. *Psychological Bulletin, 99*(1), 66-77.

Browning, D., & Boatman, B. (1977). Incest: Children at risk. *American Journal of Psychiatry, 134,* 69-72.

Burgess, A., & Holmstrom, L. (1978). Accessory to sex: Pressure, sex, and secrecy. In A. Burgess et al. (Eds.), *Sexual assault of children and adolescents.* Lexington, MA: Lexington Books.

Corwin, D. (1985, September). *Sexually abused child's disorder.* Paper presented to National Summit Conference on Diagnosing Child Sexual Abuse, Los Angeles, CA.

Courtois, C. (1979). The incest experience and its aftermath. *Victimology, 4,* 337-347.

Courtois, C. (1986, May). *Treatment for serious mental health sequelae of child sexual abuse: Post-traumatic stress disorder in children and adults.* Paper presented at the Fourth National Conference on Sexual Victimization of Children, New Orleans.

DeFrancis, V. (1969). *Protecting the child victim of sex crimes committed by adults.* Denver, CO: American Humane Association.

DeYoung, M. (1982). *The sexual victimization of children.* Jefferson, NC: McFarland.

Donaldson, M. A., & Gardner, R., Jr. (1985). Diagnosis and treatment of traumatic stress among women after childhood incest. In C. R. Figley (Ed.), *Trauma and its wake: The study and treatment of post-traumatic stress disorder* (pp. 356-377). New York: Brunner/Mazel.

Eth, S., & Pynoos, R. S. (1985). *Post-traumatic stress disorder in children.* Los Angeles, CA: American Psychiatric Association.

Finkelhor, D. (1979). *Sexually victimized children.* New York: Free Press.

Finkelhor, D. (1984). *Child sexual abuse: New theory and research.* New York: Free Press.

Finkelhor, D. (1986). *Sourcebook on child sexual abuse.* Beverly Hills, CA: Sage.

Finkelhor, D., & Browne, A. (1985). The traumatic impact of child sexual abuse: A conceptualization. *American Journal of Orthopsychiatry, 55*(4), 530-541.

Frederick, C. J. (1985). Children traumatized by catastrophic situations. In S. Eth & R. S. Pynoos (Eds.), *Post-traumatic stress disorder in children* (pp. 73-99). Los Angeles, CA: American Psychiatric Association.

Frederick, C. J. (1986). Post-traumatic stress disorder and child molestation. In A. Burgess & C. Hartman (Eds.), *Sexual exploitation of clients by mental health professionals.* New York: Praeger.

Friedrich, W. N., Urquiza, A. J., & Beilke, R. (1986). Behavioral problems in sexually abused young children. *Journal of Pediatric Psychology, 11,* 47-57.

Fromuth, M. (1986). The relationship of childhood sexual abuse with later psychological and sexual adjustment in a sample of college women. *Child Abuse and Neglect, 10*(1), 5-16.

Gelinas, D. (1983). The persisting negative effects of incest. *Psychiatry, 46,* 312-332.

Gomes-Schwartz, B., Horowitz, J., & Sauzier, M. (1985). Severity of emotional distress among sexually abused preschool, school-age and adolescent children. *Hospital & Community Psychiatry, 36*(5), 503-508.

Goodwin, J. (1982). *Sexual abuse: Incest victims and their families.* Boston, MA: John Wright-PSG.

Goodwin, J. (1985). Post-traumatic symptoms in incest victims. In S. Eth & R. S. Pynoos (Eds.), *Post-traumatic stress disorder in children* (pp. 157-168). Los Angeles, CA: American Psychiatric Association.

Green, B. L., Wilson, J. P., & Lindy, J. D. (1985). Conceptualizing post-traumatic stress disorder: A psychosocial framework. In C. R. Figley (Ed.), *Trauma and its wake: The study and treatment of post-traumatic stress disorder* (pp. 53-69). New York: Brunner/ Mazel.

Groth, N. (1979). *Men who rape.* New York: Plenum.

Herman, J. (1981). *Father-daughter incest.* Cambridge, MA: Harvard University Press.

Herman, J., & Hirschman, L. (1977). Father-daughter incest. *Signs, 2*, 735-756.

Horowitz, M. J. (1976). *Stress response syndromes.* New York: Jason Aronson.

Janoff-Bulman, R. (1985). The aftermath of victimization: Rebuilding shattered assumptions. In C. R. Figley (Ed.), *Trauma and its wake: The study and treatment of post-traumatic stress disorder* (pp. 15-35). New York: Brunner/Mazel.

Jehu, D., Klassen, C., & Gazan, M. (1985-1986). Cognitive restructuring of distorted beliefs associated with childhood sexual abuse. *Journal of Social Work and Human Sexuality, 4*, 49-69.

Jones, C., & Bentovim, A. (n.d.). *Sexual abuse of children: Fleeting trauma or lasting disaster.* Unpublished manuscript, the Hospital for Sick Children, London.

Justice, B., & Justice, R. (1979). *The broken taboo.* New York: Human Sciences Press.

Kaufman, I., Peck, A., & Tagiuri, C. (1954). The family constellation and overt incestuous relations between father and daughter. *American Journal of Orthopsychiatry, 24*, 266-279.

Kilpatrick, D. G., Amick-McMullan, A., Best, C. L., Burke, M. M., & Saunders, B. E. (1986, May). *Impact of child sexual abuse: Recent research findings.* Paper presented to the Fourth National Conference on the Sexual Victimization of Children, New Orleans.

Kinsey, A. C., Pomeroy, W. B., Martin, C. E., & Gebhard, P. H. (1953). *Sexual behavior in the human female.* Philadelphia: W. B. Saunders.

Langmade, C. J. (1983). The impact of pre- and postpubertal onset of incest experiences in adult women as measured by sex anxiety, sex guilt, sexual satisfaction and sexual behavior. *Dissertation Abstracts International, 44*, 917B. (University Microfilms No. 3592)

Lindberg, F. H., & Distad, L. J. (1985). Post-traumatic stress disorders in women who experienced childhood incest. *Child Abuse and Neglect, 9*, 329-334.

Lustig, N. et at. (1966). Incest: A family group survival pattern. *Archives of General Psychiatry, 14*, 31-40.

Meiselman, K. (1978). *Incest.* San Francisco, CA: Jossey-Bass.

Miller, J. et al. (1978). Recidivism among sexual assault victims. *American Journal of Psychiatry, 135*, 1103-1104.

Nir, Y. (1985). Post-traumatic stress disorder in children with cancer. In S. Eth & R. S. Pynoos (Eds.), *Post-traumatic stress disorder in children* (123-132). Los Angeles, CA: American Psychiatric Association.

Peters, J. (1976). Children who are victims of sexual assault and the psychology of offenders. *American Journal of Psychotherapy, 30*, 398-421.

Peters, S. D. (1988). Child sexual abuse and later psychological problems. In G. Wyatt & G. Powell (Eds.), *The lasting effects of child sexual abuse*. Newbury Park: Sage.

Peters, S. D., Wyatt, G., & Finkelhor, D. (1986). Prevalence. In D. Finkelhor & associates (Eds.), *Sourcebook on child sexual abuse* (pp. 15-59). Beverly Hills, CA: Sage.

Pynoos, R. S., & Eth, S. (1985a). Developmental perspective on psychic trauma in childhood. In C. R. Figley (Ed.), *Trauma and its wake: The study and treatment of post-traumatic stress disorder* (pp. 36-52). New York: Brunner/Mazel.

Pynoos, R. S., & Eth, S. (1985b). Children traumatized by witnessing acts of personal violence: Homicide, rape, or suicide behavior. In S. Eth & R. S. Pynoos (Eds.), *Post-traumatic stress disorder in children* (pp. 19-43). Los Angeles, CA: American Psychiatric Association.

Rogers, C., & Terry, T. (1984). Clinical intervention with boy victims of sexual abuse. In I. Stewart & J. Greer (Eds.), *Victims of sexual aggression*. New York: Van Nostrand Reinhold.

Russell, D. (1983). The incidence and prevalence of intrafamilial and extrafamilial sexual abuse of female children. *Child Abuse and Neglect, 7*, 133-146.

Russell, D. (1986). *The secret trauma: Incest in the lives of girls and women*. New York: Basic Books.

Silbert, M., & Pines, A. (1981). Sexual child abuse as an antecedent to prostitution. *Child Abuse & Neglect, 5*, 407-411.

Sloan, P., & Kaprinski, E. (1942). Effects of incest on the participants. *American Journal of Orthopsychiatry, 12*, 666-673.

Steele, B., & Alexander, H. (1981). Long-term effects of sexual abuse in childhood. In P. Mrazek & C. Kempe (Eds.), *Sexually abused children and their families*. Oxford: Pergamon.

Summit, R. (1983). The child sexual abuse accommodation syndrome. *Child Abuse & Neglect, 7*, 177-193.

Summit, R., & Kryso, J. (1978). Sexual abuse of children: A clinical spectrum. *American Journal of Orthopsychiatry, 48*, 237-251.

Terr, L. C. (1985). Children traumatized in small groups. In S. Eth & R. S. Pynoos (Eds.), *Post-traumatic stress disorder in children* (pp. 47-70). Los Angeles, CA: American Psychiatric Association.

Trimble, M. R. (1985). Post-traumatic stress disorder: History of a concept. In C. R. Figley (Ed.), *Trauma and its wake: The study and treatment of post-traumatic stress disorder* (pp. 5-14). New York: Brunner/Mazel.

Tsai, M., & Wagner, N. (1978). Therapy groups for women sexually molested as children. *Archives of Sexual Behavior, 7*, 417-429.

Tuft's New England Medical Center, Division of Child Psychiatry. (1984). *Sexually exploited children: Service and research project*. Final report for the Office of Juvenile Justice and Delinquency Prevention, U.S. Department of Justice, Washington, DC.

Weiss, M. et al. (1955). A study of girl sex victims. *Psychology Quarterly, 29*, 1-27.

Wilson, J. P., Smith, W. K., & Johnson, S. K. (1985). A comparative analysis of PTSD among various survivor groups. In C. R. Figley (Ed.), *Trauma and its wake: The study and treatment of post-traumatic stress disorder* (pp. 142-172). New York: Brunner/Mazel.

PART II

Research with Adults Molested as Children

Much of the progress made in the field of child sexual abuse has been accomplished through the use of adult survivors in research. Although limitations in recall of retrospective information have been noted, research with adults molested as children has been helpful, specifically in identifying long-term effects of abuse upon latter psychological functioning. Risk factors identified in adults and their families of origin are currently being used in longitudinal and cross-sectional studies of recent child victims.

The chapters in this section review some of the most prevalent effects of child victimization with both clinical (Briere & Runtz) and probability samples (Peters; Russell, Shurman, & Trocki; Stein, Golding, Siegel, Burnam, & Sorenson). While Russell et al. examine only intrafamilial abuse, Briere and Runtz, Peters and Stein et al. examine abuse that is perpetrated by both family and nonfamily members.

It will become apparent as you read this section that there is no uniform definition of child sexual abuse used in these chapters. For example, in order to emphasize the effects of abuse perpetrated by adults upon a young victim, Briere and Runtz examine only incidents that occurred at or before age 15, initiated by someone 5 or more years older than the victim. They exclude incidents involving noncontract abuse with adolescent peers. Following from Russell's original San Francisco sample, she and her colleagues define child sexual abuse as occurring at or before age 17, but experiences involving attempted or completed sexual contact with a relative that were wanted and with a peer less than 5 years older than the victim are excluded. The Epidemiological Catchment Area (ECA) study, from which Stein et al. extracted data for their chapter, included pressure or force to have sexual contact with a child at or before age 16, but excluded noncontact abuse. Peters, however, adapted the more broad definition established in Wyatt's research with a Los Angeles County sample for her study. This definition required that the abuse incident occurred before age 18 and involved contact abuse ranging from fondling, frottage, attempted and completed intercourse, oral sex as well as noncontact incidents (exhibitionism); and a perpetrator who was at least 5 years older than the victim or used coercion to maintain the victim's participation.

In all of the studies, subjects who did not report being abused at or before the upper age limit used were used as control groups with which to compare the abused sample on critical demographic and study variables. While the Briere and Runtz, Peters and Russell et al. samples were exclusively female, the ECA study findings, described by Stein et al., included both males and females.

Until recently, most research on child sexual abuse has failed to examine the ethnic composition of the sample. In this section, three studies, Peters, Russell et al., and Stein et al. include multiethnic samples and the latter two examine ethnic differences in the effects of child victimization. These studies illustrate how differences in the initial life experiences, socioeconomic, marital status, and other background factors for Afro-American and Hispanic women may cause even more difficulties for abuse survivors in coping with their child sexual abuse experiences.

Other noted features about the chapters are the variety of psychological problems identified in the research. Briere and Runtz describe Post-Traumatic Stress-related symptoms and longer-term problems in their sample, including dissociative experiences and suicidality. They recommend that these sequelae be labeled, "post sexual abuse trauma," and suggest that most of the problems and dynamics found in their sample were consistent with those described earlier in Finkelhor's chapter. Strategies for treatment are recommended to minimize cognitive, psychological, and sexual problems in adult survivors.

Peters examines problems with depression, depressive episodes, substance abuse, and their association with family problems that place children at risk for feelings of helplessness, low self-esteem, and a greater vulnerability in later life.

Stein et al. identify psychiatric symptomatology that met DMS III criteria in the ECA study and discuss these problems within Dohrenwend's conceptualization of stress and its effects upon coping. And, finally, Russell et al. review the impact of our society's racism upon the development of Third World women that compounds their adjustment to sexual abuse in childhood.

These chapters are thought provoking and should prove to be useful to the researcher, clinician, and policymaker.

5

Post Sexual Abuse Trauma

JOHN BRIERE
MARSHA RUNTZ

Despite a growing literature on the subject, there continues to be controversy in mental health circles regarding the effects of sexual abuse. Sexual contact between adults and children has been variously presented as a potentially positive experience for the victim (e.g., Ramey, 1979), as not inherently harmful (e.g., Constantine, 1980; Henderson, 1983), and as almost inevitably destructive (e.g., Butler, 1978; Herman, 1981). Proponents of a classical psychoanalytic view of incest often cite Freud (1962), who ultimately considered the incest reports of his female patients to be fantasies and "the expression of the typical Oedipal complex in women." In contrast, other workers (e.g., Masson, 1984; Rush, 1977) accuse Freud of covering up what were his patients' legitimate reports of sexual victimization.

Contrary to the claims of certain writers that "research is inconclusive" regarding the harmfulness of sexual victimization (Henderson, 1983, p. 34), however, most published studies indicate that a history of incest or other sexual abuse is associated with subsequent psychological and social dysfunction in adulthood, including dysphoric mood, negative cognitions, interpersonal problems, self-destructiveness, and revictimization (Browne

AUTHORS' NOTE: We would like to express our appreciation to Klinic Community Health Centre, Winnipeg, Canada, and the Crisis Resolution Unit of Harbor—UCLA Medical Center for their support of this chapter in its earlier stages. Thanks also due Cheryl Lanktree, Carmen Stukas, Sharon Sawatzky, and Annette Brodsky for their helpful comments. A version of this chapter appears in the *Journal of Interpersonal Violence*. Reprint requests should be addressed to John Briere, Ph.D., Assistant Professor of Psychiatry (Psychology), LAC/USC Medical Center, 1934 Hospital Place, Los Angeles, CA 90033.

& Finkelhor, 1986). Preliminary data (Briere, Evans, Runtz, & Wall, 1988; Urquiza & Crowley, 1986) suggest that abuse-related psychological symptomatology is often not gender-specific, and thus may be equally likely to occur in both male and female abuse victims.

As noted by several writers (e.g., Conte, 1984; Finkelhor, 1984), however, a significant proportion of the research in this area consists of summarized case reports, or is flawed by methodological problems such as small sample sizes, inadequate measures, biased sampling, and/or the absence of appropriate control groups. In the current study we attempted to address some of these difficulties by (a) selecting a random clinical sample of adult female sexual abuse victims, (b) comparing them to a group of nonabused women from the same client population, and (c) evaluating their level of symptomatology with a measure specifically designed to tap abuse-related trauma. With regard to the latter point, we were concerned that scales based on theoretical constructs (e.g., the "Depression" or "Hysteria" scales of the MMPI) might be inappropriate measures of sexual abuse effects, since postabuse trauma need not necessarily correspond to the specific patterns of disturbance associated with established psychiatric disorders.

Method

This sample consisted of 152 consecutive women requesting appointments at the crisis counseling department of an urban Canadian community health center. The average age of these women was 27.3 years, with a range of 14 to 54. In total, 49% of the subjects in this study were never married, 25% were married or living as married, and 26% were separated, divorced, or widowed. Almost all were Caucasian, and were primarily from the lower middle class. The most common presenting problems for these women were depression (33%), relationship difficulties (27%), suicidality (23%), and anxiety (14%). Clients were self-referred (22%), or were referred by social services (32%), medical practitioners (20%), or family, friends, or others (26%).

Subjects were evaluated on a protocol that elicited data on, among other areas, family background (including childhood history of sexual abuse) and presenting problems, and included a Crisis Symptom Checklist (CSC).[1] Items on the CSC were read to the subject and, according to her response, scored as 1 (present) or 0 (absent) in the past two months. The checklist consists of 24 items, which are described in Table 5.1. In the

TABLE 5.1
Differences Between Sexually Abused and Nonabused Clients

Variable	% nonabused	& abused	X^2	p
Current psychoactive mediation	14.0	31.3	6.73	.01
History of psychiatric hospitalization	22.1	19.4	0.16	ns
History of suicide attempts	33.7	50.7	4.51	.03
Battered as adult	17.6	48.9	12.83	.0003
History of rape	8.3	17.7	2.12	ns
History of drug addiction	2.3	20.9	11.19	.0005
History of alcoholism	10.5	26.9	5.89	.02
CSC Items (below)				
Insomnia	37.2	43.3	0.58	ns
Restless sleep	54.7	71.6	4.62	.03
Nightmares	23.3	53.7	15.07	.0001
Early morning awakenings	26.7	32.8	0.67	ns
Isolation	48.8	64.2	3.59	.06
Loneliness	68.6	68.7	0.00	ns
Decreased sex drive	29.1	41.8	2.69	ns
Lethargy	43.0	55.2	2.24	ns
Sadness	67.4	76.1	1.38	ns
"Spacing out"	22.1	41.8	6.87	.009
Anxiety attacks	27.9	53.7	10.54	.001
Uncontrollable crying	25.6	31.3	0.62	ns
Trouble controlling temper	18.6	38.8	7.72	.006
Dizziness	11.6	20.9	2.45	ns
Fainting	4.7	7.5	0.54	ns
Desire to hurt self	18.6	31.3	3.33	.07
Desire to hurt others	11.6	20.9	2.45	ns
Sexual problems	15.1	44.8	16.40	.0001
Fear of men	15.1	47.8	19.33	.0001
Fear of women	3.5	11.9	2.86	.09
Frequent handwashing	1.2	7.5	2.47	ns
Derealization	10.5	32.8	10.32	.001
Out of body experiences	8.1	20.9	4.15	.04
Chronic muscle tension	44.2	65.7	7.00	.008

NOTE: X^2 results reflect Yates corrections, where appropriate.

relatively few instances where a client found a CSC item confusing or unclear, it was clarified by the intake worker until a definite response could be recorded. Also examined were several psychosocial problems not covered in the CSC. Each subject was queried about (a) history of psychiatric hospitalizations, (b) previous suicide attempts, (c) self-described drug addiction and/or alcoholism, (d) victimization after age 14 through rape or battering (physical violence from a "live-in" or marital partner), and (e) current use of psychoactive medication (drugs prescribed for a psychiatric condition).

Sexual abuse was operationally defined in this study as any self-reported sexual contact (i.e., fondling to intercourse) experienced by a client before the age of 15, initiated by someone 5 or more years her senior. This definition, chosen by the authors to emphasize the relative youth of the victim and the relative power of her abuser, did not include aversive experiences between same-age peers, victimization during later adolescence (i.e., ages 15-17), or "exposure only" events (e.g., exhibitionism). Because of these restrictions, this definition falls at the conservative end of the continuum of definitions utilized by researchers in this area (Peters, Wyatt, & Finkelhor, 1986).

Results

Of the 152 walk-in clients, 67 (44.1%) had a history of sexual child abuse by the current definition, although only 26 (39% of abuse subjects) referred to abuse in their presenting complaints. There were no significant differences between abused and nonabused subjects in terms of age, marital status, or ethnicity. Since social class was not specifically indicated on the intake forms, possible SES differences could not be ascertained.

As indicated in Table 5.1, former sexual abuse victims were significantly more likely than nonabused clients to be currently taking psychoactive medication, to have a history of substance addiction, to have been victimized in an adult relationship, and to have made at least one suicide attempt in the past. Abuse victims were also more likely to report a variety of dissociative experiences, sleep problems, feelings of isolation, anxiety and fearfulness, problems with anger, sexual difficulties, and self-destructiveness.

In total, 21 of the 24 CSC items were endorsed with sufficient frequency (i.e., less than a 1:10 marginal distribution) to allow inclusion in a factor analysis. Factor analysis produced six factors with eigenvalues exceeding 1.0, accounting for 57.4% of the total symptom variance. Based on their respective item loadings after Varimax rotation, these factors were named *Dissociation* (e.g., "feeling that things are unreal"), *Sleep Disturbance* (e.g., "insomnia"), *Alienation* (e.g., "isolation"), *Sexual Difficulties* (e.g., "sexual problems"), *Anger* (e.g., "problems controlling your temper"), and *Tension* (e.g., "feeling tense all the time").[2]

Discriminant analysis, using the six unit-weighted factor scales to predict abuse history, yielded a highly significant function, $X^2 = 29.90$, $p <$ .001. As shown in Table 5.2, both ANOVA and discriminant structure coefficients indicated that clients with a history of sexual abuse scored higher on the Dissociation, Sleep Disturbance, Sexual Difficulties, Anger, and Tension scales of the CSC than did nonabused clients.

Effect size analysis of the significant univariate results (Cohen, 1977; Wolfe, 1986) indicated that sexual abuse had a relatively "small" effect on Tension, a "medium" effect on Anger, Sleep Disturbance, and Dissociation, and a "large" effect on Sexual Difficulties (see Table 5.2). Binomial effect size transformation (Wolfe, 1986) suggests that the typical abused subject had more difficulties in these areas, on average, than 71.2% of nonabused subjects.

Discussion

In this study, 44% of a random sample of female walk-in clients to a Canadian community health center crisis service reported of childhood sexual abuse.[3] As a group, sexually abused women experienced substantially greater psychological symptomatology, were more likely to be using psychoactive medication, and more frequently reported histories of suicide attempts, substance addiction, and battery as an adult than did nonabused clients.

Although dissociation was relatively common among abuse victims in the present data, few empirical studies have investigated or reported this symptom as a form of adult postabuse trauma. The most extensive literature review available to date (Browne & Finkelhor, 1986), for example, does not cite any reports of dissociative experiences among adults who were sexually abused as children (although see Blake-White & Kline, 1984; Summit, 1983, for clinical descriptions, and a nonclinical study by Briere & Runtz, 1988). We hypothesize that, in addition to its known relationship to anxiety, dissociation may initially function as a coping technique, later becoming an semiautonomous symptom. For example, an abused child may learn to dissociate from her body as an adaptive means of escaping sensory input during victimization, and may eventually generalize this "going away" defense to other aversive and anxiety-provoking experiences during adolescence and adulthood. Clinical experience suggests

TABLE 5.2
Means and Statistical Results for CSC Scales According to Sexual Abuse History

Scale	Means[1]		ANOVA		DFA	Effect size	
	no abuse (n = 86)	abuse (n = 67)	F(1,150)	p	c²[2]	d[3]	%[4]
Dissociation	.188	.343	12.05	.0007	.60	.6	73
Sleep Disturbance	.369	.513	7.80	.006	.48	.5	69
Alienation	.612	.697	2.03	ns	.25	—	—
Sexual Difficulties	.200	.448	22.26	.0001	.81	.8	79
Anger	.165	.303	8.49	.004	.50	.5	69
Tension	.347	.485	4.87	.03	.38	.4	66

1. CSC scale scores were formed by averaging across all items per scale, and thus range from 0 to 10. May be interpreted as the average proportion of items per scale answered affirmatively per group.
2. Discriminant function structure coefficients, considered meaningful (Italicized) at $|c| \geq .35$.
3. Effect size estimate, based on F statistic (.2 – .4 = "small", .5 – .7 = "medium", $\geq .8$ = "large"; Cohen, 1977)
4. Percentage of nonabused subjects with less symptomatology on this scale than the average abused subject, based on binomial effect size.

that this defense has both voluntary and involuntary components—the latter of which are often experienced by the victim as a serious mental health problem.

The current study also indicates that, as a group, clients with sexual abuse histories experience more anxiety-related problems than do their nonabused peers. Such symptomatology may represent, in part, conditioned responses to victimization that persist into adulthood in a manner similar to chronic rape trauma (Burgess & Holmstrom, 1974). Recent research, for example, views rape as "an *in vivo* classical conditioning situation," where aspects of the assault become conditioned stimuli that evoke subsequent anxiety reactions in other circumstances (Kilpatrick, Resick, & Veronen, 1981, p. 110). In the context of abuse, sexual stimuli are likely to become associated with pain and/or psychological trauma, resulting in conditioned anxiety, phobias, "sexual dysfunctions," and other negative responses to sexual events as the victim matures (Jehu et al., 1984-1985). Finally, the sleep disturbance and somatic complaints reported in the present chapter and elsewhere may arise, in part, from such conditioned anxiety and associated autonomic arousal (Briere & Runtz, 1988).

The anger found among former abuse victims in the current study parallels the experiences of many rape victims (Brickman & Briere, 1984; Burgess & Holstrom, 1974). This affect is thought to result from the betrayal, powerlessness, and stigmatization intrinsic to many instances of childhood sexual abuse (Finkelhor & Browne, 1985), evoking a chronic experience of rage. Such anger may be directed toward self (e.g., self-mutilation, suicidality) or toward others (e.g., aggression, criminal acts), producing "acting out" behavior in response to a variety of interpersonal stimuli (e.g., Runtz & Briere, 1986).

Given the current findings and related studies, postabuse trauma might be viewed as a form of chronic Rape Trauma Syndrome (Burgess & Holmstrom, 1974), where sexual victimization takes place in childhood rather than at a later age. More broadly, one may argue that both rape and sexual abuse effects represent varieties of what is commonly referred to as Post-Traumatic Stress Disorder (PTSD; American Psychiatric Association, 1987). Lindberg and Distad (1985a), Blake-White and Kline (1984), and Goodwin (1984), for example, demonstrate that the long-term trauma associated with childhood incest experiences often satisfy current diagnostic criteria for "chronic" or "delayed" PTSD, leading Lindberg and Distad (1985a, p. 334) to conclude that "people, whether they are victims of incest, rape, war or terrorism, have characteristic ways of reacting to gross stress."

As noted by Finkelhor (this volume), however, a number of the problems of former sexual abuse victims cannot be neatly subsumed within the diagnosis of PTSD. In the present instance, for example, sexual abuse survivors were more likely than nonabused subjects to report previous suicide attempts, in agreement with data from other samples of adults who were sexually victimized as children (Bagley & Ramsay, 1985; Briere, in press; Briere & Runtz, 1986, 1987). In a similar vein, former sexual abuse victims more frequently described drug addiction, alcoholism, and having been revictimized in an adult relationship, as has also been found in other studies (Briere, in press; Fromuth, 1986; Herman, 1981; McCord, 1985; Peters, 1984; Russell, 1986; Runtz, 1987). Finkelhor and Browne (1985) trace these problems to the low self-esteem and interpersonal vulnerability that arise from perceived powerlessness and stigmatization—dynamics they believe to be intrinsic to the abuse process. The victim's perception of her or his powerlessness and lack of self-worth may motivate certain extreme behaviors as "solutions" to other problems. Suicide attempts, for example, may involve not only self-destructiveness, but also a relatively dramatic "cry for help" (Briere & Corne, 1985; Farberow & Schneidman, 1961) based on the expectation that extraordinary measures are required to gain attention and support from others (Briere & Runtz, 1986). Similarly, alcoholism and drug addiction in the abuse survivor may additionally function as a sort of chemically induced dissociation, invoked as a chronic coping response to aversive affects, memories, and situations.

In other places (Briere, 1985, 1988) we note that many of the problems of adults who experienced extended or severe sexual abuse in childhood (e.g., the substance abuse, self-destructiveness, and chronic anger found in the present study, as well as the ambivalence, need for attention, intense and unstable relationships, and so on noted by clinicians such as Butler, Gelinas, or Herman) may cause them to be seen as personality disorders (especially "Borderline" and Histrionic") in current psychiatric nomenclature. We question the need for or appropriateness of multiple psychiatric labels (i.e., PTSD, Borderline Personality Disorder, Hysteria), with their associated stigma and etiologic assumptions, to define the specific constellation of psychological disturbance arising from severe childhood sexual victimization. Instead, we suggest the more global notion of "post sexual abuse trauma" to describe these long-term effects. This latter construct refers to those experiences and behaviors that were initially adaptive responses, accurate perceptions, or conditioned reactions to abuse during childhood, but that elaborated and generalized over time to become "symptoms" and/or contextually inappropriate components of the victim's adult personality (see Summit, 1983, for a further description of the victim's "accommodation" to sexual abuse). The developmental and adaptive aspects of such post sexual abuse trauma distinguish it, to some extent, from the more static aspects of "delayed PTSD."

Implications for
Mental Health Practice

To the extent that the present data can be generalized to other clinical groups it appears that childhood sexual victimization is associated with a variety of psychological and social problems among psychotherapy clients. The implications of such data for mental health practice are major. Extrapolating from recent prevalence studies (e.g., Russell, 1983; Wyatt, 1985), it is probable that at least one-third of adult women and perhaps half that many men have had actual sexual contact with a substantially older person as a child. Making the conservative assumption that only 20% of sexual abuse victims suffer major long-term effects,[4] it is likely that a large number of individuals (over 6% of the female population in the current calculation) experience significant psychological symptomatology in adult-hood as a direct result of sexual victimization in childhood.

The persistence of such effects in so many individuals, as well as the 44% incidence rate in the current clinical sample, suggests that clinicians be routinely vigilant to the possibility of unresolved sexual abuse trauma in those persons requesting mental health services. The present data, along with a recent nonclinical study (Briere & Runtz, 1988), indicate that the index of suspicion should be especially high when client complaints include elements of dissociation, somatization, and dysphoria, in combination with sexual and/or interpersonal dysfunction.[5] Unfortunately, as noted by various writers (e.g., Butler, 1978; Herman, 1981; Summit, 1983), mental health practitioners are unlikely to ask routinely about sexual abuse and, when they are told of such a history, may discount or even disbelieve their clients. This tendency to avoid abuse issues during the assessment phase of treatment may have serious consequences, since many clients will not volunteer victimization experiences unless specifically asked. In the present study, for example, only 39% of former abuse victims identified themselves as such prior to direct questioning by the intake clinician. Since "recognition of sexual abuse . . . is entirely dependent on the individual's inherent willingness to entertain the possibility that the condition may exist" (Sgroi, 1975, p. 20), wide dissemination of data on the incidence and specific effects of childhood sexual abuse may be necessary to increase clinicians' awareness of post sexual abuse trauma in adults.

As important as is the clinical identification of abuse-related symptomatology in adult clients, however, one of the ultimate values of this undertaking concerns its impact on actual therapeutic practice. Although several authors describe victim-based therapies for adults with sexual abuse histories (e.g., Briere, 1988; Courtois & Watts, 1982; Herman, 1981; Lindberg & Distad, 1985a), work in this area remains in its infancy. Data from the present study and current literature do suggest certain treatment applications, however, as briefly outlined below.

PTSD-related effects. As has been discussed, a number of postabuse symptoms (e.g., the dissociation, flashbacks, nightmares, and sleep disturbance noted in the present chapter) may arise from conditioned responses to early victimization experiences. Many of these symptoms are characteristic of Post-traumatic Stress Disorder, and therefore may respond to interventions specifically designed to ameliorate this syndrome (Lindberg & Distad, 1985a). Clinicians who work with PTSD sufferers stress the importance of (a) emotional catharsis, and (b) repeatedly "replaying" the aversive memories until "the victim can honestly say that the memory is not as frequent, the physical distress is not as great, and the intensity of the memory has decreased" (Burgess & Holmstrom, 1979, p. 331). The net effect of this procedure may be loosely equivalent to that of systematic desensitization (Wolfe, 1969), such that anxious arousal to abuse-related cues is counterconditioned through the repeated evocation of painful memories in a safe, supportive therapeutic environment.

Cognitive effects. In addition to classically conditioned responses and their elaborations over time, the long-term effects of sexual abuse appear to include negative thoughts, assumptions, and perceptions regarding self, others, and the environment. For example, the recent literature and current data suggest that many abuse survivors experience guilt, low self-esteem, distrust of others, and helplessness (e.g., Courtois, 1979; Gold, 1986; Jehu et al., 1984-1985; Wyatt & Mickey, this volume). Finkelhor and Browne (1985) trace these reactions to a variety of traumagenic factors that arise from sexual victimization, including betrayal, powerlessness, and stigmatization. Such experiences during childhood cognitive development may produce not only the depression and anxiety cited in many studies, but also may motivate the self-destructive and/or archaic coping behaviors found here and elsewhere (e.g., suicidality, substance abuse, delinquency, and "promiscuity"). Acknowledging these long-term sequelae, Jehu, Klassen, and Gazan (1985-1986) describe a "cognitive restructuring" program that attempts to alter the distorted and/or unrealistic beliefs of the sexual abuse survivor. Jehu et al. specifically focus on key cognitions such as the notions that the client is to blame for his or her victimization, that he or she is helpless and worthless, and that his or her future is hopeless.

Other writers also address the sexual abuse victim's tendency toward self-derogating perceptions and attributions, although they may not subscribe to a cognitive therapy perspective per se. A common way in which this is done is to provide education to the abuse survivor regarding the general dynamics of childhood sexual victimization, with special attention to the victim's powerlessness and lack of culpability at the time of the abuse (Courtois & Watts, 1982; Herman, 1981; Lindberg & Distad, 1985a, 1985b; Meiselman, 1978). Such procedures seek to externalize the victim's shame, guilt, and rage by placing the responsibility on the perpetrator, and/or on society at large (e.g., Brickman, 1984). Finally, several writers suggest that the cognitive changes outlined above are best accomplished in group therapy, where mutual disclosure and support lead to decreased stigmatization and isolation, increased awareness of communalities of experience, and the *in vivo* debunking of social myths regarding responsibility and blame (Gelinas, 1981; Herman, 1981; Johnson, 1985; Tsai & Wagner, 1978).

Implications for the psychotherapeutic process. Regardless of what form treatment takes, the current data and related research suggest that psychotherapy for post sexual abuse trauma incorporate certain elements. First, and perhaps by definition, clinical interventions are likely to be most effective if they directly address early victimization experiences, as opposed to solely "here and now" concerns. Second, client "transference" probably plays an important part in psychotherapy for postabuse trauma. Most loosely defined, this refers to the abuse survivor's tendency to perceive or evaluate the client-therapist relationship through cognitive schemata derived from the original victim-abuser relationship. Thus the client may fear derogation, exploitation, or betrayal from the therapist—expectations that may motivate situationally inappropriate affects or behaviors such as avoidance, fear, rage, or (paradoxically) idealization and acquiescence. In this "projected" interpersonal context, the clinician must strive to ensure that the therapeutic relationship does not recapitulate the traumagenic dynamics of the original abuse. Among other aspects of sound clinical practice, this involves the avoidance of authoritarian or exploitative therapist behaviors, the establishment of clear therapeutic limits and boundaries, and the development of a supportive relationship that reinforces client independence and self-acceptance.

In summary, the present chapter describes the results of a study linking childhood sexual victimization to adult psychosocial disturbance in a sample of female psychotherapy clients. These sequelae appear to involve (a) classically conditioned emotional responses that generalize and elaborate over time; (b) negative cognitions and perceptions regarding self, others, and the future; and (c) archaic coping behaviors that cease to be adaptive in the postabuse environment. We join other writers in suggesting that, despite the commonness of childhood sexual victimization in our society, most helping professionals are relatively unaware of potential child abuse effects in the adult clients they serve. It is our belief that this "blind spot" supports a critical underestimation of the role of aversive childhood experiences in the development of adult psychopathology, despite the intuitive notion that hurt children may eventually become hurt adults. As this state of affairs changes, it is likely that our current understanding of certain psychological disorders will change as well, perhaps leading to new and more effective psychotherapeutic approaches and techniques.

NOTES

1. The CSC has since been updated and expanded, and renamed the Trauma Symptom Checklist (TSC-33). Given the greater breadth and established psychometric qualities of the TSC-33 (Briere, & Runtz, 1987), we suggest its use over the CSC in future research.

2. Factor structure and exact wording of the CSC is available from the first author.

3. Although the current sample was derived from an urban Canadian population, clinical and research experience with individuals from both America and Canada offer little reason to doubt the representativeness of these data to other North American clinical groups. A number of the current studies in the literature, in fact, are based on Canadian samples (e.g., Bagley & Ramsay, 1985; Briere & Runtz, 1986; Gold, 1986; Jehu et al., 1985-1986; Runtz, 1987).

4. The accuracy of this estimate is difficult to assess, especially given the arbitrariness of labels such as "major" or "serious" in describing sexual abuse effects. Russell (1986) reports that over 50% of the intrafamilial sexual abuse victims in her sample described "some" or "great" long-term effects. Browne and Finkelhor (1986, p. 72), on the other hand, suggest that "under one-fifth (of female sexual abuse victims) evidence serious pathology."

5. Interestingly, Freud described equivalent symptoms in his study of Hysteria, which he initially attributed to the effects of child molestation. Later, of course, he withdrew this formulation in favor of his "Oedipal" theory, which viewed his patients' abuse disclosures as "Untrue . . . derived from fantasies and not from real occurrences" (1962, p. 584).

REFERENCES

American Psychiatric Association. (1987). *Diagnostic and statistical manual of mental disorders* (3rd. ed., rev.).

Bagley, C., & Ramsay, R. (1985, February). *Disrupted childhood and vulnerability to sexual assault: Long-term sequels with implications for counseling.* Paper presented at the conference on Counseling the Sexual Abuse Survivor, Winnipeg, Canada.

Blake-White, J., & Kline, C. M. (1984, September). Treating the dissociative process in adult victims of childhood incest. *Social Casework: The Journal of Contemporary Social Work,* pp. 394-402.

Brickman, J. (1984). Feminist, nonsexist and traditional models of therapy: Implications for working with incest. *Women and Therapy, 3,* 49-67.

Brickman, J., & Briere, J. (1984). Incidence of rape and sexual assault in an urban Canadian population. *International Journal of Women's Studies, 7,* 195-206.

Briere, J. (1985, April). *The effects of childhood sexual abuse on later psychological functioning: Defining a post-sexual abuse syndrome.* Paper presented at the Third National Conference on Sexual Victimization of Children, Washington, DC.

Briere, J. (1988). *Therapy for adults molested as children: Beyond survival.* New York: Springer.

Briere, J. (in press). The long-term clinical correlates of childhood sexual victimization. *Annals of the New York Academy of Sciences.*

Briere, J., & Corne, S. (1985). Previous psychiatric hospitalizations and current suicidal behavior in crisis line callers. *Crisis Intervention, 14,* 3-10.

Briere, J., Evans, D., Runtz, M., & Wall, T. (1988). Symptomology in men who were molested as children: A comparison study. *American Journal of Orthopsychiatry, 58,* 457-461.

Briere, J., & Runtz, M. (1986). Suicidal thoughts and behavior in sexual abuse survivors. *Canadian Journal of Behavioural Sciences, 18,* 413-423.

Briere, J., & Runtz, M. (1987, July) *A brief measure of victimization effects: The Trauma Symptom Checklist (TSC-33).* Paper presented at the Third National Family Violence Research Conference, Durham, NH.

Briere, J., & Runtz, M. (1988). Symptomatology associated with childhood sexual victimization in a non-clinical adult sample. *Child Abuse & Neglect, 12,* 51-59.

Browne, A., & Finkelhor, D. (1986). The impact of child sexual abuse: A review of the research. *Psychological Bulletin, 99,* 66-77.

Burgess, A. W., & Holmstrom, L. L. (1974). Rape trauma syndrome. *American Journal of Psychiatry, 131,* 981-986.

Burgess, A. W., & Holmstrom, L. L. (1979). *Rape: Crisis and recovery.* Bowie, MD: Robert J. Brady.

Butler, S. (1978). *Conspiracy of silence: The trauma of incest.* San Francisco: Volcano.

Cohen, J. (1977). *Statistical power analysis for behavioral sciences* (rev. ed.). New York: Academic Press.

Constantine, L. L. (1980). Effects of early sexual experiences: A review and synthesis of research. In L. L. Constantine & F. M. Martinson (Eds.), *Children and sex: New findings, new perspectives* (pp. 217-244). Boston: Little, Brown.

Conte, J. R. (1984, November). *The effects of sexual abuse on children: A critique and suggestions for further research.* Paper presented at the Third International Institute of Victimology, Lisbon, Portugal.

Courtois, C. (1979). Characteristics of a volunteer sample of adult women who experienced incest in childhood or adolescence. *Dissertation Abstracts International, 40,* 3194A-3195A.

Courtois, C., & Watts, D. (1982). Counseling adult women who experienced incest in childhood or adolescence. *Personnel and Guidance Journal, 60,* 275-279.

Farberow, N. L., & Schneidman, E. D. (1961). *The cry for help.* New York: McGraw Hill.

Finkelhor, D. (1984). *Designing studies on the impact and treatment of child sexual abuse.* A publication of the Family Violence Research Program, University of New Hampshire.

Finkelhor, D., & Browne, A. (1985). The traumatic impact of child sexual abuse: A conceptualization. *American Journal of Orthopsychiatry, 55,* 530-541.

Freud, S. (1962). The etiology of hysteria. In J. Strachley (Ed. & Trans.), *The complete psychological works of Sigmund Freud.* London: Hogarth. (Original work published 1933)

Fromuth, M. E. (1986). The relationship of childhood sexual abuse with later psychological and sexual adjustment in a sample of college women. *Child Abuse & Neglect, 10,* 5-15.

Gelinas, D. J. (1981). Identification and treatment of incest victims. In E. Howell & M. Bayes (Eds.), *Women and mental health.* New York: Basic Books.

Gold, E. R. (1986). Long-term effects of sexual victimization in childhood: An attributional approach. *Journal of Consulting and Clinical Psychology, 54,* 471-475.

Goodwin, J. (1984). Incest victims exhibit Post Traumatic Stress Disorder. *Clinical Psychiatry News, 12,* 13.

Henderson, J. (1983). Is incest harmful? *Canadian Journal of Psychiatry, 28,* 34-39.

Herman, J. (1981). *Father-daughter incest.* Cambridge, MA: Harvard University Press.

Jehu, D., Gazan, M., & Klassen, C. (1984-1985). Common therapeutic targets among women who were sexually abused. *Journal of Social Work and Human Sexuality, 3,* 25-45.

Jehu, D., Klassen, C., & Gazen, M. (1985-1986). Cognitive restructuring of distorted beliefs associated with childhood sexual abuse. *Journal of Social Work and Human Sexuality, 4,* 49-69.

Johnson, M. E. (1985). *What characteristics of adult incest victims suggest that group therapy is an effective treatment modality?* Unpublished manuscript, University of California, Los Angeles, School of Nursing.

Kilpatrick, D., Resick, P., & Veronen, L. (1981). The effects of a rape experience: A longitudinal study: *Journal of Social Issues, 37,* 105-122.

Lindberg, F. H., & Distad, L. H. (1985a). Post-traumatic stress disorder in women who experienced childhood incest. *Child Abuse and Neglect, 9,* 329-334.

Lindberg, F. H., & Distad, L. J. (1985b). Survival responses to incest: Adolescents in crisis. *Child Abuse & Neglect, 9,* 521-526.

Masson, J. M. (1984). *The assault on truth: Freud's suppression of the seduction theory.* New York: Farrar, Straus, Giroux.

McCord, J. (1985). Long-term adjustment in female survivors of incest: An exploratory study. *Dissertation Abstracts International, 46,* 650B.

Meiselman, K. C. (1978). *Incest: A psychological study of causes and effects with treatment recommendations.* San Francisco: Jossey-Bass.

Peters, S. D. (1984). *The relationship between childhood sexual victimizations and adult depression among Afro-American and white women.* Unpublished doctoral dissertation, University of California, Los Angeles.

Peters, S. D., Wyatt, G. E., & Finkelhor, D. (1986). Prevalence. In D. Finkelhor (Ed.), *A sourcebook on child sexual abuse* (pp. 15-59). Beverly Hills, CA: Sage.

Ramey, J. (1979). Dealing with the last taboo. *SEICUS, 7,* 1-2, 6-7.

Runtz, M. (1987). *The psychosocial adjustment of women who were sexually and physically abused during childhood and early adulthood: A focus on revictimization.* Unpublished master's thesis, University of Manitoba, Winnipeg, Canada.

Runtz, M. T., & Briere, J. (1986). Adolescent "acting out" and childhood history of sexual abuse. *Journal of Interpersonal Violence, 1,* 326-334.

Rush, F. (1977). The Freudian cover-up. *Chrysalis,* 31-45.

Russell, D.E.H. (1983). The incidence and prevalence of intrafamilial and extrafamilial sexual abuse of female children. *Child Abuse & Neglect, 7,* 133-146.

Russell, D.E.H. (1986). *The secret trauma: Incest in the lives of girls and women.* New York: Basic Books.

Sgroi, S. M. (1975). Sexual molestation of children: The last frontier in child abuse. *Children Today, 4,* 18-21.

Summit, R. T. (1983). The child sexual abuse accommodations syndrome. *Child Abuse & Neglect, 7,* 177-193.

Tsai, M., & Wagner, N. (1978). Therapy groups for women sexually molested as children. *Archives of Sexual Behavior, 7,* 417-429.

Urquiza, A. J., & Crowley, C. (1986, May). *Sex differences in the survivors of childhood sexual abuse.* Paper presented at the Fourth National Conference on the Sexual Victimization of Children, New Orleans, LA.

Wolfe, F. M. (1986). *Meta-analysis: Quantitative methods for research synthesis.* Beverly Hills, CA: Sage.

Wolpe, J. (1969). *The practice of behavior therapy.* New York: Penguin.

Wyatt, G. E. (1985). The sexual abuse of Afro-American and white-American women in childhood. *Child Abuse & Neglect, 9,* 507-519.

6

Child Sexual Abuse and Later Psychological Problems

Child sexual abuse has always been a controversial topic. Historically, there has been considerable reluctance to believe victims, and doubts have been raised about the negative effects of early abuse experiences. In recent years, however, knowledge about child sexual abuse has increased dramatically. As was evident from the literature reviewed in Chapter 1, it is now clear that the prevalence of such abuse is much greater than had been previously believed, with between 15% and 45% of women having experienced at least one incident of sexual abuse involving physical contact before the age of 18 (Bagley & Ramsay, 1985; Finkelhor, 1979; Fromuth, 1983; Russell, 1983; Wyatt, 1985).

There is also growing evidence of the harmful effects of child sexual abuse. Some of this evidence derives from studies involving relatively small samples of highly specific populations, such as follow-up studies of sexually abused children (Nakishima & Cakus, 1977) or observations of adult women in psychotherapy (Herman, 1981; Tsai & Wagner, 1978). Consequently, these studies cannot provide information about the effects of abuse

AUTHOR'S NOTE: This research was conducted as part of my doctoral dissertation and was presented at the 93rd annual meeting of the American Psychological Association, in Los Angeles, August 1985. I wish to thank Gail E. Wyatt, Ph.D., for her support and guidance throughout the project, and Keith Nuechterlein, Ph.D., and Don Guthrie, Ph.D., for their assistance with data analysis. Correspondence regarding this article should be addressed to Stefanie D. Peters, Ph.D., Barrington Psychiatric Center, Suite 320, 1990 S. Bundy Drive, Los Angeles, CA 90025.

among the larger population of women, particularly those whose abuse experiences have remained hidden. Furthermore, few of the studies cited above include comparison groups of nonabused women, so it has often not been possible to establish definitely that the problems being observed are more common among abuse victims.

Several very recent studies have endeavored to overcome these limitations by making use of the large-scale survey approach to studying the long-term consequences of sexual abuse. The results of these studies indicate that sexually abused women do exhibit poorer psychological adjustment (Fromuth, 1983; Seidner & Calhoun, 1984) and a greater degree of mental health problems (Bagley & Ramsay, 1985; Briere & Runtz, this volume; Sedney & Brooks, 1984) compared to nonabused women.

The purpose of the present study was to assess the long-term consequences of child sexual abuse among a community sample of adult women. Depression and substance abuse were chosen as the primary outcome variables because they represent problems that are frequently observed among abuse victims (Benward & Densen-Gerber, 1975; Herman, 1981; Tsai & Wagner, 1978). A question of particular interest was whether "noncontact" abuse experiences, such as seeing an exhibitionist, had the same impact as abuse that involved physical contact between victim and perpetrator. An additional goal was to examine the influence of family characteristics associated with the risk of abuse. The demonstrated risk factors for sexual abuse—such as lack of closeness with parents (Finkelhor, 1984)—represent deficiencies within the family that may themselves contribute to later psychological difficulty. However, most researchers have not accounted for the influence of family background when assessing the association between sexual abuse and adult outcomes.

Three hypotheses were set forth. First, women who experienced contact abuse prior to age 18 were expected to exhibit greater psychological difficulty as adults than women who experienced no abuse or only noncontact abuse. Second, among women with a history of contact abuse, the severity of the abuse would be related to the degree of psychological difficulty. Third, it was predicted that the effects of sexual abuse on adult difficulty would remain significant after controlling for family characteristics associated with abuse.

Method

Subjects

Recruitment. The present study arose from a larger study of sexual socialization and sexual experiences among a sample of 126 Afro-American and 122 White women, ages 18 to 36, in Los Angeles County. Participants in the original study were recruited through random-digit dialing, and took part in an extensive face-to-face interview, which included questions on both voluntary and abusive sexual experiences. Complete descriptions of the procedures for the original study are presented elsewhere (Wyatt, 1985; Wyatt & Mickey, this volume).

Women who had participated in the original study were sent a letter describing the present study. This was followed by a telephone call to determine their willingness to complete an additional interview. Of the original sample of 248 women, 122 were interviewed for the present study, 67 could not be located, and 39 declined to participate. The remaining 20 women were not contacted due to their concerns about confidentiality or their previously expressed wishes not to participate in other research efforts.

The overall rate of attrition from the original sample, regardless of cause, was 51%. Among those women who could be contacted regarding the study, the response rate was 76%.

Sample. The data presented in this chapter are derived from a total sample of 119 women—50 Afro-American women and 69 White women. An additional 3 women completed interviews but were excluded from the sample due to a history of psychotic symptomatology suggestive of schizophrenia. The exclusion was made in order to reduce some of the heterogeneity among the women who reported periods of depression. Table 6.1 presents the demographic characteristics of the women in the sample at the time they were interviewed.

Measures

Interview. A two-part structured interview was developed for use in this study. The first section focused on the subject's life up to the age of 17 and was designed to assess family characteristics believed to be associated with vulnerability to sexual abuse. These included demographic characteristics, family structure, and the quality of relationships with parents and siblings.

TABLE 6.1
Demographic Characteristics of Subjects, by Ethnicity

Variable	Afro-American Women (N = 50)		White Women (N = 69)	
	N	%	N	%[a]
Education				
Less than high school	7	14	6	9
High school	17	34	29	42
Partial college	16	32	18	26
College graduate	6	12	8	12
Postgraduate education	4	8	8	12
Marital Status				
Married	20	40	29	42
Separated	3	6	6	9
Divorced	9	18	17	24
Widowed	1	2	0	—
Never Married	17	34	17	24
Monthly Household Income[b]				
$ 0-$ 999	14	28	8	12
$1,000-$1,999	18	36	20	29
$2,000-$2,999	10	20	18	26
$3,000-$3,999	5	10	10	14
$4,000-and above	3	6	12	17
Refused to give information	0	—	1	1
Presence of Children				
Yes	42	84	32	46
No	8	16	37	54

a. Percentages do not always total to 100 due to rounding error.
b. Includes partner's income if subject was married or cohabiting.

The second portion of the interview assessed problems with depression, alcohol, and drug abuse since the age of 18. Questions concerning depression and alcohol abuse were developed based on the corresponding sections of the Schedule for Affective Disorders and Schizophrenia, Lifetime version (SADS-L; Endicott & Spitzer, 1979). Screening questions on mania and psychotic symptoms were also included to identify subjects whose symtomology was more suggestive of bipolar disorder or schizophrenia. Administration of the entire SADS-L would have been impracticable because of limited resources. Since the SADS-L provides only a loosely structured inquiry about drug abuse, questions in this area were adapted from the NIMH Diagnostic Interview Schedule (DIS; Robins, Helzer, Croughan, & Ratcliff, 1981).

The Research Diagnostic Criteria (RDC; Spitzer, Endicott, & Robins, 1978) were used to determine whether the symptoms described by the subjects met the criteria for major or minor depressive episodes, alcohol abuse, or probable drug abuse. However, because the SADS-L was not administered in its entirety, it was not possible to make differential diagnoses, but to determine only the presence of the identified problems.

The reliability of the entire SADS-L in assessing history of depressive episodes has been established in two recent studies of clinical samples (Andreasen et al., 1981; Mazure & Gershon, 1979). The SADS-L has also been used successfully in studies of multiethnic community samples (Vernon & Roberts, 1982; Weissman & Myers, 1978).

Interviewer reliability was assessed for two aspects of the interview: categorization of depressive episodes and rating of degree of impaired functioning when depressed. I reviewed ten randomly selected interviews by each of the interviewers. For each interviewer, reliability was computed for categorization of depressive episodes as major, minor, or not meeting RDC criteria. This yielded kappa coefficients ranging from .75 to .83. Reliability of impairment ratings was assessed by Pearson correlations, which ranged from .90 to .96.

Beck Depression Inventory—Short Form (BDI-SF; Beck, Rial, & Rickles, 1974). The BDI-SF is a 13-item self-report measure of the intensity of current depressive symptomology. It has been shown to correlate highly with the original 21-item BDI (Gould, 1982) and with clinicians' ratings (Beck et al., 1974).

History of sexual abuse. Information concerning subjects' abuse history, or the lack of such a history, was obtained from data collected in the original study of sexual experiences. A description of the methods used in collecting these data can be found in Wyatt (1985). For each incident of sexual abuse reported by a subject, the following information was made available for use in this research: (1) the sexual activity involved; (2) the relationship of the perpetrator to the subject; (3) the perpetrator's age; (4) the subject's age; (5) the total number of occurrences with this perpetrator; and (6) the duration and frequency of the abuse.

The availability of previously collected abuse data had several major advantages. First, the subjects were spared having to describe their abuse experiences over again. Second, subjects' responses concerning psycho- logical difficulties were not influenced by discussion of sexual abuse within the same interview. Third, the use of previously collected data made it possible for the interviewers in the present study to be blind to whether or not each subject had been abused.

The definition of sexual abuse used in this study specified three criteria. To be classified as sexual abuse, each incident must have:

(1) occurred before the subject was 18 years old;
(2) involved intentional and unambiguous sexual behavior of a physical (rather than merely verbal) nature;
(3) involved a perpetrator who either was at least 5 years older than the victim or used some type of coercion to secure her participation.

This definition encompassed noncontact incidents where the perpetrator exposed his genitals, but excluded noncontact incidents where only a verbal solicitation occurred. Sexual activity involving contact ranged from fondling of the breasts, buttocks, or genitals to vaginal intercourse or oral sex. Voluntary sex play with peers during childhood was not considered to be sexual abuse, nor were voluntary sexual relationships with older partners when the subjects were adolescent.

Procedure

Interview. All subjects were given the choice of being interviewed at their homes, at UCLA, or at a medical clinic that was conveniently located for many of the Afro-American women.

Consent forms described the nature and purpose of the study and informed the subjects that information collected in the original study on certain types of childhood and adolescent sexual experiences would be released to this investigator. Interviews lasted from 45 to 90 minutes, after which subjects completed the BDI-SF. Subjects received a payment of $10 for their participation, as well as reimbursement for parking expenses.

Interviewers. Interviews were conducted by two Afro-American and three White women. Four of these women were advanced graduate students in clinical psychology, and the fifth had extensive experience in survey research. Interviewers took part in a month-long training period that included pilot interviews with volunteers recruited through an advertisement in the UCLA campus newspaper. All training interviews were audiotaped and carefully monitored, with additional training provided where necessary.

Results

Prevalence and Characteristics
of Sexual Abuse Experiences

Of the 119 women in this sample, 71 (60%) reported at least one incident of sexual abuse prior to age 18. A total of 128 incidents involving different perpetrators were reported, and 36 of the 71 women (51%) had been abused by two or more separate perpetrators. In total, 60% of the incidents involved physical contact, ranging from fondling to oral sex and vaginal intercourse. Strangers made up the majority (79%) of perpetrators in noncontact incidents. Contact abuse experiences, on the other hand, generally involved someone known to the victim, either an acquaintance (45%) or a family member (35%). All of the perpetrators were male. Of the 76 incidents of contact abuse, 3 (4%) involved biological fathers and an additional 9 (12%) were committed by a stepfather or mother's boyfriend. Among the contact abuse incidents, 29% involved repeated occurrences with the same perpetrator, with the duration ranging from 1 week to 12 years. The age at which the abuse took place ranged from 2 to 17, with 51% of contact incidents and 37% of noncontact incidents occurring when the subject was 12 or younger.

For the analyses to follow, the sample was divided into three groups, based on abuse history before the age of 18:

(1) No abuse—Women who reported no sexual abuse (40%; $N = 48$).
(2) Noncontact abuse—Women who reported *only* noncontact experiences (14%; $N = 17$).
(3) Contact abuse—Women who reported at least one incident of abuse involving bodily contact (46%; $N = 54$). This group includes women who experienced both contact and noncontact abuse.

For the original sample of 248 women in Wyatt's (1985) study of sexual experiences, the figures are almost identical: 38% no abuse, 17% noncontact abuse, and 45% contact abuse. Although there was considerable attrition of women from the original sample to the subsample involved in this study, subject loss appears to have been evenly distributed across abuse groups.

Abuse History and Current
Demographic Characteristics

Demographic characteristics such as income, marital status, and SES have been found to be related to the occurrence of depression (Hirschfeld &

TABLE 6.2

Comparison of Contact, Noncontact, and No Abuse Groups
on Selected Mental Health Indicators

Indicator	% of women reporting each indicator, by abuse group			X^2
	Contact	Noncontact	None	
At least one depressive episode	85	59	66	6.88**
Suicide attempt[a]	21	18	6	3.52
Sought professional help[a]	56	80	59	2.04
Psychiatric hospitalization[b]	20	25	0	4.79*
Definite alcohol abuse	22	6	6	13.13***
Probable drug abuse	31	12	12	6.32**

a. Asked only of women who reported at least one depressive episode ($N = 88$).
b. Asked only of women who sought help for depression ($N = 52$).
*$p < .10$; **$p < .05$; ***$p < .01$.

Cross, 1982). Prior to testing the specific hypotheses concerning the long-term consequences of sexual abuse, the three abuse groups—contact, noncontact, and no abuse—were compared on the following characteristics: age, education, income, SES (computed according to Hollingshead's 1975 index), marital status, and the presence of children. These comparisons revealed no significant differences between groups, indicating that demographic characteristics would not confound the relationship between abuse and later psychological problems.

Sexual Abuse and
Psychological Difficulty

The first hypothesis predicted that women who experienced contact abuse would exhibit greater psychological difficulty as adults than women who experienced no abuse or only noncontact abuse. To test this hypothesis, the three abuse groups were compared on a number of indicators of depression and substance abuse (see Tables 6.2 and 6.3).

Women in the contact abuse group were significantly more likely than women in either the noncontact or no abuse groups to have experienced alcohol abuse [$X^2 (2, N = 118) = 13.13, p < .01$], probable drug abuse [$X^2 (2, N = 118) = 6.32, p < .05$], and at least one major depressive episode since the age of 18 [$X^2 (2, N = 119) = 6.90, p < .05$]. A Kruskal-Wallis test of rank scores also demonstrated a significantly higher number of major depressive episodes among the contact abuse group as compared to the other two

TABLE 6.3
Means and Standard Deviations for Contact, Noncontact, and
No Abuse Groups on Selected Indicators of Depression

Variable	Abuse Group		
	Contact	Noncontact	None
Current mood ratings[a]			
M	4.06	2.18	2.77
SD	5.20	2.86	2.93
N	54	17	48
Age-adjusted number of major depressive episodes[b]			
M	1.59	.39	.68
SD	2.97	.88	1.80
N	54	17	48
Age-adjusted number of minor depressive episodes[b]			
M	.85	.51	.25
SD	2.08	1.46	.93
N	54	17	48
Ratings of impairment[c]			
M	2.63	2.30	2.53
SD	1.44	.82	1.41
N	46	10	32

a. Higher scores indicate greater depression.
b. Total number of episodes was divided by the subject's current age minus 18 in order to compensate for the range in ages among the participants. The distributions for both major and minor episodes were highly positively skewed, necessitating the use of nonparametric statistics.
c. Higher scores indicate greater impairment.

groups $[X^2 (2, N = 119) = 8.92, p < .01]$, although there was no significant difference for number of minor episodes. Scores on the BDI-SF, indicating current depressed mood, were in the expected direction, but did not attain statistical significance $[F(2, 116) = 1.93, p = .15]$.

Among those women who had been depressed, abuse history did not affect the degree of impairment in functioning or the likelihood of seeking professional help, being hospitalized, or attempting suicide.

Severity of Sexual Abuse

The second hypothesis concerned the relationship between the severity of sexual abuse and the degree of psychological difficulty among women who experienced contact abuse. An Index of Psychological Difficulty (IPD) was constructed by summing scores on the following six items:

(1) Number of major depressive episodes: 0 = none; 1 = low; 2 = moderate; 3 = high.
(2) History of suicide attempt: 0 = no; 1 = yes.
(3) History of psychiatric hospitalization: 0 = no; 1 = yes.
(4) Current depressed mood: 0 = nondepressed; 1 = mild depression; 2 = moderate to severe depression (based on cut-offs given in Beck et al., 1974).
(5) Alcohol abuse: 0 = none; 1 = some problems; 2 = definite abuse.
(6) Drug abuse: 0 = none; 1 = some problems; 2 = probable abuse.

IPD scores ranged from 0 to 11, with 64% of the sample scoring 3 or less.

Based on the literature, six aspects of the individual's abuse experience(s) were selected as indicators of severity: (1) the total number of contact abuse incidents with different perpetrators; (2) the most serious sexual behavior that occurred; (3) the duration of the longest incident with a given perpetrator; (4) the maximum frequency of abuse; (5) the age at which the last incident of contact abuse occurred; and (6) whether the abuse involved a relative. (Information concerning the degree of coercion involved in the abuse experiences had not been coded at the time this research was conducted, and so was not available for use in these analyses.)

Among the 54 women who experienced contact abuse, a stepwise multiple regression was conducted to assess the relationship of severity of abuse to IPD scores. Independent variables were the six indicators of severity. The results of this analysis are summarized in Table 6.4.

Number of contact abuse incidents emerged as the strongest predictor of IPD scores, with a higher number of incidents associated with greater psychological difficulty. The duration of the abuse and being older when the last abuse incident occurred were also related to greater difficulty in adulthood. Taken together, these three aspects of the abuse experience account for over 25% of the variance in IPD scores.

Relative Contributions of Sexual Abuse and Family Characteristics

So far, we have examined the associations between sexual abuse in childhood and adolescence and psychological difficulty in adulthood. However, the risk of sexual abuse has been linked to certain family characteristics, which may themselves produce psychological problems later in life. This raises a critical question of whether the apparent long-term consequences of sexual abuse are merely an artifact of underlying deficiencies in family relationships.

TABLE 6.4

Stepwise Multiple Regression—Severity of Abuse and
Psychological Difficulty

Step	Variable Entered	Zero-order Correlation[a]	Multiple R	R^2
1	Number of contact abuse incidents	.43	.43	.18
2	Duration	.37	.48	.23
3	Age at last abuse	.34	.52	.27

a. Zero-order correlations between IPD scores and other aspects of abuse are: type of sexual activity, r = .18; frequency of abuse. r = .28; abuse by a relative, r = .17.

The third hypothesis predicted that the effects of sexual abuse on psychological difficulty in adulthood would remain significant after controlling for the influence of family characteristics associated with abuse. Previous analyses (reported in detail in Peters, 1984) had identified lack of maternal warmth as the family characteristic most strongly associated with the occurrence and severity of contact abuse. The maternal warmth scale was derived from eight items assessing aspects of the mother-daughter relationship during childhood and adolescence.

The first test of this hypothesis addressed the question of whether differences between the three abuse groups—contact, noncontact, and no abuse —were due to differences in the quality of the mother-daughter relationship. An analysis of covariance demonstrated that, after adjusting for the level of maternal warmth, the three abuse groups differed significantly in IPD scores [F(2, 114) = 4.02, $p < .05$]. Post-hoc comparisons of means indicated that the contact abuse group exhibited a significantly higher level of psychological difficulty than either the noncontact or the no abuse groups.

The second test of the hypothesis involved only the women who had experienced contact abuse and assessed the relative contributions of maternal warmth and severity of abuse to prediction of psychological difficulty in adulthood. Maternal warmth and three aspects of abuse—number of incidents, age at last abuse incident, and duration—were entered into a stepwise multiple regression with IPD scores as the dependent variable. The results of this analysis are summarized in Table 6.5. Maternal warmth did emerge as the strongest predictor of psychological difficulty in adulthood. However, when two abuse variables—duration and number of incidents—were added into the equation, the percentage of variance in IPD

TABLE 6.5

Stepwise Multiple Regression Assessing the Influence of Abuse and Maternal Warmth on Psychological Difficulty

Step	Variable Entered	Zero-order Correlation	Multiple R	R^2
1	Maternal warmth	−.50	.50	.25
2	Duration of abuse	.37	.56	.32
3	Number of contact abuse incidents	.43	.59	.35

scores that could be explained by the independent variables increased from 25% to 35%.

Discussion

The findings of this study demonstrate a significant association between child sexual abuse experiences and later psychological difficulty in a community sample of adult women. Women with a history of contact abuse were more likely to experience problems with depression and substance abuse and reported a greater number of depressive episodes, as compared to women with a history of no abuse or only noncontact abuse. The degree of psychological difficulty in adulthood was related to specific aspects of the abuse experiences—the number of incidents, the duration of the abuse, and being older when the abuse ended. Furthermore, the relationship of sexual abuse to psychological difficulty remained significant after controlling for the influence of maternal warmth.

These data provide empirical support for clinical observations concerning the prevalence of mental health problems among women who were victims of sexual abuse while they were growing up (Benward & Densen-Gerber, 1975; Herman, 1981; Nakishima & Cakus, 1977; Tsai & Wagner, 1978; Westermeyer, 1978). The findings are also highly consistent with those of other empirical studies that have compared abused and nonabused women. Several studies of nonclinical samples (Bagley & Ramsay, 1985; Briere & Runtz, this volume; Sedney & Brooks, 1984) have found significantly greater problems with depression among abused women. Additionally, Briere (1984) reported a greater likelihood of substance abuse among abused as compared to nonabused women within a clinical sample of psychotherapy patients. The rapidly accumulating evidence from empirical studies suggests that the negative psychological consequences of child sexual abuse are not limited to those women who are sufficiently distressed to seek professional help, but rather are widespread among victims in general.

The present study also examined the effect of specific aspects of the abuse experience on later psychological problems. A unique contribution is the finding that abuse histories limited to only noncontact experiences are not associated with depressive episodes and substance abuse in adulthood. Several studies have identified only a single "abused" group that includes women with only noncontact experiences (Fromuth, 1983; Sedney & Brooks, 1984; Seidner & Calhoun, 1984), a decision that may have attenuated differences between the abused and nonabused groups.

Among women with a history of contact abuse, the aspects of abuse most strongly associated with later psychological problems were the number of incidents and the duration of the longest incident. These findings are highly consistent with the results of two other recent studies of nonclinical samples looking at similar outcome measures. In these studies, number of incidents and duration were linked with poorer mental health as measured by a composite index of psychiatric disturbance (Bagley & Ramsay, 1985) and scores on a Chronic Depression subscale of the Hopkins Symptom Checklist (Briere & Runtz, in press). (The term *number of perpetrators* as used by Briere and Runtz is equivalent to the term *number of incidents* used by this author [J. Briere, personal communication, April, 1986].)

The results of this study also suggest that abuse occurring at older ages contributes to greater psychological difficulty. Tsai, Feldman-Summers, and Edgar (1979) reported a similar finding and suggested that older victims may suffer more negative consequences because they are more aware of the sexual meaning of the abuse experiences and more likely to feel responsible for its occurrence.

Finally, the results of this study suggest that the long-term psychological effects of sexual abuse are not merely artifacts of underlying deficiencies in family relationships. In this sample, the strongest predictor of the risk of sexual abuse was lack of maternal warmth while growing up, a construct that other researchers have consistently found to be associated with later mental health problems, particularly depression (Crook, Raskin, & Elliott, 1981; Jacobson, Fasman, & DiMascio, 1975; Parker, 1983). However, controlling for the effects of maternal warmth did not eliminate the significant relationships between abuse experiences and later psychological problems.

Before considering the implications of these results, several cautions are in order. First, although the sample contains a wider range of demographic characteristics than studies using only college students (e.g., Fromuth, 1983; Sedney & Brooks, 1984; Seidner & Calhoun, 1984), it cannot be assumed to be representative of the general population. In particular, younger Afro-American women are underrepresented due to a high rate of attrition among this group from the original study to the sample used in the present study (see Peters, 1984). Second, the sample may not be fully representative of the general population in terms of their abuse experiences. It is possible, for instance, that very severely abused women were reluctant to participate in a study of this type. The final caution concerns the high rate of depression reported in the present study. This appears to be the result of several factors: (1) the wording of the recruitment letter may have generated greater interest among women who had been depressed; (2) the use of only the partial SADS-L interview may have resulted in failure to differentiate depression from other types of psychological problems; and (3) subjects may have used the term "depression" to describe many types of distress, a pattern common among laypersons (Mountjoy & Roth, 1982). However, the general overestimation of depression should not affect the comparisons reported here because these factors would most likely have had the same influence on abused and nonabused women.

Although there is growing evidence linking child sexual abuse to later psychological difficulty, little attention has been given to the question of how abuse experiences exert such an effect over the span of so many years. In this sample, for instance, the amount of time elapsed since the last incident of contact abuse averaged almost 16 years. I propose that both sexual abuse and the associated family characteristics are likely to interfere with the development of self-esteem and mastery, and these deficits, in turn, increase the likelihood of psychological problems later in life. A model of these interrelationships can be developed by integrating the findings of this and other studies of sexual abuse with the literature from other areas.

Studies of parent-child relationships have consistently demonstrated a link between lack of maternal warmth and low self-esteem in children (Elrod & Crase, 1980; Growe, 1980; Sears, 1970). This may help to explain the finding in the abuse literature that lack of maternal warmth is associated with an increased risk of sexual abuse (Bagley & Ramsay, 1985; Finkelhor, 1984; Fromuth, 1983; Peters, 1984). Children with low self-esteem may be more likely to be chosen as targets by molesters and, once chosen, may be less successful in fending off the assault. The experience of being sexually abused generates powerful feelings of helplessness (Summit, 1983) that further erode the victim's self-esteem and sense of mastery. It is these enduring changes in a woman's experience of herself and her capabilities that create a greater vulnerability to psychological problems later in life.

The findings of the present study are consistent with such a model. These results suggest that it is primarily the experience of being repeatedly abused—whether by different persons on separate occasions or by the same person over a period of time—that is associated with more severe psychological problems in adulthood. According to an attributional analysis, repeated victimization would be more likely to produce internal stable attributions about the causes of the abuse (Abramson, Seligman, & Teasdale, 1978). These attributions would then lead to feelings of helplessness and vulnerability to later psychological distress.

The task facing both researchers and clinicians is to develop an understanding of how sexual abuse interacts with other aspects of a woman's childhood experiences to create this vulnerability. Recent prevalence studies indicate that sexual abuse is widespread among women in the general population (Russell, 1983; Wyatt, 1985), and prevalence rates may be even higher among clinical populations (Benward & Densen-Gerber, 1975; Briere, 1984). However, women entering psychotherapy do not generally disclose that they were sexually abused while growing up (Westermeyer, 1978). Therefore, clinicians must take the initiative in asking about sexual abuse history and identifying unresolved feelings that may have contributed to the client's present problems.

REFERENCES

Abramson, L., Seligman, M., & Teasdale, J. (1978). Learned helplessness in humans: Critique and reformulation. *Journal of Abnormal Psychology, 87,* 49-74.

Andreasen, N. C., Grove, W. M., Shapiro, R. W., Keller, M. B., Hirschfeld, R.M.A., & McDonald-Scott, P. (1981). Reliability of lifetime diagnosis: A multicenter collaborative perspective. *Archives of General Psychiatry, 38,* 400-405.

Bagley, C., & Ramsay, R. (1985, February). *Disrupted childhood and vulnerability to sexual assault: Long-term sequels with implications for counseling.* Paper presented to Conference on Counseling the Sexual Abuse Survivor, Winnipeg, Canada.

Beck, A. T., Rial, W. Y., & Rickels, K. (1974). Short form of Depression Inventory: Cross-validation. *Psychological Reports, 34,* 1184-1186.

Benward, J., & Densen-Gerber, J. (1975). Incest as a causative factor in antisocial behavior: An exploratory study. *Contemporary Drug Problems, 4,* 323-340.

Briere, J. (1984). *The effects of childhood sexual abuse on later psychological functioning: Defining a post-sexual abuse syndrome.* Paper presented at the Third National Conference on Sexual Victimization of Children, Washington, DC.

Crook, T., Raskin, A., & Elliott, J. (1981). Parent-child relationships and adult depression. *Child Development, 52,* 950-957.

Elrod, M. M., & Crase, S. J. (1980). Sex differences in self-esteem and parental behavior. *Psychological Reports, 46,* 719-727.

Endicott, J., & Spitzer, R. L. (1979). Use of the Research Diagnostic Criteria and the Schedule for Affective Disorders and Schizophrenia to study affective disorders. *American Journal of Psychiatry, 136,* 52-56.

Finkelhor, D. (1979). *Sexuality victimized children.* New York: Free Press.

Finkelhor, D. (1984). *Child sexual abuse: New theory and research.* New York: Free Press.

Fromuth, M. E. (1983). *The long term psychological impact of childhood sexual abuse.* Unpublished doctoral dissertation, Auburn University.

Gould, J. (1982). A psychometric investigation of the standard and short form Beck Depression Inventory. *Psychological Reports, 51,* 1167-1170.

Growe, G. A. (1980). Parental behavior and self-esteem in children. *Psychological Reports, 47,* 499-502.

Herman, J. L. (1981). *Father-daughter incest.* Cambridge, MA: Harvard University Press.

Hirschfeld, R.M.A, & Cross, C. K. (1982). Epidemiology of affective disorders: Psychosocial risk factors. *Archives of General Psychiatry, 39,* 35-46.

Hollingshead, A. B. (1975). *Four-factor index of social position.* Unpublished manuscript, Yale University, New Haven, CT.

Jacobson, S., Fasman, J., & DiMascio, A. (1975). Deprivation in the childhood of depressed women. *Journal of Nervous and Mental Disease, 160,* 5-14.

Mazure, C., & Gershon, E. S. (1979). Blindness and reliability in lifetime psychiatric diagnosis. *Archives of General Psychiatry, 36,* 521-525.

Mountjoy, C. Q., & Roth, M. (1982). Studies in the relationship between depressive disorders and anxiety states: Part I. Rating scales. *Journal of Affective Disorders, 4,* 127-147.

Nakishima, I. I., & Cakus, G. E. (1977). Incest: Review and clinical experience. *Pediatrics, 60,* 696-701.

Parker, G. (1981). Parental reports of depressives: An investigation of several explanations. *Journal of Affective Disorders, 3,* 131-140.

Parker, G. (1983). Parental "affectionless control" as an antecedent to adult depression: A risk factor delineated. *Archives of General Psychiatry, 40,* 956-960.

Peters, S. D. (1984). *The relationship between childhood sexual victimization and adult depression among Afro-American and white women.* Unpublished doctoral dissertation, University of California at Los Angeles.

Robins, L. N., Helzer, J. E., Croughan, J., & Ratcliff, K. S. (1981). National Institute of Mental Health Diagnostic Interview Schedule: Its history, characteristics, and validity. *Archives of General Psychiatry, 38,* 381-389.

Russell, D.E.H. (1983). The incidence and prevalence of intrafamilial and extrafamilial sexual abuse of female children. *Child Abuse and Neglect, 7,* 133-146.

Sears, R. R. (1970). Relation of early socialization experiences to self-concepts and gender role in middle childhood. *Child Development, 41,* 267-289.

Sedney, M. A., & Brooks, B. (1984). Factors associated with a history of childhood sexual experience in a nonclinical female population. *Journal of the American Academy of Child Psychiatry, 23,* 215-218.

Seidner, A. L., & Calhoun, K. S. (1984, August). *Childhood sexual abuse: Factors related to differential adult adjustment.* Paper presented at the Second Annual National Family Violence Research Conference, Durham, NH.

Spitzer, R. L., Endicott, J., & Robins, E. (1978). *Research Diagnostic Criteria.* New York: Biometrics Research Division, Evaluation Section, New York State Psychiatric Institute.

Summit, R. C. (1983). The child sexual abuse accommodation syndrome. *Child Abuse and Neglect, 7,* 177-193.

Tsai, M., Feldman-Summers, S., & Edgar, M. (1979). Childhood molestation: Variables related to differential impacts on psychosexual functioning in adult women. *Journal of Abnormal Psychology, 88,* 407-417.

Tsai, M., & Wagner, N. N. (1978). Therapy groups for women sexually molested as children. *Archives of Sexual Behavior, 7,* 417-427.

Vernon, S. W., & Roberts, R. E. (1982). Use of the SADS-RDC in a tri-ethnic community survey. *Archives of General Psychiatry, 39,* 47-52.

Weissman, M. M., & Myers, J. K. (1978). Affective disorders in the U.S. urban community: The use of Research Diagnostic Criteria in an epidemiological survey. *Archives of General Psychiatry, 35,* 1304-1311.

Westermeyer, J. (1978). Incest in psychiatric practice: A description of patients and incestuous relationships. *Journal of Clinical Psychiatry, 39,* 643-648.

Wyatt, G. E. (1985). The sexual abuse of Afro-American and White women in childhood. *Child Abuse and Neglect, 9,* 507-519.

7

The Long-Term Effects of Incestuous Abuse

A Comparison of Afro-American and White American Victims

DIANA E. H. RUSSELL
RACHEL A. SCHURMAN
KAREN TROCKI

Most child sexual abuse research to date has focused on the White community. Although several studies have included racial minorities in their sample populations (e.g., DeFrancis, 1969; Meiselman, 1978; Weinberg, 1955), they fail to "grasp the opportunity to examine the differences between these two groups" (Pierce & Pierce, 1984). Other studies have been undertaken in areas where few minorities live (e.g., Finkelhor, 1979) or have been limited to White respondents (e.g., Herman, 1981). The resulting dearth of information about child sexual victimization in minority communities is appropriately lamented by Lois Pierce and Robert Pierce (1984) and Gail Wyatt (1985, 1986) in their pioneering research on the effect of ethnicity on childhood sexual abuse.

That the experiences of White victims are assumed to be the norm for all minority victims is evident in the lack of ethnicity-based child sexual abuse research. But the assumption that data on Whites accurately reflect the experiences of the members of all other groups denies the role of cultural

AUTHORS' NOTE: Correspondence regarding this chapter should be addressed to Dr. Diana Russell, Department of Social Sciences, 5000 MacArthur Blvd, Oakland, CA 94613.

119

differences in people's lives, denies the fact that racism has an impact, and reflects the White bias of most researchers in this field.

This chapter will focus on a comparison of the effects of incestuous abuse reported by Afro-American and White American women. Although Russell (1986) found that there were no statistically significant differences in the *prevalence* of incestuous abuse for Afro-American and White women in her San Francisco survey, it is possible that women from these groups nevertheless report different effects as a result of their abuse experiences. This analysis constitutes a first step in determining whether current clinical and social service practices of treating all incest victims similarly— regardless of ethnicity—is appropriate.

Data

A probability sample of 930 women residents of San Francisco were interviewed during the summer of 1978 about any experience of incestuous abuse they might have had before the age of 18.[1] (For a more detailed description of the methodology of this survey, see Russell, 1986.) *Incestuous abuse* was defined as any kind of exploitive sexual contact or attempt at contact that occurred between relatives, no matter how distant the relationship, before the victim turned 18 years old. Experiences involving sexual contact or attempted contact with a relative that were wanted *and* with a peer were regarded as nonexploitive, and hence did not meet our definition of abuse. (An example would be sex play between cousins or siblings of approximately the same ages.) An age difference of less than 5 years was the criterion for a peer relationship.

Representativeness of Afro-American and White Respondents

Using a self-reported definition of ethnicity, Afro-American women constituted 10% of our sample of 930, only slightly lower than their representation in the larger San Francisco community. (According to the 1980 census, 11% of the San Francisco population was Afro-American.) However, 67% of our sample was White—10% higher than the percentage of Whites in the city. Most of this difference was due to an undersampling of Asians, the reasons for which are discussed elsewhere (see Russell, 1986).

To have increased the number of minority women without increasing our overall sample size we would have had to oversample minorities substantially, as did Wyatt (1985). Because our major objective was to ascertain the prevalence of different kinds of sexual abuse for the entire San Francisco female population, it was important to have our sample reflect as closely as possible the true demographic composition of that city.

As Myers (1982) and Wyatt (1985) have pointed out, when Afro-Americans are included in studies along with Whites, they are rarely comparable in terms of social class. This is not necessarily because of biased sampling methods. Rather, it may reflect the fact that centuries of racism have resulted in Afro-Americans being seriously underrepresented in the middle and upper classes. These class dissimilarities make it difficult to ascertain whether other differences found are due to social class or to ethnicity, or to some combination of both of these variables. Our survey data are no exception in this respect.

By all nine measures of social class used in our survey, significantly more of the Afro-American than the White respondents were from the lower social class (see Table 7.1). In addition, the Afro-American and White respondents differed in numerous other ways, for example, in the type of family structure in which they were raised, their religion, their marital and maternal status, as well as in their employment situations. There may also have been psychological differences between our Afro-American and White respondents, for example, in self-concept, socialization, sense of control over the environment, or experiences of discrimination (e.g., see Ladner, 1971; Powell, 1983), but our study did not attempt to ascertain these.

Incest Victims

In total, 110 (or 17%) of the White women in our sample were incestuously abused before the age of 18; the comparable figure for Afro-American women was 14 (16%). Of these 124 women, 18 had been victimized by more than one relative. (Of these women, 2 were Afro-American and 16 were White.) So as not to exclude these multiple experiences, our analysis will focus on the 150 different *cases* of incestuous abuse rather than on the 124 victimized women.

Despite the small number of Afro-American incest victims in our sample, statistically significant differences in the reported effects of the incestuous abuse emerged from our comparison of the two groups of women. The paucity of scientifically sound information in this area makes it important that all valid, available data be explored.

TABLE 7.1

Comparison of Afro-American and White Respondents
in Russell's San Francisco Survey

Social Class	Afro-American Women N = 90		White Women N = 627
	%	%	X^{2a}
Father had lower-class occupation	46	16	31.35***
Father had eighth grade or less education	61	26	28.40***
Mother had lower-class occupation	79	36	36.26***
Mother had eighth grade or less education	40	24	9.45**
Respondent had high school or less education	61	36	21.52***
Respondent had lower-class occupation	59	18	69.38***
Respondent's total household income in 1977 was less than $7,500	62	32	32.25***
Respondent's husband had lower-class occupation	63	15	24.92***
Respondent's husband had eighth grade or less education	22	6	9.49**
Other Social Variables			
Reared in city environment	64	48	8.26**
Reared by both biological parents	53	84	50.24***
Reared by mother only	32	8	52.14***
Mother worked most of time during respondent's childhood years	47	15	53.29***
Protestant upbringing	75	44	31.91***
Protestant religious preference at time of interview	61	24	52.90***
Born in the United States	96	83	5.37*
Divorced or separated at time of interview	30	18	7.49**
Raised at least one child	74	44	28.97***
Unemployed, on welfare, or disabled at time of interview	19	8	11.41***
	Age in Years		t-value
Mean age at birth of first child	20.5	25.0	6.97*** (334 df)

a. All chi-squares are 2×2 comparisons with 1 df.
*p < .05; **p < .01; ***p < .001.

Methods

Measuring Long- and Short-Term Effects

Two types of measures are relevant for analyzing the impact of incestuous abuse: *subjective* measures, which reflect the victim's own

FIGURE 7.1

Negative Life Experiences Scale

---

(1) Serious sexual assault (at least one experience other than incestuous abuse)
(2) Marital rape
(3) Wife beating
(4) Early childbearing (at the age of 19 or younger)
(5) Motherhood without marriage (the woman had never married but had raised one or more children)
(6) Separation or divorce
(7) Poverty (a total household income below $7,500 at the time of the interview)
(8) Downward social mobility (the woman had a lower occupational status than her mother)
(9) Downward social mobility (the woman had a lower educational status than her mother)

NOTE: Mean scores were obtained for each woman by making a simple count of one for each of the nine items on the scale, then dividing the total by the number of items for which pertinent information was available. Missing data or inapplicable items (such as, for example, marital rape or divorce for women who had never married) did not lower a woman's score.

perception of how the abuse has affected her life, and *objective* measures, which reflect possible effects of incestuous abuse that the victims did not necessarily mention. Two different subjective measures of impact were used in this study. The first was based on the victims' responses to the following question:

(1) Overall, how upset were you by this experience—extremely upset, very upset, somewhat upset, not very upset, or not at all upset?

The second attempted to ascertain longer-term effects by asking victims:

(2) Looking back on it now, how much impact would you say this experience has had on your life—a *great* effect, *some* effect, a *little* effect, or *no* effect?

The objective measure of impact used here is a "negative life experiences" scale. This nine-factor scale includes three measures of repeated victimization, three measures of instability in marital and reproductive life, two measures of downward social mobility, and one measure of poverty at the time of the interview (see Figure 7.1). Based on a frequency distribution of scores on this summary scale, women were divided into three roughly equal groups: (1) those with the "best" outcomes (i.e., relatively few of these negative life experiences); (2) those with intermediate outcomes; and (3) those with the "worst" outcomes (i.e., many of these negative life experiences). (For more detail on the actual construction and coding of this scale, see Russell, 1986.)

Findings

Subjective Measures of Impact

Over twice the percentage of experiences of incestuous abuse reported by Afro-American women as White women were described as extremely upsetting (63% versus 30%), and proportionally fewer of the experiences reported by Afro-American women than White women were described as not very or not at all upsetting (13% versus 23%) ($X^2 = 8.28$, 1 df, p < .01).

Similar differences were apparent with our long-term effects measure. Whereas 44% of the experiences of incestuous abuse reported by Afro-American women were described as having *great* long-term effects, only 22% of the experiences reported by White women were described as having a comparable impact ($X^2 \sim 4.77$, 1 df, p < .05). Interestingly, Wyatt (1986) also found that "a greater percentage of White women reported no lasting effects" when compared with Afro-American women in her Los Angeles sample.

In all Russell's previous analyses of her qualitative incest data, she has not differentiated between the responses of incest victims from different ethnic groups. Because there is so little specific information about Afro-American incest victims in the literature in general, a few examples follow of the answers of the Afro-American women in our sample to the questions about the impact of incest victimization on their lives.

Thirty-nine-year-old Kate was 14 when her biological father called her his baby and put his hand on her breast.

[Upset?] Extremely upset. [Effect on your life?] A great effect. It's affected how I feel about him up till today. I feel guilty now because he's old and needs lots of attention and I don't feel anything for him and I can't give it to him. Men can't be trusted. I told my daughters so that they would be able to tell me if it happened with them, and it did.

Ellen was 15 years old when her 30-year-old brother tried to touch her genitals when she was asleep. She was 24 when interviewed.

[Upset?] Extremely upset. [Effect on your life?] Some effect. It really hurt me. About a year ago I dreamt about it and I woke up crying. Afterward I was afraid for a man to touch me. I think it affected me a great deal. It affected me when I started having intercourse. I think about what happened and I get a cold standoffish feeling. It turned me off. I'm barely getting over it now. I think about what happened and I freeze up.

Twenty-five-year-old Eileen was only 5 when her uncle, who was in his 30s, tried to force her onto the bed to have intercourse.

[Upset?] Extremely upset. Then, just a little; now, it really bothers me extremely. [Effect on your life?] Some effect. I don't trust men at all. I feel that most of the time when you meet someone they're after sex. They don't look at you as a person nor do they care how you feel.

Mabel was 13 the one time her adoptive father raped her. She was 58 at the time of the interview.

[Upset?] Extremely upset. [Effect on your life?] A great effect. It affected my relationships with men. Even when I found a decent boyfriend, I'd figure that he was out to do something to me because of what had been done to me by my father. I thought badly of men in general for a long time. [Which of all your experiences was the most upsetting?] The first experience I had in my life when I was 13 was the most upsetting. It affected my trust in people—in parents, in men. What happens to you when you're young upsets you more than at any other time.

Forty-three-year-old Dorothy was 13 when she was raped by her 28-year-old brother-in-law.

[Upset?] Extremely upset. [Effect on your life?] A great effect. I'm sure I drove my husband to drinking because my view of sex is that it's obscene. I can't stand to see people kissing. After having my baby, it got worse. I couldn't have sex at all. If the experiences hadn't been so close to home, it wouldn't have been so bad. Men only have one thing in mind and that's to mutilate the body. I've been to several psychiatrists but it doesn't seem to go away.

When she was 16, Dorothy was molested by another 26-year-old brother-in-law.

[Upset?] Extremely upset. [Effect on your life?] A great effect. It was a terrible experience. I was afraid to tell anyone because they would say it was my fault. Sometimes now when I wake up, I think some man is standing at my bed. If a strange man says something to me when I go out, I'm liable to turn around and cut or stab him. It's so deep-seated, even now at 43 I'm still affected. I can't seem to get over it. I'm paranoid.

TABLE 7.2

Outcome on the Negative Life
Experiences Scale by Ethnicity (in percentages)

Outcome	Afro-American Women N = 90		White Women N = 627	
	Victims (14)	Nonvictims (76)	Victims (110)	Nonvictims (517)
Best	7	30	41	63
Intermediate	7	25	27	21
Worst	86	45	32	16

Comparisons: (1) Differences between White and Afro-American victims (X^2 = 15.35, 2 df, p < .001).
(2) Differences between Afro-American victims and nonvictims (X^2 = 7.95, 2 df, p < .02).
(3) Differences between White victims and nonvictims (X^2 = 21.55, 2 df, p < .001).

Objective Measures of Impact

Because the experiences of Afro-American and White women are shaped by such different forces (e.g., the former are subject to racial discrimination, affecting their access to income, education, and employment opportunities), it is not meaningful simply to compare Afro-American and White victims when analyzing the negative life experiences (NLE) scale described above. Rather, one must add a new control group, composed of nonvictims, to capture the potential impact of incestuous abuse on later life. (We use the word *potential* because it is impossible to know for sure whether the incestuous abuse is the source of reported negative life experiences, or whether there are some other contributing factors. We have little reason to believe, however, that victims would differ from nonvictims as a *group* in any other way than the incest experience.)

Table 7.2 presents the NLE scale, stratified by ethnicity, and whether or not the respondent was a victim of incest. This table shows that Afro-American incest victims are significantly more likely to fall into the "worst outcome" group on the NLE scale than either White victims (86% versus 32%, X^2 = 15.35, 2 df, p < .001) or than Afro-American women who were not incestuously abused as children (86% versus 45%, X^2 = 7.95, 2 df, p < .02). Similarly, Whites who were victims of incestuous abuse as children were twice as likely as Whites who were never victimized to be in the worst outcome category (32% compared with 16%, X^2 = 21.55, 2 df, p < .001).

The other end of the spectrum is equally telling. Relatively few victims of incest (Afro-American *or* White) were in the best outcome category of the

NLE scale compared with their nonvictimized peers. Most striking are the differences for Afro-American women. Whereas only 7% of Afro-American incest victims could be described as having best outcomes, the comparable figure for Afro-American nonincest victims was over four times greater—or 30%! (X^2 = 4.52, 1 df, p < .05.) The fact that fewer than one-third of Afro-American nonvictims fell into this best outcome category is also sobering information.

To try to understand *why* Afro-American women reported more upset, greater long-term effects, and more negative life experiences as a result of incestuous abuse than White women, we examined in what ways, if any, their sexual abuse experiences differed. A number of variables were analyzed, including the severity of the abuse, its frequency and duration, the degree of force or violence involved, several measures related to age (i.e., age at onset, age disparity between victim and perpetrator, and age of perpetrator), and the relationship between the victim and perpetrator.

Severity

Incestuous abuse of Afro-American incest victims was over three times more likely than incestuous abuse of White victims to be at the *very severe* level. (Experiences involving oral, anal, or vaginal intercourse were considered *very severe* abuse, those involving genital fondling or attempted fondling, *severe* abuse, and more minor acts of sexual contact or attempted contact, *least severe* abuse.) Whereas 56% of the experiences reported by Afro-American incest victims involved some form of intercourse or attempted intercourse, the same was true of less than one-fifth (18%) of the experiences reported by White incest victims. Conversely, the experiences of White women were over twice as likely as the experiences of Afro-American women to be at the *least severe* level: 41% versus 19% (X^2 = 12.32, 2 df, p < .01).

In contrast to our findings, Wyatt (1985, p. 514) found no significant relationship between ethnicity and severity of child sexual abuse involving contact. One explanation for this difference may be that Wyatt's analysis was not confined to incestuous abuse, but included cases of extrafamilial child sexual abuse as well.

Pierce and Pierce (1984) also found some differences in the type of abuse reported by White and Afro-American victims, with White victims more likely to have been subjected to oral sex, and Afro-American victims, to intercourse. However, their data were even less comparable to ours than Wyatt's since they are based only on substantiated cases of child sexual

TABLE 7.3

Perpetrator-Victim Relationship by Ethnicity (in percentages)

Perpetrator	Afro-American Women N = 14[a]		White Women N = 129[a]	
Biological Father	7	} 28%	16	} 24%
Stepfather[b]	21		8	
Brother	14		12	
Grandfather	0		9	
Uncle	43		26	
First Male Cousin	0		14	
Female Relative	0		5	
Other Male Relative	14		11	
Total %	99		101	

a. If a woman was sexually assaulted by more than one of the same type of relative (e.g., by 2 uncles), she is included only once. Hence the total for Afro-American victims is 14 rather than 16, and for White women it is 129 rather than 134.

b. Includes 1 adoptive father and 1 foster father.

Overall table ($X^2 = 8.54$, 7 df, $p < .30$).

Father comparison only ($X^2 = 4.66$, 1 df, $p < .05$).

abuse reported to a child abuse hotline. (The finding concerning oral sex was significant at the < 0.001 level, while that concerning intercourse was only a trend [1984, p. 6].) In our survey, the only three cases involving oral sex occurred to White victims. All nine Afro-American cases of very severe abuse involved completed vaginal intercourse (5) or attempted intercourse (4).

Type of Incest Perpetrator

For the sample as a whole, incestuous abuse by a father was found to be significantly more traumatic than sexual abuse by other relatives (Russell, 1986). With our small sample size of only 14 Afro-American victims, it is not surprising that the differences revealed in the overall perpetrator-victim relationship by ethnicity do not reach statistical significance. Nonetheless, some interesting trends did emerge (see Table 7.3). Whereas White incest victims were over twice as likely to be abused by their biological fathers as Afro-American victims (16% versus 7%), just the opposite was true with respect to stepfathers: 21% of Afro-American victims were abused by stepfathers compared with 8% of Whites (father comparison only $X^2 = 4.66$, 1 df, $p < .05$).[2]

In trying to explain similar findings in her Los Angeles study, Wyatt (1985, p. 517) pointed out that stepfathers are more common in Afro-

American families, and biological fathers in White families. Although we cannot test this hypothesis directly with our data (our data indicate only the number of women who were *raised* by a stepfather, not the number who had ever lived with one), it seems highly plausible that the observed differences are related to this difference in family structure.

Table 7.3 also shows that Afro-American girls were more likely to have been victimized by uncles—a finding that reached statistical significance in the Pierce and Pierce (1984, p. 7) study. White victims were more likely to be abused by grandfathers, male cousins, and female perpetrators.

Force or Violence
Accompanying Incestuous Abuse

A quarter of the Afro-American incest victims reported that verbal threats accompanied the abuse, compared to only 6% of White victims (X^2 = 4.68, 1 df, p < .03). When the use of physical force, verbal threats, and weapons are combined into a single measure of force or violence, Afro-American victims were more likely to be subjected to force or violence than White victims. Specifically, 57% of the cases of incestuous abuse by Afro-American perpetrators involved the use of some degree of physical force or violence compared to 33% of the cases of incestuous abuse by perpetrators (X^2 = 4.53, 1 df, p < .05).

Age at Onset of Victimization

Consistent with the findings of Wyatt (1985, p. 515), the mean age of onset for incest victimization in our study was younger for White girls than for Afro-American girls: 10.7 years and 12.6 years, respectively (t-value = 2.16, 145 df, p < .05). Incest victimization of girls aged 9 and younger was twice as frequent for White girls as for Afro-American girls (35% versus 19%). However, this difference was not significant at < 0.05 level (X^2 = 2.53, 1 df, p < .15).

Age of Incest Perpetrator

Although the mean ages of Afro-American and White incest perpetrators at the time they abused their relatives was very similar (34.6 years and 33.7 years, respectively), the age distribution giving rise to these means varies significantly by ethnicity. For instance, whereas only 13% of Afro-American perpetrators were 25 or under at the time of the abuse, fully 39% of White perpetrators fell into this age category (see Table 7.4). Interest-

TABLE 7.4

Age of Incest Perpetrator by Ethnicity (in percentages)

Age of Perpetrator	Incidents Involving Afro-American Women N = 16	Incidents Involving White Women N = 132
Less than 18	13	26
18 to 25	0	13
26 to 35	38	17
36 to 45	44	20
46 to 55	6	10
55 Plus	0	15
Total	101	101

NOTE: Missing observations: 2 for White women;
(X^2 = 12.69, 5 df, p < .05).

ingly, the vast majority of Afro-American incest perpetrators (82%) were between the ages of 26 and 45 when they began the incestuous abuse compared to only 37% of the White incest perpetrators. White incest perpetrators were, in contrast, more evenly distributed across the age spectrum (X^2 = 12.69, 5 df, p < .05).

Age Disparity Between Victim and Perpetrator

Age disparity has frequently been found to be associated with trauma (Browne & Finkelhor, 1986; Finkelhor, 1979; Russell, 1986). Given our findings on the age of perpetrators, it is not surprising that nearly three times as many of the incest experiences reported by White victims as Afro-American victims occurred with perpetrators who were less than 9 years older than them. Incest experiences reported by Afro-American victims, by contrast, were more likely to have occurred with perpetrators who were at least 10 years older than they were. However, these associations did not reach statistical significance (X^2 = 5.97, 3 df, p < .12).

Other Factors

Three other variables that were associated with trauma when examining victims from all ethnic groups were the frequency of the abuse, the period of time over which it occurred, and whether or not the woman had been victimized by more than one relative on different occasions. There were no differences between Afro-American and White victims with regard to any of these factors.

Discussion

It seems likely that some of the findings reported above may explain why more Afro-American incest victims than White incest victims reported being extremely upset by the abuse and suffering from greater long-term effects. Specifically, Afro-American victims were more likely than White victims to be abused at the *very severe* level in terms of the sex acts involved, the abuse was more likely to be accompanied by force, and the perpetrator was more likely to be middle-aged at the time of the abuse rather than younger or older. These three factors were also associated with the degree of trauma reported by women from all ethnic groups combined (Russell, 1986). Although Afro-American victims were not more likely than their White counterparts to be abused by a father, they were more often abused by their uncles, and less often by their grandfathers, first cousins, and female perpetrators—the three types of perpetrators associated with the least traumatic abuse in our survey (Russell, 1986).

Other factors that are unique to the life circumstances of Afro-American women in this culture may also play a part in their reporting more trauma as a result of incestuous abuse than White women. For example, the trauma of incestuous abuse may be compounded by the trauma of being born and raised as an Afro-American female in a racist and sexist culture (see, for example, Jackson, 1973; Ladner, 1971; Powell, 1979, 1983).

While this analysis may shed some light on why Afro-American incest victims reported more trauma than White victims did, it does not explain why they were more likely to be abused at the *very severe* level and with more force in the first place. How might these findings be explained?

It is widely believed that there is an association between social class and violence, and some empirical studies have supported this belief (e.g., Straus, Gelles, & Steinmetz, 1980). Since our Afro-American respondents were disproportionately from the lower class, could this explain why Afro-American incest victims were more forcefully and severely sexually abused?

Using what we consider to be our best measures of social class background—the education and occupational status of the incest victims' fathers—no association was found between social class and the severity of the incestuous abuse or the force that accompanied the abuse. Nor was there an association between these variables when victims were compared with nonincest victims within each of these two ethnic groups. So this hypothesis is not supported by our survey data.

Another possible explanation may center around the issue of consanguinity—that is, whether or not the perpetrator was a blood relative. When looking at victims from all ethnic backgrounds, for example, we found that incest perpetrated by non-blood relatives was more likely to be at the *very severe* level than the abuse perpetrated by blood relatives ($X^2 = 12.40$, 4 df, p $<$ .02). Non-blood relatives were also significantly more likely to use force or violence when committing the abuse ($X^2 = 13.57$, 6 df, p $<$ .03). The fact that fewer Afro-American victims than White victims were abused by consanguineal relatives in our sample may thus explain (at least in part) the observed differences in severity and the use of force or violence.

Since the mean age at onset for incest victimization was older for Afro-American girls than for White girls, it could also be that there is an association between age at onset, severity, and use of force. Although analysis revealed a statistically significant relationship between these variables for all incest victims, regardless of ethnicity, it was not in the direction that would support this hypothesis. Girls who were sexually abused at the *least severe* level had the oldest mean age—12.1 years compared to 11.6 years for the *very severely* abused and 10.0 years for the *severely* abused.

A final explanation for why Afro-American women reported incestuous abuse at a more severe level than White women may relate to the age of the perpetrator. We noted that the vast majority of Afro-American incest perpetrators were between the ages of 26 and 45, with a mere 6% being older than 45 years. Analysis of our data on all incest victims reveals that severity did indeed decline as age increased—at least when our *severe* and *very severe* categories are combined. (Whereas the mean age [at onset] for perpetrators of *severe* and *very severe* incestuous abuse was 29 years, the comparable figure for the perpetrators of *least severe* abuse was 41 years.) So our findings that younger perpetrators more often abused their victims with greater severity, and that the overwhelming majority of the Afro-American incest perpetrators were relatively young (94% were under the age of 45), may help to explain why the Afro-American victims were more often sexually abused at a more severe level.

In summary, Afro-American incest victims in our San Francisco probability sample reported greater trauma as a result of the abuse than White incest victims. Possible reasons for this finding were discussed, including the fact that the abuse to which Afro-American victims were subjected was more severe in terms of the sexual acts involved, was accompanied by more force, and their incest perpetrators were more likely to be of an age associated with higher levels of trauma. In addition, we suggested that the trauma of being raised an Afro-American female in a racist and sexist society may compound the effects of the abuse. Finally, we attempted to explain why Afro-American victims may have been sexually assaulted with more force and at a more severe level.

Our analysis affirms the importance of ethnicity as a factor to be considered by researchers, clinicians, and laypeople alike. It also indicates the need for further research on the long-term effects of incestuous abuse of Afro-American women.

NOTES

1. This survey was funded by the National Institute of Mental Health (Grant RO1MH28960) and the National Center on Child Abuse and Neglect (Grant 90-CA-813/01).
2. Pierce and Pierce (1984, pp. 7-8) also found that Afro-American children were significantly less likely to be abused by their biological fathers. However, abuse by stepfathers was unrelated to the victim's race in their study.

REFERENCES

Browne, A., & Finkelhor, D. (1986). The impact of child sexual abuse: A review of the research. *Psychological Bulletin, 99*(1).

DeFrancis, V. (1969). *Protecting the child victim of sex crimes committed by adults.* Denver, CO: American Humane Association, Children's Division.

Finkelhor, D. (1979). *Sexually victimized children.* New York: Free Press.

Herman, J. (1981). *Father-daughter incest.* Cambridge, MA: Harvard University Press.

Jackson, J. (1973). Black women in a racist society. In C. V. Willie, B. Kramer, & B. Brown (Eds.), *Racism and mental health.* Pittsburgh: University of Pittsburgh Press.

Ladner, J. (1971). *Tomorrow's tomorrow: The Black woman.* Garden City, NY: Doubleday.

Meiselman, K. C. (1978). *Incest.* San Francisco: Jossey-Bass.

Myers, H. (1982). Research on the Afro-American family: A critical review. In B. Bass, G. Wyatt, & G. Powell (Eds.), *The Afro-American family: Assessment, treatment, and research issues.* New York: Grune & Stratton.

Pierce, L., & Pierce, R. (1984). *Race as a factor in childhood sexual abuse.* Paper presented at the Second National Family Violence Research Conference, Durham, NH.

Powell, G. (1979). Growing up Black and female. In C. Kopp (Ed.), *Becoming female: Perspectives on development.* New York: Plenum.

Powell, G. (1983). Coping with adversity: The psychosocial development of Afro-American children. In G. Powell, J. Yamamoto, A. Romero, & A. Morales (Eds.), *The psychosocial development of minority group children*. New York: Bruner/Mazel.

Russell, D.E.H. (1986). *The secret trauma: Incest in the lives of girls and women*. New York: Basic Books.

Straus, M. A., Gelles, R. J., & Steinmetz, S. K. (1980). *Behind closed doors: Violence in the American family*. Garden City, NY: Doubleday.

Weinberg, S. K. (1976). *Incest behavior* (rev. ed.). Secaucus, NJ: Citadel.

Wyatt, G. E. (1985). The sexual abuse of Afro-American and white women in childhood. *Child Abuse and Neglect: The International Journal, 9*, 507-519.

Wyatt, G. E. (1986). *The aftermath of child sexual abuse: The victim's experience*. Unpublished manuscript.

8

Long-Term Psychological Sequelae of Child Sexual Abuse

The Los Angeles Epidemiologic Catchment Area Study

JUDITH A. STEIN
JACQUELINE M. GOLDING
JUDITH M. SIEGEL
M. AUDREY BURNAM
SUSAN B. SORENSON

Research on the psychological aftermath of child sexual abuse has evolved significantly over the years. Like the "three generations of research" of psychiatric epidemiology in general (Weissman & Klerman, 1978), sexual abuse research shows three generations of growth. The first generation reported generally univariate or bivariate rates of psychological reactions among treated populations (usually White women) with symptom checklists, clinical evaluations, and open-ended questions. Treatment studies are subject to selection bias, however, because most sexual abuse victims do

AUTHORS' NOTE: This research was supported by the Epidemiologic Catchment Area Program (UO1 MH 35865) and by supplemental funds from the National Center for the Prevention and Control of Rape (Grant MH 35865-03). Jacqueline M. Golding and Susan B. Sorenson were supported by a Psychiatric Epidemiology Training Grant (USPHS MH 14664). The Epidemiologic Catchment Area Program is a series of five epidemiologic research studies performed by independent research teams in collaboration with staff of the Division of Biometry and Epidemiology of the National Institute of Mental Health (NIMH). The NIMH principal collaborators are Darrel A. Regier, Ben Z. Locke, and Jack D. Burke, Jr.; the NIMH project officer is William J. Huber. The principal investigators and coinvestigators from the five sites are Yale University, UO1 MH 34224—Jerome K. Myers, Myrna M. Weissman, and Gary L. Tischler; Johns Hopkins University, UO1 MH 33870—Morton Kramer and Sam not seek professional treatment (DiVasto et al., 1984; Golding, Stein, Siegel, Burnam & Sorensen, in press; Herold, Mantle, & Zemitis, 1979). Moreover, those who use services probably have higher rates of psychological symptomatology than nonutilizers, leading to an overestimation of psychological dysfunction among the sexually abused. Also problematic, symptom scales are often unstandardized, have unknown psychometric properties, and are unable o make specific psychiatric diagnoses. Similarly, clinical ratings tend to be unreliable and of questionable validity (Spitzer & Fleiss, 1974; Zubin, 1967).

Second generation studies, in contrast, assess psychological symptomatology among representative samples using structured interviews. For example, using a structured interview and symptom checklist, Peters (1984) interviewed 119 abused and nonabused women randomly selected from Los Angeles community households. These studies offer important advances methodologically, although they are limited somewhat by their inability to make specific psychiatric diagnoses.

More recently, a third generation is emerging that estimates prevalence of specific DSM-III diagnoses among representative community respondents using multivariate techniques. For example, an earlier analysis of the present data examined the prevalence and predictors of nine specific psychiatric disorders among abused and nonabused community respondents (Burnam et al., in press). This research extends previous work by including over 3,000 randomly selected community residents, with about equal proportions of males and females, and Hispanics and non-Hispanic Whites. This large sample allows generalization to sexually abused persons whether or not they seek treatment, permits gender and ethnic comparisons, and allows some multivariate analyses that are typically not possible. This chapter presents data on child sexual abuse from this recent, primarily "third generation" study—the Los Angeles ECA study.

Purpose of this Study

This study estimates lifetime and current (prior six months) prevalence of psychological reactions to child sexual abuse (CSA) by gender and ethnicity (Hispanic versus non-Hispanic White) in a representative,

Shapiro; Washington University, St. Louis, UO1 MH 33883—Lee N. Robins and John H. Helzer; Duke University, UO1 MH 35386—Dan Blazer and Linda George; University of California, Los Angeles, UO1 MH 35865—Marvin Karno, Richard L. Hough, Javier I. Escobar, M. Audrey Burnam, and Dianne M. Timbers. We gratefully acknowledge the work of Vivian Barnett Brown, Cynthia Telles, and Dianne Timbers in the development of the sexual abuse instrument. Requests for reprints should be sent to Judith A. Stein, Island Mental Health Center, Coupeville, WA 98239.

community sample. We examine the prevalence of 15 psychological symptoms attributed to sexual abuse among respondents with CSA and 11 specific psychiatric disorders among those abused as children and the unabused. Current symptoms and diagnoses reflect long-term sequelae (*at least* two years after the abuse) because CSA is defined as before age 16, and respondents were at least 18 years old.

Method

These data are from a supplement to the Los Angeles Epidemiologic Catchment Area (ECA) study, one of five sites of the NIMH-initiated collaborative ECA program. The ECA program's primary goals are to estimate the prevalence and incidence of specific psychiatric disorders and to examine patterns of health service utilization. Los Angeles respondents were also asked a series of questions regarding lifetime sexual abuse. The design and methodology of the ECA surveys are described elsewhere (Eaton & Kessler, 1985; Regier et al., 1984).

Sample

The sample consists of 3,132 adults (age 18 or older) from two Los Angeles mental health catchment areas. The East Los Angeles catchment area contains predominantly Hispanic Americans (83%) whereas the Venice/Culver City catchment area contains largely non-Hispanic Whites (63%) but also many Hispanics (21%). Almost 90% of the Hispanic Americans in these catchment areas are of Mexican cultural or ethnic origin. Respondents chose whether to take the interview in English or Spanish; the instrument allowed easy switching.

A two-stage probability technique selected a sample of 3,132 adults (age 18 or older), with census blocks and households as primary and secondary sampling units, respectively. Within each catchment area, every household had an equal probability of selection, with one adult randomly selected from each household (Kish, 1965). Respondents were interviewed in person, yielding a 68% completion rate. Data were weighted to adjust for this sampling design and for nonresponse.

Measures

Sexual abuse. The sexual abuse instrument was developed at the Los Angeles ECA site, in collaboration with NIMH, to estimate lifetime sexual abuse prevalence and its circumstances. Sexual abuse was assessed with the question, "In your lifetime, has anyone ever tried to pressure or force you to have sexual contact? By sexual contact I mean their touching your sexual parts, your touching their sexual parts, or sexual intercourse." Those answering affirmatively (n = 447) were asked if they had ever been forced or pressured for sexual contact before age 16 (CSA) or older (adult sexual assault; ASA) and their age at first incident. Because we were assessing incidents in adulthood and childhood, we needed a sexual abuse definition appropriate for both. Our definition excluded some types of commonly defined CSA (e.g., noncontact exposure) and conservatively limited CSA to incidents before age 16. Abuse was coded as either present or absent. Age of perpetrator was not ascertained.

The prevalence of CSA for the total sample (weighted for sampling design and nonresponse) was 5.3%. Rates were higher for non-Hispanic Whites (8.7%) versus Hispanics (3.0%), women (6.8%) versus men (3.8%), and younger persons at the time of interview (6.5%) versus older persons (3.9%; Siegel, Sorenson, Golding, Burnam, & Stein, 1987). Prevalence of ASA is presented elsewhere (Sorenson, Stein, Siegel, Golding & Burnam, 1987).

Emotional/behavioral reactions. Abused respondents were asked the following fifteen questions about their emotional and behavioral reactions to sexual abuse: "Think about how being sexually pressured or forced affected your life. Did it ever cause you to

(1)   Become fearful of people or situations that didn't used to frighten you?
(2)   Stop doing things that you did or stop going places that you went before?
(3)   Become afraid of having sexual relations?
(4)   Have less sexual interest?
(5)   Have less pleasurable sexual relations?
(6)   Feel dishonored or spoiled?
(7)   Feel guilty?
(8)   Feel sad, blue, or depressed?
(9)   Feel angry?
(10) Feel tense, nervous, or anxious?
(11) Have trouble sleeping?
(12) Lose or increase your appetite?
(13) Drink more alcohol or use more drugs?
(14) Become afraid of being alone?
(15) Anything else?"

Analyses estimated lifetime and current prevalence (prior six months) of each symptom among the 82 respondents abused as children, reclassifying open-ended responses where possible. Prevalence of emotional reactions to lifetime sexual abuse is examined elsewhere (Siegel, Golding, Stein, Sorenson, & Burnam, 1988).

Psychiatric disorder. Psychiatric disorders based on DSM-III criteria were assessed using the NIMH Diagnostic Interview Schedule (DIS; Robins, Helzer, Croughan, & Ratcliff, 1981), a highly structured instrument administered by lay interviewers that generates diagnoses from computer algorithms based on self-reported signs and symptoms. Generally, the DIS has adequate test-retest reliability, good to fair validity among patient populations (Robins et al., 1981; Robins, Helzer, Ratcliff, & Seyfried, 1982), and is the preferred method for generating specific diagnoses from survey data collected by lay interviewers.

The DIS assesses lifetime presence of each disorder, age of onset of disorder, and current diagnoses for four prevalence periods (within the past two weeks, the past month, the past six months, and the past year). Analyses reported here are based on lifetime and six-month (current) diagnoses. We examined the following DIS/DSM-III diagnostic categories and specific disorders making up each category: substance use disorders (alcohol or drug abuse/dependence), schizophrenic disorders (schizophrenia or schizophreniform disorder); affective disorder (mania, major depression, or dysthymia); and anxiety disorder (panic disorder, phobia, or obsessive-compulsive disorder). Antisocial personality disorder was also examined, but anorexia nervosa and somatization disorder were excluded from analyses because of two few cases; dysthymia was excluded from analyses involving age because the DIS does not ascertain its age of onset. Diagnostic exclusions based on hierarchical ordering of disorders for multiple psychiatric diagnoses were not applied because of limited data on underlying assumptions and appropriate guidelines for operationalizing DSM-III exclusion rules. Prevalence of disorder was estimated for the 82 respondents with CSA and the 2,601 unabused respondents.

Demographics. We examined gender, age, ethnicity, and education. Ethnicity was classified as Hispanic (121 abused in childhood or adulthood; 19 abused in childhood only), non-Hispanic White (284, childhood or adulthood; 56 childhood only), or other (42, childhood or adulthood; 7, childhood only).[1] Education served as an indicator of socioeconomic status because it was highly correlated with income ($r = .39$, $p = .0001$) and job status ($r = .55$, $p = .0001$) but had fewer missing cases than the latter two variables. Education was dichotomized at each ethnic group's median years of education completed (10 for Hispanics; 14 for non-Hispanic Whites and for others). Age at interview was dichotomized at 18 to 39 versus 40 or

TABLE 8.1
Demographic Characteristics of Sexually Abused Respondents

| | Respondents with any lifetime sexual abuse | | | | Respondents with child sexual abuse only | | | |
	Non-Hispanic White	Hispanic	other	total	Non-Hispanic White	Hispanic	other	total
Men								
18-39	63	33	15	111	15	6	5	26
40+	28	6	3	37	5	0	0	5
Total	91	39	18	148	20	6	5	31
Women								
18-39	126	60	20	206	20	10	2	32
40+	66	22	3	91	16	3	0	19
Total	192	82	23	297	36	13	2	51
Total	283	121	41	445	56	19	7	82

NOTE: Unweighted sample sizes are shown. Two respondents are omitted because of missing demographic data.

older. Table 8.1 shows the demographic characteristics of respondents with any lifetime sexual abuse and with CSA only (no adult sexual abuse).

Our analyses are based on the 82 respondents abused in childhood only, excluding those abused in adulthood or both childhood *and* adulthood. This conservative procedure separates the experiences of adult assault from those of child abuse, permitting more conclusive statements about the psychological sequelae of CSA. The 2,601 nonabused respondents formed the comparison group. For brevity, CSA or its equivalent refers here to those abused in childhood only.

Results

Psychological Symptoms

Lifetime prevalence. Table 8.2 shows the percentage of respondents with CSA attributing each of the fourteen possible psychological symptoms to their abuse by gender and ethnicity. All tests were calculated with 95% confidence intervals and standard errors adjusted for the clustered sampling design (Shah, 1981).

Over 75% of respondents had experienced at least one symptom, with anxiety (49.9%), anger (47.9%), guilt (47.5%), and depression (45.2%) most commonly reported. Least frequent symptoms were increased substance

TABLE 8.2
Lifetime Prevalence of Emotional Reactions to Child Sexual Abuse
by Gender and Ethnicity

	Total (n = 75)	Men (n = 30)	Women (n = 44)	Hispanics (n = 16)	Non-Hispanic Whites (n = 53)
Any symptom	75.6(5.9)	65.9(9.3)	82.8(6.9)	85.5(8.3)	72.6(7.5)
Fearful	33.1(6.6)	17.8(7.1)	44.9(10.2)	60.3(13.6)	26.0(6.2)
Behavioral restriction	24.5(6.2)	9.3(5.6)	36.1(8.2)	34.2(13.2)	23.0(7.1)
Afraid of sex	27.3(6.0)	16.9(9.0)	34.9(6.6)	32.0(13.4)	25.8(6.8)
Less sexual interest	24.4(5.3)	14.1(7.0)	31.9(6.4)	57.4(10.5)	16.3(5.2)*
Less sexual pleasure	27.4(6.0)	16.3(7.5)	35.5(7.4)	40.4(14.5)	23.5(6.9)
Dishonored	40.3(5.9)	32.5(10.0)	46.1(7.1)	46.9(14.4)	39.2(8.0)
Guilty	47.5(6.7)	36.8(10.9)	55.4(9.0)	36.6(12.3)	50.0(8.9)
Depressed	45.2(6.4)	34.2(9.8)	53.3(8.8)	60.0(13.5)	39.3(8.3)
Angry	47.9(6.2)	40.2(9.6)	53.6(9.1)	67.0(12.6)	42.8(8.0)
Anxious	49.9(6.5)	39.4(9.3)	57.4(8.8)	42.2(12.7)	50.1(8.0)
Insomnia	28.0(6.2)	15.8(9.0)	37.0(8.0)	33.4(11.4)	25.4(7.5)
Appetite disturbance	8.9(3.6)	3.9(3.8)	12.7(5.7)	24.3(11.9)	5.3(2.9)
Increased substance use	4.0(1.8)	0.0(0.0)	6.9(2.7)*	0.0(00.0)	5.5(2.4)*
Afraid to be alone	15.8(4.1)	1.7(1.7)	26.1(6.4)*	29.2(13.0)	11.7(4.0)

NOTE: Percentages are shown, followed by standard errors in parentheses.
*Gender or ethnic difference, $p < .05$.

use (4.0%), appetite disturbance (8.9%), and fear of being alone (15.8%). Women reported significantly more substance use (6.9% versus 0%) and fear of being alone (26.1% versus 1.7%) than men. Hispanics reported loss of sexual interest significantly more often (57.4% versus 16.3%) and substance use less often (0% versus 5.5%) than non-Hispanic Whites.

Current prevalence. Table 8.3 presents the prevalence of symptoms six months prior to the interview by gender and ethnicity. Because CSA is defined as before age 16 and respondents were 18 years or older, six-month prevalence implies persistence for *at least* two years. Mean age at *first* sexual abuse incident was 9.71 years, with women ($M = 8.79$) reporting first incidents earlier than men ($M = 11.0$, $p < .05$). Age of first abuse did not differ significantly by ethnicity ($M = 10.31$, Hispanics; $M = 9.44$, non-Hispanic Whites). Similarly, mean age at *most recent* abuse incident was

TABLE 8.3

Six-Month Prevalence of Emotional Reactions Attributed to Child
Sexual Abuse by Gender and Ethnicity

	Total (n = 75)	Men (n = 30)	Women (n = 45)	Hispanic (n = 16)	Non-Hispanic White (n = 53)
Any symptom	19.6(5.1)	11.1(8.5)	25.7(7.1)	14.3(10.2)	20.8(6.5)
Fearful	1.7(1.1)	0.0(0.0)	3.0(2.2)	0.0(0.0)	2.3(1.6)
Behavioral restriction	0.0(0.0)	0.0(0.0)	0.0(0.0)	0.0(0.0)	0.0(0.0)
Afraid of sex	4.9(2.4)	0.0(0.0)	8.5(4.4)	0.0(0.0)	5.0(2.9)
Less sexual interest	3.6(2.1)	0.0(0.0)	6.3(3.7)	0.0(0.0)	5.0(2.9)
Less sexual pleasure	4.2(2.2)	0.0(0.0)	7.4(4.0)	0.0(0.0)	4.1(2.6)
Dishonored	8.4(4.9)	8.6(8.1)	8.2(5.3)	0.0(0.0)	11.6(6.9)
Guilty	10.5(5.1)	8.9(8.3)	11.7(5.9)	0.0(0.0)	12.6(7.0)
Depressed	12.5(5.3)	8.9(8.3)	15.1(6.3)	5.5(5.5)	13.7(7.1)
Angry	14.8(4.8)	11.1(8.5)	17.5(6.4)	14.3(10.2)	16.0(5.9)
Anxious	10.6(5.2)	9.1(8.5)	11.7(5.8)	0.0(0.0)	14.3(7.2)*
Insomnia	3.9(2.7)	0.0(0.0)	6.7(4.7)	0.0(0.0)	5.3(3.7)
Appetite disturbance	0.0(0.0)	0.0(0.0)	0.0(0.0)	0.0(0.0)	0.0(0.0)
substance use	0.0(0.0)	0.0(0.0)	0.0(0.0)	0.0(0.0)	0.0(0.0)
Afraid to be alone	1.4(1.0)	0.0(0.0)	2.4(1.8)	0.0(0.0)	1.9(1.4)

*Hispanics differ from non-Hispanic Whites, $p < .05$.

12.49, suggesting that current symptoms were generally attributed to an incident occurring over five years earlier.

Nearly 20% of the sample reported at least one current symptom. The most commonly reported lifetime symptoms—anger, depression, anxiety, and guilt—were also most common in the six months preceding the interview (14.8%, 12.5%, 10.6%, 10.5%, respectively). Sexual disturbance was also persistent, with about 20% experiencing one or more symptom six months prior to the interview. Non-Hispanic Whites reported significantly more anxiety than Hispanics (14.3% versus 0%). Current symptoms did not differ significantly by gender.

Psychiatric Diagnosis

Lifetime prevalence. Table 8.4 presents the lifetime prevalence of 11 specific psychiatric disorders and five disorder groups by gender and

TABLE 8.4

Lifetime Prevalence of Psychiatric Disorders by Child Sexual Abuse

	All Respondents		Men		Women		Hispanics		Non-Hispanic Whites	
	Not Abused	Abused During Childhood	Not Abused	Abused During Childhood	Not Abused	Abused During Childhood	Not Abused	Abused During Childhood	Not Abused	Abused During Childhood
	(n = 2601)	(n = 82)	(n = 1294)	(n = 31)	(n = 1307)	(n = 51)	(n = 1289)	(n = 19)	(n = 1010)	(n = 56)
Substance Use Disorders	16.5(0.8)	36.6(6.5)*	26.7(1.3)	55.4(10.3)*	6.0(0.7)	24.1(5.9)	16.8(1.3)	32.7(11.9)*	18.1(1.4)	35.7(7.8)
Alcohol abuse/dependence	13.8(0.7)	26.7(5.3)*	23.2(1.3)	35.7(9.8)	4.1(0.6)	20.8(5.5)*	15.7(1.2)	24.5(11.4)	13.1(1.2)	26.4(6.2)
Drug abuse/dependence	5.5(0.5)	26.2(6.2)	7.8(0.8)	44.9(10.0)*	3.1(0.6)	13.7(3.5)*	3.3(0.5)	27.6(11.6)*	9.2(1.0)	24.5(6.4)*
Schizophrenic Disorders	0.4(0.1)	3.0(1.7)	0.4(0.2)	0.0(0.0)	0.5(2.9)	5.0(2.9)	0.4(0.2)	0.0(0.0)	0.5(0.2)	2.6(1.8)
Schizophrenia	0.4(0.1)	1.8(1.3)	0.4(0.2)	0.0(0.0)	0.4(0.1)	3.1(2.3)	0.4(0.2)	0.0(0.0)	0.5(0.2)	1.0(1.0)
Schizophrenia disorder	0.1(0.0)	1.1(1.1)	0.0(0.0)	0.0(0.0)	0.1(0.1)	1.9(1.8)	0.1(0.1)	0.0(0.0)	0.1(0.1)	1.6(1.6)
Affective Disorders	7.0(0.6)	20.5(3.7)	5.9(0.7)	13.8(5.6)	8.3(0.8)	24.9(5.8)*	5.9(0.7)	41.2(10.6)*	8.6(1.1)	12.7(3.0)
Mania	0.2(0.1)	0.7(0.7)	0.4(0.2)	0.0(0.0)	0.2(0.1)	1.2(1.2)	0.0(0.0)	0.0(0.0)	0.6(0.2)	1.0(1.0)
Major depressive disorder	4.7(0.5)	18.6(3.6)	3.9(0.5)	13.8(5.6)	5.5(0.7)	21.9(5.6)*	3.6(0.6)	32.6(10.5)*	6.1(0.9)	12.7(3.0)
Dysthymia	3.7(0.4)	10.7(3.4)	3.0(0.6)	10.6(4.8)	4.4(0.6)	10.8(4.6)	3.9(0.6)	27.0(11.1)*	3.4(0.6)	4.9(2.6)
Anxiety Disorders	10.9(0.7)	29.5(6.5)*	8.0(0.9)	18.2(7.9)	13.9(1.1)	36.5(7.1)*	12.2(1.1)	39.2(12.4)*	9.8(0.9)	25.4(6.6)*
Phobia	9.7(0.7)	23.2(5.3)*	7.0(0.8)	6.5(4.5)	12.5(1.1)	34.2(7.0)*	11.3(1.1)	39.2(12.4)*	8.1(0.9)	18.2(5.8)
Panic disorder	0.8(0.2)	8.1(3.0)*	0.3(0.1)	8.4(4.9)	1.3(0.4)	7.8(4.2)	1.0(0.3)	10.1(9.3)	0.8(0.3)	5.5(2.8)
Obsessive compulsive disorder	1.4(0.2)	6.9(3.3)	1.3(0.3)	6.4(4.8)	1.5(9.3)	7.2(4.3)	1.0(0.3)	15.3(10.2)	2.0(0.4)	3.5(2.7)
Antisocial Personality Disorder	2.4(0.3)	9.1(2.9)*	4.2(0.5)	12.6(5.9)	0.6(0.2)	6.8(2.9)	3.1(0.4)	7.8(5.7)	2.1(0.4)	10.3(3.5)*
Any Diagnosis	29.0(1.0)	63.6(6.9)*	34.0(1.5)	71.2(9.7)*	24.0(1.5)	58.6(7.7)*	31.0(1.5)	71.2(9.3)*	28.7(1.7)	59.9(8.6)*

NOTE: Percentages are shown, followed by standard errors in parentheses. Respondents who were sexually abused during adulthood are omitted from this analysis.

*Respondents with childhood sexual abuse differ from those with no sexual abuse, $p < .05$.

143

ethnicity among respondents with CSA and among the nonabused. Confidence intervals (as described above) tested group differences.

Respondents abused during childhood were significantly more likely than the nonabused to have at least one lifetime DIS diagnosis (63.6% versus 29.0%), and to have higher prevalence of substance abuse (36.6% versus 16.5%), alcohol abuse/dependence (26.7% versus 13.8%), drug abuse/dependence (26.2% versus 5.5%), affective disorder (20.5% versus 7.0%), major depressive disorder (18.6% versus 4.7%), anxiety disorder (29.2% versus 10.9%), phobia (23.2% versus 9.7%), panic disorder (8.1% versus 0.8%) and antisocial personality disorder (9.1% versus 2.4%). The two groups did not differ in lifetime prevalence of schizophrenia, schizophreniform disorder, mania, dysthymia, or obsessive compulsive disorder.

Abused men had significantly higher rates of drug abuse/dependence, substance abuse/dependence, and any diagnosis compared to their nonabused counterparts; abused women had higher rates of all disorders except antisocial personality, including any disorder. Abused non-Hispanic Whites had elevated rates of any diagnosis, drug abuse/dependence, anxiety, and antisocial personality disorders, whereas abused Hispanics had significantly higher rates of drug abuse/dependence, affective disorder, major depression, anxiety, phobia, dysthymia, and any lifetime diagnosis compared to the unabused.

Current prevalence. Table 8.5 shows current (prior six months) psychiatric disorder prevalence by gender and ethnicity among respondents with CSA and among the unabused.

Respondents abused before age 16 were significantly more likely to have a psychiatric disorder in the preceding six months than the nonabused (36.5% versus 13.7%). They also had a higher prevalence of affective disorder (13.4% versus 2.4%), major depression (13.4% versus 2.1%), anxiety (20.8% versus 5.6%), and panic disorder (6.8% versus 0.6%) than the nonabused. Again, current prevalence reflects long-term responses an average of 5 years after the most recent abuse. Of respondents with current major depression (n = 14) or panic disorder (n = 6), 93% and 83%, respectively, were first abused before disorder onset.

Men with CSA were significantly more likely than their nonabused counterparts to have a current disorder and drug abuse/dependence; abused women were more likely to have any current diagnosis, affective disorder, major depression, and anxiety. Abused non-Hispanic Whites showed increased rates of anxiety whereas abused Hispanics had elevated rates of any current diagnosis, affective disorder, and major depression.

TABLE 8.5
Current[a] Prevalence of Psychiatric Disorders by Child Sexual Abuse

	All Respondents		Men		Women		Hispanics		Non-Hispanic Whites	
	Not Abused	Abused During Childhood	Not Abused	Abused During Childhood	Not Abused	Abused During Childhood	Not Abused	Abused During Childhood	Not Abused	Abused During Childhood
	(n = 2601)	(n = 82)	(n = 1294)	(n = 31)	(n = 1307)	(n = 51)	(n = 1289)	(n = 19)	(n = 1010)	(n = 56)
Substance Use Disorders	6.0(0.6)	11.9(3.0)	10.0(1.1)	24.0(6.3)	1.9(0.5)	3.9(2.3)	6.3(0.9)	8.0(5.9)	6.2(0.9)	8.8(3.6)
Alcohol abuse/ dependence	4.6(0.5)	6.9(2.3)	7.7(0.9)	12.6(4.7)	1.4(0.4)	3.1(2.2)	5.2(0.8)	0.0(0.0)	4.2(0.8)	6.2(3.1)
Drug abuse/ dependence	2.0(0.3)	8.2(2.8)	3.3(0.6)	17.6(6.7)*	0.7(0.2)	2.0(1.4)	1.5(0.4)	8.0(5.9)	3.2(0.6)	7.0(3.3)
Schizophrenic Disorders[a]	0.3(1.1)	3.0(1.7)	0.3(0.2)	0.0(0.0)	0.2(0.1)	5.0(2.9)	0.3(0.2)	0.0(0.0)	0.3(0.2)	2.6(1.8)
Schizophrenia	0.3(1.1)	1.8(1.3)	0.3(0.2)	0.0(0.0)	0.2(0.1)	3.1(2.3)	0.3(0.2)	0.0(0.0)	0.3(0.2)	1.0(1.0)
Schizophrenia disorder	0.0(0.0)	1.1(1.1)	0.0(0.0)	0.0(0.0)	0.1(0.1)	1.9(1.8)	0.1(0.1)	0.0(0.0)	0.0(0.0)	1.6(1.6)
Affective Disorders	2.4(0.4)	13.4(3.8)*	1.9(0.4)	8.5(4.3)	3.0(0.5)	16.6(6.1)*	2.2(0.5)	32.6(10.5)*	3.0(0.6)	7.0(2.5)
Mania	0.1(0.0)	0.0(0.0)	0.2(0.1)	0.0(0.0)	0.1(0.1)	0.0(0.0)	0.0(0.0)	0.0(0.0)	0.3(0.2)	0.0(0.0)
Major depressive disorder	2.1(0.3)	13.4(3.8)*	1.6(0.4)	8.5(4.3)	2.5(0.5)	16.6(6.1)*	2.0(0.5)	32.6(10.5)*	2.4(0.4)	7.0(2.5)
Anxiety Disorders	5.6(0.5)	20.8(5.0)*	2.7(0.4)	16.6(7.1)	8.7(0.8)	23.7(6.4)*	6.7(0.8)	26.7(11.5)	4.8(0.6)	18.3(6.1)*
Phobia	5.0(0.4)	14.3(4.4)	2.3(0.4)	6.5(4.5)	7.8(0.8)	19.4(6.4)	6.3(0.8)	26.7(11.5)	3.9(0.5)	11.9(5.0)
Panic disorder	0.6(0.2)	6.8(2.8)	0.2(0.1)	5.2(3.8)	0.9(0.3)	7.8(4.2)	0.7(0.3)	10.1(9.3)	0.6(0.2)	3.7(2.2)
Obsessive compulsive disorder	0.5(0.1)	4.1(2.4)	0.3(0.2)	4.8(4.7)	0.6(0.2)	3.7(2.6)	0.3(0.2)	5.2(5.1)	0.6(0.3)	2.6(2.6)
Antisocial Personality Disorder	0.6(0.2)	0.7(0.7)	1.2(0.3)	0.0(0.0)*	0.1(0.0)	1.2(1.1)	1.3(0.3)	0.0(0.0)	0.4(0.2)	0.0(0.0)
Any Diagnosis	13.7(0.7)	36.5(5.7)*	14.2(1.1)	42.2(8.5)*	13.1(1.0)	36.7(7.4)*	15.3(1.1)	49.7(10.4)*	13.2(1.2)	29.5(7.3)

NOTE: Percentages are shown, followed by standard errors in parentheses. Respondents who were sexually abused during adulthood are omitted from this analysis.

a. Within six months prior to interview.

*Respondents with childhood sexual abuse differ from those with no sexual abuse, $p < .05$.

Multivariate associations. To determine whether demographics or adult sexual abuse account for the CSA-psychiatric disorder association, we estimated multiple logistic regression models using the SAS CATMOD procedure (SAS Institute, 1985).[2] CSA (coded as present or absent) predicted each psychiatric disorder significantly associated with CSA in bivariate analyses. Adult sexual abuse, adult *and* child sexual abuse, gender, age, ethnicity, and education were controls. As shown in Table 8.6, all associations of CSA with both lifetime and current psychiatric disorder except two remained significant when controlling other sexual abuses and demographic variables; associations of CSA with both current drug abuse/dependence and current panic disorder were significant before but not after adjusting for design effects.

Discussion

These findings strongly suggest that CSA has persisting psychological consequences in the form of both symptomatology attributed to the abuse and DIS-DSM-III psychiatric diagnoses. Three-fourths of the abused reported symptoms of distress, with about half reporting anxiety, anger, guilt, or depression, similar to earlier findings for lifetime sexual abuse (Siegel et al., 1988). Our rates for guilt and appetite disturbances are lower than those reported previously (DeFrancis, 1969; Peters, 1984), although our 50% lifetime anxiety rate associated with CSA is within the range reported in previous studies (Anderson, Bach, & Griffith, 1981; Briere, 1984; Peters, 1976; Sedney & Brooks, 1984). The high depression and sexual disturbance rates among the abused are consistent with previous findings that such reactions are common (Bagley & Ramsay, 1985; Briere, 1984; Briere & Runtz, 1985; Peters, 1984; Sedney & Brooks, 1984; Tsai, Feldman-Summers, & Edgar, 1979).

Substance use disorders, major depression, phobia, panic disorder, and antisocial personality also showed elevated prevalence among those abused as children—even when gender, ethnicity, age, and education were controlled—consistent with earlier results for any sexual abuse (childhood or adulthood; Burnam et al., in press). Our 27% lifetime alcohol abuse/dependence and 26% lifetime drug abuse/dependence rates among the abused are consistent with community (Peters, 1984) and clinical studies (Briere, 1984; Herman, 1981). Our 29% lifetime anxiety rate is markedly lower than the estimated 59% among college women (Sedney & Brooks, 1984) and the

40% to 83% range among clinical samples (Anderson et al., 1981; DeFrancis, 1969), perhaps because we did not assess generalized anxiety or Post-Traumatic Stress Disorders. Our rate is higher, however, than the 19% for somatic anxiety reported by Bagley and Ramsay (1985). The lifetime depression rate of 19% is consistent with a 15% community estimate (Bagley & Ramsay, 1985) and an 18% depression hospitalization rate among students (Sedney & Brooks, 1984), but is markedly lower than Sedney and Brooks's 65% estimate for depression symptoms. Divergent findings may be due to differences in sample sources, CSA definitions, or dependent measures.

Strikingly, the most commonly reported psychological reactions were also highly prevalent at the time of the interview. Nearly one in five respondents with CSA reported at least one current symptom; more than 10% had current symptoms of anxiety, anger, guilt, or depression. Furthermore, the abused had elevated current rates of major depression, panic disorder, and any DIS diagnosis. Our 15% rate for current depression is similar to Bagley and Ramsay's (1985) 17% rate for depression symptoms within the past week. Sexual abuse preceded onset of major depression and panic disorder in nearly all cases, consistent with sexual abuse predicting later onset of almost all disorders except two (Burnam et al., in press) and with increased depression incidence and depressive episodes over time among sexually abused community respondents with physical contact (Peters, 1984). The associations of CSA with almost all current disorders after controlling gender, ethnicity, age, and education eliminates demographic differences as an explanation for these relationships.

This study suggests that childhood sexual abuse may trigger onset of major depressive disorder, alcohol abuse or dependence, drug abuse or dependence, phobia, and panic disorder. The lack of association for schizophrenic disorders, mania, or obsessive compulsive disorder may reflect low base rates for those diagnoses or significant genetic predispositions, particularly for schizophrenic and bipolar disorders (Kendler, 1983; Mendlewicz & Rainer, 1974). Perhaps CSA more strongly influences disorders in which psychosocial stress appears to play a larger role than genetic predisposition.

These findings are especially dramatic because they imply long-term psychological sequelae of at least two years since the last abuse and, on average, eight years after the first sexual abuse incident and five years after the most recent incident. Unfortunately, however, these data cannot determine whether symptoms attributed initially to the abuse recurred in

TABLE 8.6
Psychiatric Diagnosis as a Function of Sexual Abuse

	Any Lifetime Diagnosis	Lifetime Substance Abuse/ Dependence	Lifetime Alcohol Abuse/ Dependence	Lifetime Drug Abuse/ Dependence	Lifetime Affective Disorder	Lifetime Major Depressive Disorder
Intercept	-1.65***	-.75**	.25	-1.38***	.45	.32
Child Abuse[1]	.75***	.63***	.60***	.74*	.53**	.68**
Adult Abuse[1]	.59***	.57***	.50***	.62***	.53***	.57***
Child and Adult Abuse[1]	.89***	.70***	.54**	.83***	.69**	.78*
Gender[1]	-.22***	-.77***	-.90***	-.36***	.21***	.23**
Age	.01***	.02***	.01***	.06***	.01*	.02**
Ethnicity						
Non-Hispanic White[2]	-.18**	-.11	-.33***	.50***	.12	.22
Other[2]	.06	-.26***	-.03	-.86***	-.16	-.24*
Education	-.04	-.07	-.16*	.14	.11	.22**

	Lifetime Dysthymia	Lifetime Anxiety Disorder	Lifetime Phobia	Lifetime Panic Disorder	Lifetime Antisocial Personality Disorder
Intercept	2.49***	.16	.44	3.29***	1.40*
Child Abuse[1]	.59*	.62**	.54**	1.23*	.77**
Adult Abuse[1]	.47**	.49***	.38**	.82*	.38
Child and Adult Abuse[1]	-.16	.85***	.88***	.65	.74*

148

Gender	.18*	.28***	.31***	.50*	– .74***	
Age	– .00	.00	.00	– .02	.03***	
Ethnicity						
Non-Hispanic White[2]	– .14	–.18*	–.25**	– .19	– .57*	
Other[2]	.13	.07	.18*	– .25	– .37*	
Education	– .07	–.00	–.03	.27	– .25*	

	Any Current Diagnosis	Current Drug Abuse/ Dependence	Current Affective Disorder	Current Major Depressive Disorder	Current Anxiety Disorder	Current Panic Disorder
Intercept	– .56*	–.32	.84*	.69*	.89***	3.72***
Child Abuse[1]	.67***	.60	.88**	.97**	.77**	1.36
Adult Abuse[1]	.52***	.41	.72***	.74***	.49***	.42
Child and Adult Abuse[1]	.77***	.60	.79	.83	.83***	.77
Gender	– .06	–.60***	.15	.15	.47***	.51
Age	.01***	.09***	.01**	.02**	.00	– .02
Ethnicity						
Non-Hispanic White[2]	– .26***	.30	–.10	– .10	– .28*	– .34
Other[2]	– .02	–.61***	–.13	– .04	.04	.04
Education	– .15**	–.05	–.03	.01	.01	– .07

NOTE: Logistic regression coefficients are shown. Significance levels are adjusted for the clustered sampling design (see text).

1. Compated to respondents with no sexual abuse.

2. Compared to Hispanic respondents.

$*p < .05$; $**p < .01$; $***p < .001$.

response to other events. Moreover, this study did not ascertain whether the psychiatric disorders are attributable to the abuse, although the disorders showing increased current prevalence (i.e., major depression and panic disorder) are consistent with symptoms most frequently and persistently attributed to CSA (i.e., depression, guilt, and anxiety). While not conclusive, these findings highlight the pervasiveness of psychological symptomatology and psychiatric diagnosis years after CSA and suggest the possibility of their long-term persistence.

Gender comparisons revealed abused men having "acting out" lifetime and current diagnoses, such as drug abuse/dependence. Abused women, in contrast, had higher prevalence of all lifetime disorders except antisocial personality and higher current prevalence of any disorder, affective disorder, major depression, and anxiety. The conclusion that women experience greater psychopathology after CSA is consistent with the finding that female gender predicts fear/anxiety among all abused respondents (Siegel et al., 1988). Gender differences may be due to the small number of men in the sample or the variations in abuse circumstances among men and women.

Abused Hispanics had increased lifetime prevalence of any DIS diagnosis, drug abuse/dependence, major depression, anxiety, phobia, and affective disorder. Abused non-Hispanic Whites had elevated lifetime prevalence of any disorder, drug abuse/dependence, anxiety, and antisocial personality.disorder. Abused non-Hispanic Whites also had higher current prevalence of anxiety disorder whereas abused Hispanics had higher current prevalence of any diagnosis, affective disorder, and major depression. These findings, particularly noteworthy because of the small number of abused Hispanics, suggest that abused Hispanics may be at increased risk for many lifetime and current psychiatric disorders relative to abused non-Hispanic Whites.

Further analyses should explore the consistency and source of these differences. Potential ethnic differences in abuse circumstances or the predominance of women among abused Hispanics versus non-Hispanic Whites may help explain these patterns. Alternatively, CSA may exacerbate socioeconomic difficulties related to minority status, particularly for less acculturated and undocumented persons reluctant to seek treatment or report to police. Our finding of lower mean education level among Hispanics versus non-Hispanic Whites is consistent with this possibility. Perhaps the interaction of these factors and the CSA compromises children's already limited cognitive, emotional, and verbal abilities at the time of the assault, as well as their ability to integrate, resolve, and cope with the experiences in the long term. Future research should assess the relative contribution of alternative explanations such as these.

As a third generation study, this research extends previous work by examining prevalence of specific DIS/DSM-III psychiatric disorders and psychiatric symptomatology in a large random community sample of abused and nonabused respondents. Analyses with sufficient numbers of men and Hispanics revealed dramatic gender and ethnic differences undetectable in previous studies. Like other cross-sectional studies, however, this research relies on retrospective data, potentially confounding its findings through "effort after meaning" (Brown, 1974). This possibility is less likely for psychiatric diagnoses than for symptoms attributed to the abuse, however, because the interview schedule assessed disorder and sexual abuse separately. Alternatively, a third, unexplored factor may increase the risk for both sexual abuse and psychopathology, although multivariate analyses ruled out confounding by gender, ethnicity, education, and age at interview. The possibility of confounding by a third variable is underscored by Burnam et al.'s (in press) finding that later onset of depression, phobia, and drug abuse/dependence was elevated among the abused both before and after the first abuse. More detailed analyses of these data are needed to explore their possible competing explanations.

A fruitful avenue for future research may be toward third generation sexual abuse studies, obtaining DSM-III psychiatric diagnoses from community samples with sufficient numbers of men and minorities to permit gender and ethnic comparisons. Additionally, findings may be refined substantially by incorporating multivariate analyses and examining mediating or confounding variables. Finally, sexual abuse research may benefit greatly by focusing on theory development and testing. With the accumulation of findings on psychological sequelae, research in sexual abuse research is transcending description, seeking to explain *why* certain persons are at increased risk for psychopathology. To this end, theory development and testing are essential.

Recently, Dohrenwend (1983) outlined five alternative models of life stress processes that appear promising for guiding sexual abuse research. The ECA data are consistent with three models—proneness, vulnerability, and additive burden. Higher rates of major depression, drug abuse/dependence, antisocial personality, and phobia among the abused compared to the unabused (Burnam et al., in press) support the proneness model. Increased prevalence of disorder among abused versus nonabused women and abused versus nonabused Hispanics reported here supports the vulnerability model. Finally, increased prevalence of disorder among the abused versus the nonabused, all women versus all men, and all Hispanics versus all non-Hispanic Whites supports the additive burden model. Advances in sexual abuse research may come more readily by formally testing competing theories of sexual abuse sequelae, delineating the most promising theory for specific disorders or symptoms.

In conclusion, this is a time of refinement and maturation for sexual abuse research. Methodologically advanced, theory-driven research is in the forefront. This approach will elaborate on the rich, descriptive data currently available, generating explanations of why and under what conditions people who are sexually abused as children are at increased risk for psychopathology.

NOTES

1. Sample sizes are sometimes slightly smaller because of missing data. Analyses by ethnicity compared non-Hispanic Whites and Hispanics only because of too few respondents in the "other" category.

2. Linear models of the same form (Holt, 1977) estimated design effects for adjusting the chi-squares for each regression coefficient in the CATMOD model conservatively (Leaf et al., 1985).

REFERENCES

Anderson, S. C., Bach, C. M., & Griffith, S. (1981, April). *Psychosocial sequelae in intrafamilial victims of sexual assault and abuse.* Paper presented at the Third International Conference on Child Abuse and Neglect, Amsterdam, The Netherlands.

Bagley, C., & Ramsey, R. (1985). Sexual abuse in childhood: Psychosocial outcomes and implications for social work practice. *Social Work Practice in Sexual Problems, 4*, 33-47.

Briere, J. (1984). *The effects of childhood sexual abuse on later psychological functioning: Defining a "post-sexual-abuse syndrome."* Paper presented at the Third National Conference on Sexual Victimization of Children, Washington, DC.

Briere, J., & Runtz, M. (1985). *Symptomatology associated with prior sexual abuse in a non-clinical sample.* Paper presented at the meeting of the American Psychological Association, Los Angeles, CA.

Brown, G. W. (1974). Meaning, measurement and stress of life events. In B. S. Dohrenwend & B. P. Dohrenwend (Eds.), *Stressful life events: Their nature and effects.* New York: John Wiley.

Burnam, M. A., Stein, J. A., Golding, J. M., Siegel, J. M., Sorenson, S. B., Forsythe, A. B., & Telles, C. A. (in press). Sexual assault and mental disorders in a community population. *Journal of Consulting and Clinical Psychology.*

DeFrancis, V. (1969). *Protecting the child victim of sex crimes committed by adults.* Denver, CO: American Humane Association.

DiVasto, P. V., Kaufman, A., Rosner, L., Jackson, R., Christy, J., Pearson, S., & Burgett, T. (1984). The prevalence of sexually stressful events among females in the general population. *Archives of Sexual Behavior, 13*(1), 59-67.

Dohrenwend, B. P. (1983). *Alternative social psychological models of relations between life stress and illness.* Paper presented at the American Public Health Association, Dallas, TX.

Eaton, K. W., & Kessler, L. G. (1985). *Epidemiologic field methods in psychiatry: The NIMH Epidemiologic Catchment Area Program.* New York: Academic Press.

Golding, J. M., Stein, J. A., Siegel, J. M., Burnam, M. A., & Sorenson, S. B. (in press). Sexual assault history and use of health and mental health services. *American Journal of Community Psychology.*

Herman, J. L. (1981). *Father-daughter incest.* Cambridge, MA: Harvard University Press.

Herold, E. S., Mantle, D., & Zemitis, O. (1979). A study of sexual offenses against females. *Adolescence, 14*(53), 65-72.

Holt, M. M. (1977). *SURREGR: Standard errors of regression coefficients from sample survey data.* Research Triangle Park, NC: Research Triangle Institute. (Revised 1982 by B. V. Shah.)

Kendler. (1983). Overview: A current perspective on twin studies of schizophrenia. *American Journal of Psychiatry, 140*(11), 1413-1425.

Kish, L. (1965). *Survey sampling.* New York: John Wiley.

Leaf, P. J., Livingston, M. M., Tischler, G. L., Weissman, M. M., Holzer, C. E., & Myers, J. K. (1985). Contact with health professionals for the treatment of psychiatric and emotional problems. *Medical Care, 23,* 1322-1337.

Mendlewicz, J., & Rainer, J. D. (1974). Morbidity risk and genetic transmission in manic-depressive illness. *American Journal of Human Genetics, 26,* 692-701.

Peters, J. J. (1976). Children who are victims of sexual assault and the psychology of offenders. *American Journal of Psychotherapy, 30,* 398-421.

Peters, S. D. (1984). *The relationship between childhood sexual victimization and adult depression among Afro-American and White women.* Unpublished doctoral dissertation, University of California, Los Angeles.

Regier, D. A., Myers, J. K., Kramer, M., Robins, L. N., Blazer, D. G., Hough, R. L., Eaton, W. W., & Locke, B. Z. (1984). The NIMH Epidemiologic Catchment Area program. *Archives of General Psychiatry, 41*(10), 934-941.

Robins, L. N., Helzer, J. E., Croughan, J., & Ratcliff, K. S. (1981). National Institute of Mental Health diagnostic interview schedule. *Archives of General Psychiatry, 48,* 381-389.

Robins, L. N., Helzer, J. E., Ratcliff, K. S., & Seyfried, W. (1982). Validity of the diagnostic interview schedule, version II: DSM-III diagnoses. *Psychological Medicine, 12,* 855-870.

SAS Institute, Inc. (1985). *SAS user's guide: Statistics, Version 5 Edition.* Cary, NC: Author.

Sedney, M. A., & Brooks, B. (1984). Factors associated with a history of childhood sexual experience in a nonclinical female population. *Journal of the American Academy of Child Psychiatry, 23,* 215-218.

Shah, B. V. (1981). *SESUDAAN: Standard errors program for computing of standardized rates from sample survey data.* Research Triangle Park, NC: Research Triangle Institute.

Siegel, J. M., Golding, J. M., Stein, J. A., Sorenson, S. B., & Burnam, M. A. (1988). *Psychological reactions to sexual assault.* Unpublished manuscript.

Siegel, J. M., Sorenson, S. B., Golding, J. M., Burnam, M. A., & Stein, J. A. (1987). The prevalence of childhood sexual assault: The Los Angeles Epidemiologic Catchment Area project. *American Journal of Epidemiology, 126,* 1141-1153.

Sorenson, S. B., Stein, J. A., Siegel, J. M., Golding, J. M., & Burnam, M. A. (1987). Prevalence of adult sexual assault. The Los Angeles Epidemiologic Catchment Area project. *American Journal of Epidemiology, 126,* 1154-1164.

Spitzer, R. L., & Fleiss, J. L. (1974). A re-analysis of the reliability of psychiatric diagnosis. *British Journal of Psychiatry, 125,* 341-347.

Tsai, M., Feldman-Summers, S., & Edgar, M. (1979). Childhood molestation variables related to differential impact of psychosexual functioning in adult women. *Journal of Abnormal Psychology, 88,* 407-417.

Weissman, M. M., & Klerman, G. L. (1978). Epidemiology of mental disorders. *Archives of General Psychiatry, 35,* 705-712.

Zubin, J. (1967). Classification of the behavior disorders. In P. R. Farnsworth & O. McNemar (Eds.), *Annual review of psychology* (pp. 373-406). Palo Alto, CA.

PART III

Research with Child Victims

This section includes three chapters regarding the impact of intrafamilial and extrafamilial sexual abuse on children. The first contribution by Conte and Schuerman describes one of the first research projects funded by the National Center for Prevention and Control of Rape to examine the differential effects of sexual abuse. Although the authors discuss some of the methodological shortcomings of research with child victims, there are many noteworthy aspects of this study that should be highlighted. First, this study included a substantial number of abused and nonabused children. Second, a variety of measures were used and data were collected from more than one source. This multimeasure, multisource approach is especially useful in research with children. The results clearly indicate that the clinical sample of abused and nonabused children differed behaviorally and psychologically.

The discussion of the social costs of child sexual abuse provides some policy implications that need to be considered. The methodological limitations discussed will be of particular interest to those who conduct research with child victims. This chapter can also be useful to clinicians who need to establish guidelines for evaluating other studies on child victims and conclusions that can be drawn from them, given the research design.

There are few studies that focus on the coping mechanisms that children use to adapt to the trauma of sexual abuse. However, such studies are crucial in order to understand the lasting effects of sexual abuse and to devise effective treatment programs. Friedrich's chapter proposes that the adaptational processes are dependent on many factors, the foremost being the developmental stage of the child and the individual coping style. He provides a scholarly discussion of child development from an ecological perspective and reviews some of the major issues in child development, namely, coping and adaptation manifested in sexually abused children's behavior.

The author's findings indicate that sexualization is a persistent behavioral response among these children. The chapter stresses the importance of developmental and family variables in assessing the outcome of sexual abuse and suggests the importance of more than one assessment during the course of treatment.

The third chapter in this section is an extension of Friedrich's findings regarding the persistence of sexualization. Judith Becker's work on adult sex offenders is well known. This chapter, however, focuses on juvenile sex offenders with a history of sexual abuse. Although she emphasizes the fact that most children who are abused do not perpetrate sexual abuse upon others, she does suggest that there may be a relationship between a history of sexual victimization and the development of a deviant sexual interest. Becker reviews some pertinent data on male sex abuse victims, particularly the issue of sexual adjustment, and presents some theoretical conceptualizations regarding the etiology of deviant sexual behavior.

For those readers who are particularly interested in the evaluation and treatment of adolescent sex offenders, the program at the Sexual Behavior Clinic at the New York State Psychiatric Institute is described. It should be noted that minority group clients are overrepresented in their client population and may not be similar to adolescent offenders in other programs.

Finally, the suggestion for future research on adolescent sex offenders is of particular importance for prevention. The numbers of adolescent sex offenders are substantial and it appears that male rather than female child victims are most often abused by juveniles. More longitudinal research with child adolescent victims is needed to enhance the valuable contribution made by these chapters.

9

The Effects of Sexual Abuse on Children

A Multidimensional View

JON R. CONTE
JOHN R. SCHUERMAN

The effects of childhood sexual experiences on children and adults victimized as children have been an interest of mental health professionals for some time. Although the number of reports dealing with some aspect of this interest has greatly increased of late, there has been a steady flow of publications over the last thirty years or so (for reviews, see Browne & Finkelhor, 1986; Conte, 1985; Mrazek & Mrazek, 1981). Among the effects of childhood sexual abuse reported in this literature are depression, guilt, learning difficulties, sexual promiscuity, runaway behavior, somatic complaints (e.g., headaches or stomach aches), and changes in normal behavior (e.g., regression to the behavior of a younger child) (Burgess, Groth, & McCarland, 1981), hysterical seizures (Goodwin, Simms, & Bergman, 1979), phobias, nightmares, and compulsive rituals (Weiss, Rogers, Darwin, & Dutton, 1955), and self-destructive behaviors (Carroll, Schaffer, Spensely, & Abramowitz, 1980; DeYoung, 1982; Yorukoglu & Kemph, 1966).

Until very recently, much of the literature describing the effects of sexual abuse has consisted of clinical reports in which the presumed effects are

AUTHORS' NOTE: Correspondence to the first author should be directed to 969 East 60th Street, Chicago, IL 60637. A version of this chapter appeared in the *Journal of Interpersonal Violence.*

anecdotally presented, often in relatively small samples, without actual measurement of the effects reported. While such reports are useful in providing a context for discovery, without measurement or control procedures they fail to demonstrate with any certainty what the actual functioning of children is and what may account for such functioning.

More important, such reports also appear open to numerous sources of bias. For example, one of the studies often cited as indicating that sexual abuse produces no long-term negative effects is the early study by Bender and Gruett (1952). In this clinical report of fifteen cases, the authors conclude that most had good adjustment some years after the abuse. However, in actually reading the fifteen brief case reports, it appears that only two of the cases reflected good adjustment. The remainder experienced a range of problems, including a successful suicide, repeated hospitalizations, and drug and alcohol abuse. This early report illustrates the problems that accompany clinical case reports. Without actual data describing the effects, variation in effects across cases, and change in the effects across time, it is difficult to determine how reliable or representative the findings are, nor is it always possible to understand the basis of the authors' conclusions.

Recent research efforts have tended to employ some kind of "psychological" test to describe empirically the effects of sexual abuse along a number of dimensions of child behavior. For example, among the measures employed by the Tufts New England Medical Center (Tufts, 1984) study was the Louisville Behavior Checklist (Miller, 1981), a multi-item, multifactor measure of psychopathology in children. Comparing sexually abused preschoolers (N = 30) with the norms provided with the Louisville for nonabused children and children in psychiatric care, the sexually abused children presented significantly more behavioral disturbances than nonabused children on 11 of 18 test scales and significantly less behavioral disturbance than children in psychiatric care on 15 of 18 scales. Sexually abused school age children (N = 58) presented significantly more behavioral disturbance than nonabused children on all but two scales (somatic behavior and lack of socially valued interpersonal skills). School age abused children presented significantly less behavioral disturbance than school age children under psychiatric care on all scales except inappropriate sexual behavior.

Using the Achenbach Child Behavior Checklist, Friedrich, Urquiza, and Beilke (1986) report that approximately 40% of males and 45% of females in a sample of 64 sexually abused children present elevated scores on the Internalizing factor (includes items such as fearful, inhibited, depressed). In total, 40% of males and 37% of females presented elevated scores on an Externalizing factor (includes items such as aggressive, antisocial, and uncontrolled behavior).

This chapter will summarize the results of a large research project describing the effects of sexual abuse on children. (See also Conte, Berliner, & Schuerman, 1986; Conte, Schuerman, & Berliner, in preparation; Conte & Schuerman, 1987.)

Methodology

The data reported here were collected as part of a study funded by the National Center for the Prevention and Control of Rape at the National Institute of Mental Health and was a collaborative effort of the School of Social Service Administration at the University of Chicago and the Sexual Assault Center (SAC) at Harborview Medical Center in Seattle. The project's purpose was twofold: (1) to describe the effects of sexual abuse on children and (2) to identify factors associated with differential effects (Conte et al., 1986). Children 4 to 17 years of age seen at SAC between September 1983 and May 1985 believed to have been sexually abused were eligible for the study. Children who had been removed from their homes and placed in substitute care, whose parent(s) refused permission for participation in the study, or whose parent was regarded by the social worker as emotionally unable to complete data collection (e.g., because of extreme emotional upset) were excluded from the study. Children were also excluded if the agency social worker believed that abuse had not occurred. Data were collected at or near the time of disclosure of the abuse from the child's parent (nonoffending), the social worker, and the child if she or he was over 12 years of age. Data were also collected from the parent twelve months later.

Sample

In total, 369 sexually abused children constitute the abused sample. The majority of these children (58%) were seen within six months of the last incident of sexual abuse. In terms of the duration of the abuse, 25% of the children had been abused one time, 44% for a limited period of time, and 25% chronically (in 6% of the cases duration was not clear during the intake assessment). The offender was a stranger in 4%, an acquaintance of the child or family in 30%, a natural or stepparent in 29%, other relative in 23%,

TABLE 9.1

Comparison of Families of Abused and Not Abused Children

	Abused	Not Abused	Significance
Education of Parent			
Professional	2%	20%	
Four yr. college	8%	30%	
1-3 yrs. college	32%	34%	
High school grad	38%	15%	Mann Whitney U
10-11 years	13%	1%	W = 75410.5
7-9 years	7%	—	P = .0001
less than 7	1%	—	
Family Income			
over $60,000	2%	7%	
$50-59,000	2%	8%	
$40-49,000	4%	17%	Mann Whitney U
$30-39,000	15%	19%	W = –9.8
$20-29,000	25%	25%	P = .0001
$10-19,000	19%	18%	
Less than $9,999	32%	6%	
Number dependent on family income	3.9	3.6	t = 2.45. P = .02
Number of children	2.5	1.9	t = 6.52. P = .0001
Marital status child's parents			
Married/living with someone	53%	72%	Chi^2 = 40.7
Separated	16%	4%	P = .0001
Divorced	23%	16%	
Not married/living w/someone	8%	7%	
Mean age of child	8.8	8.1	t = 1.81 NS
Sex of child			
Male	23%	42%	
Female	77%	57%	
Mean number of stressful events	2.0	1.2	t = 6.72, P = .0001
Mean number of events rated stressful	1.2	.7	t = 6.03, P = .0001
Mean negative parent outlook	.97	.83	t = 4.26, P = .0001
Mean social desirability score	5.4	4.8	t = 3.97, P = .0001
Mean support index	8.3	9.4	t = 6.68, P = .0001

babysitter in 7%, parent's partner in .5%, and other in 2% of the cases. Overall, 83% of the sample is Caucasian, 8% Black, 2% Hispanic, 3% Native American, 2% Asian, and 2% other.

In total, 318 children were recruited from the community to serve as a comparison sample. Table 9.1 presents comparative data on the samples, including demographic data (e.g., age of child, family income, and number of children in family) and data describing certain events or phenomena potentially influencing parent report of child behavior. These include the number of significant life events occurring in the child's life in the previous year, the number of these events that the parent believed were stressful, a variable that describes the general life outlook of the parent (e.g., I do not handle stress well, I am usually happy, or I have close friends whom I trust), and a measure of the tendency to give socially appropriate responses.

As can be seen in Table 9.1, the differences between the abused and comparison groups on these variables are all significantly different, except for age of child. These variables were used as control variables in subsequent analyses (see, Conte & Schuerman, 1987).

Measurement

Data for this report come from two of the measures of the effects of sexual abuse. The Symptom Checklist is a 38-item checklist completed by the social worker within seven days of the last case contact and was based on all information obtained during the intake/assessment process. The Checklist was based on a review of the symptoms or effects of sexual abuse most frequently reported in the literature. The social worker's completion of the Checklist was based on what the child and parent said during interviews and on collateral information, but was not based on information provided by the parent on the parent completed Child Behavior Profile. Sample Checklist items include behavioral regression, depression, somatic complaints, and withdrawal from usual activities. These are aspects of functioning generally regarded as indicative of stress reactions or problematic functioning.

The parent completed Child Behavior Profile obtained information from the nonoffending parent on demographic and other information (e.g., number of stressful life events) and asked the parent to indicate how characteristic (using a five-point scale from never to almost always) each of 110 behaviors are for the child (e.g., can't fall asleep, or aggressive behaviors such as yelling, hitting, and breaking things). The Child Behavior Profile was developed during a pretest phase in which two measures of child behavior were compared. Results of this research failed to support use of one measure over the other (Conte et al., 1986). Consequently, the Profile was developed by selecting items from the two measures that most discriminated between abused and not abused children. Additional items were also added based on current understanding about the effects of sexual abuse.

Procedures

Parents were referred to or brought their child to the Sexual Assault Center (SAC) for assessment, consultation, and (in some cases) short-term treatment. When a parent brought a child to SAC, she was asked to complete the Child Behavior Profile while waiting to see the social worker. In rare cases, the parent took the Profile home and returned it by mail or at the next appointment. After the social worker interviewed the child, parent, and (on occasion) others, the nature and process of the study were reviewed with the parent. The research procedures allowed a social worker to rule out any parent for whom participation in the study would be an undue burden (e.g., those who were very upset).

Social worker compliance with the study varied across workers and time. Data were not collected on parent refusal rates or on the number of cases ruled out by the social workers. However, of the total number of cases (1,338) eligible for the study during the study period and meeting all study criteria (age, victim not removed from home, and parent or significant other of the child available to complete data collection), all instruments were completed on 369 (28%).

The assessment process varied in terms of number of interviews and persons interviewed depending on the case. Social workers completed a 38-item Symptom Checklist and a Clinical Assessment Form (CAF), which summarized information about a large number of aspects of the abuse and abuse context (e.g., the relationship between victim and offender or the victim's coping during the abuse). Social workers completed the Checklist based on interviews with the child, parent, and collateral contacts.

Results

Reliability

At the time of the study, it was the policy of the Sexual Assault Center not to ask clients to engage in activities that had no direct meaning or utility for them. Consequently, reliability studies were difficult to conduct under this policy. Several reliability studies were completed by obtaining the participation of other sexual abuse programs. These have been reported elsewhere (Conte & Schuerman, 1987).

TABLE 9.2

Rank Ordering of Symptoms of 369 Sexually Abused Children
(caseworker completed symptom checklist)

	Type of Impact	%
Low self-esteem	33	
Fearful abuse stimuli	31	
Emotional upset	23	
Nightmares/sleep disorders	20	
Repressed anger/hostility	19	
Depression	19	
Withdrawal from activities	15	
Academic problems	15	
Daydreaming, loss of memory, inability to concentrate	14	
Overly compliant/anxious to please	14	
Behavior regression	14	
Aggressive behavior	14	
Generalized fear	12	
Psychosomatic complaints	10	
Nonacademic behavior problems	9	
Inability to form or maintain relationships	8	
Body image problems	8	
Age-inappropriate sexual behavior	7	
Inappropriate/destructive peer relationships	7	
Suicidal thoughts/statements		6
Indiscriminate affection giving or receiving		6
Panic/anxiety attacks		6
Obsessional or repetitive thoughts		5
Places self in dangerous situations		5
Excessive autonomic arousal		5
Minor problems with police		3
Drug/alcohol abuse		2
Shoplifting/stealing		2
Violent fantasies		2
Runs away/takes off		2
Sexually victimizes others		2
Suicidal attempts		2
Hurts self physically		1
Ritualistic behavior		1
Prostitution		.9
Eating disorders		.9
Major problems with police		.3
Psychotic episodes		0

Effects of Sexual Abuse

Symptom Checklist. Table 9.2 presents the proportion of the abused sample exhibiting each of the symptoms on the Symptom Checklist. The average number of symptoms (Social Worker Score) exhibited by abused children in this sample was 3.5. There was considerable variation in number of symptoms across the sample. Overall, 27% had four or more, 13% three, 14% two, 17% one, and 21% had no symptoms.

Child Behavior Profile. Items from the parent completed Profile were scored with higher scores indicating more of a problem for that item. In total, 40 items were dropped due to little variation (e.g., 84% of abused and 92% of not abused children were described as "never" sexually active and 97% of the abused and 100% of the nonabused children were described as "never" having tried to kill self). The 70 behaviors from the Profile for the abused sample were factor analyzed using principal axis factoring with varimax rotation resulting in eight factors: poor self-esteem, aggressive, fearful, conscientious, concentration problems, withdrawal, acting out, and anxious to please/tries too hard. A summary score (Parent Score) was created by adding the ratings for the 70 items.

Differences between abused and comparison children on these factors are all statistically significant. As is often the case with behavioral checklists, the factor analysis was somewhat disappointing. The eight factors account for 43% of the variance among the items and the communalities tend to be low, ranging from 0.15 to 0.67. Most of the communalities are below 0.5.

We decided to create a series of clinical dimensions from items on the Profile due to the relatively poor results of the factor analysis and a belief that the factor analysis failed to describe many of the problems thought to be clinically important in understanding the functioning of abused children. Characteristics of children from the original 110-item Profile were conceptually grouped into clusters based in part on the factor analysis, clinical judgment, and the clinical literature on child sexual abuse. This resulted in twelve dimensions of child behavior. Items were included in only one dimension, except for the last dimension (posttraumatic stress) that was made up of items in other dimensions. Differences between abused and not abused children on the twelve clinical dimensions are all statistically significant. Tables 9.3 and 9.4 present the factors and clinical dimensions, sample items from the Profile making up that factor or dimension, and the alpha coefficients.

Demographic Differences Between Samples

Since the abused and comparison samples differed on a number of the control variables (e.g., negative parent outlook), the differences between samples in symptoms cannot be taken as evidence for the effects of sexual abuse. To shed some light on the importance of these control variables, data for the abused sample and the ten comparative variables were entered into a series of multiple regression analyses with each of the Profile factors, clinical dimensions, and the Profile-based Parent Score and the Checklist-based Social Worker Score as dependent variables. The resulting regression equations indicate that a number of the comparative variables are associated with variation in the dependent measures. Most notable in this regard are the number of life stresses experienced by the child, age of child, and a tendency for the child's parent to have a negative outlook on life. Depending on measure of child functioning, the control variables in the final regression equations explain between 3% and 28% of the variance.[1]

TABLE 9.3
Eight Factors from the Child Behavior Profile with Sample Items
and Alpha Coefficients

Factors	
Self-esteem (alpha = .80) (e.g., feels inferior, self-critical)	Withdrawal (alpha = .51) (e.g., shy or socially isolated, or withdraws from usual activities or friends)
Aggression (alpha = .74) (e.g., aggressive behavior, bullies other kids)	Acting out (alpha = .38) (e.g., runs away, takes off, or hangs around with a bad crowd)
Fearful (alpha = .77) (e.g., afraid of being alone, cling to parents)	Anxious to please/tries too hard ` (alpha = .46) (e.g., overly complaint, too anxious to please, or overly affectionate)
Conscientious (alpha = .64) (e.g., conscientious, able to concentrate responds quickly to directions)	
Concentration problems (alpha = .42) (e.g., easily frustrated able to concentrate, or daydreams, excessive memory loss, unable to concentrate)	

A second set of regressions were run on the combined abused and comparison samples, entering first the control variables in the previous equations and then entering a dummy variable representing whether the child was abused or not abused. The sample dummy remains in the regression equation explaining a significant amount of the remaining variance (after controlling for demographic and other differences between samples) on all measures, except on the following factors: aggressive, withdrawal, acting out, and anxious to please/tries too hard. This indicates that for most measures of child functioning reported here, the observed differences in the functioning of abused and nonabused children are not solely attributable to differences between samples on the control variables used in the study.

TABLE 9.4

Clinical Dimensions of Child Behavior Profile with Sample Items and Alpha Coefficients

Factors

Concentration problems
(alpha = .83)
(e.g., academic problems or day dreams excessively, memory loss, unable to concentrate)

Nervous/emotional
(alpha = .87)
(e.g., excessive activity, restless, moods change quickly or is able to relax)

Aggression
(alpha = .84)
(e.g., aggressive behavior, [e.g., yelling, hitting, breaking things] or uncontrolled, unruly, defiant)

Depression
(alpha = .32)
(e.g., has difficulty communicating or talking or depressed or very unhappy)

Withdrawn
(alpha = .79)
(e.g., spends time with friends or other children or withdraws from usual activities)

Behavioral regression
(alpha = .72)
(e.g., has difficulty waiting his or her turn or clings to parents)

Somatic complaints
(alpha = .52)
(e.g., can't fall asleep or dizziness or faintness)

Body image/self-esteem problems
(alpha = .70)
(e.g., overly concerned about cleanliness or does not like her or his body, feels inferior)

Character/personality style difficulties
(alpha = .83)
(e.g., nice or pleasant disposition or overly complaint, too anxious to please)

Fear
(alpha = .75)
(e.g., afraid of the dark or generalized fears [e.g., afraid of leaving home, riding in car])

Antisocial
(alpha = .64)
(e.g., hangs around with bad crowd or runs away, takes off)

Posttraumatic stress
(alpha = .88)
(e.g., can't fall asleep, moods change quickly, or has panic or anxiety attacks)

Agreement Among Measures

The correlations among the various measures of child functioning vary considerably. For example, the correlations of Social Worker Score and the Profile factors vary from very low to moderately low ($r = .005$ to $.25$)

and for Social Worker Score and the Profile clinical dimensions from moderate to high correlations (r = .24 to .88). The correlation of Social Worker Score and Parent Score is moderate (r = .28, N = 310, p = .0001).

Discussion

Theoretical Work

While the description of broad areas of human functioning on which abused and not abused children appear different does have clinical implications, the atheoretical approach taken to date to such descriptions has many limitations. Sexually abused children appear to be functioning considerably different than do children who have not been abused. These differences in functioning in the study summarized above do not appear to be due solely to demographic and other differences in samples.

The field lacks a theory that explains the relationship among aspects of human functioning affected by abuse or a theory that explains how abuse influences human behavior. Even a validated conceptual model that links aspects of human functioning because they share functional relationships, are topographically similar, or are otherwise associated, would benefit research and clinical practice.

The empirical classification of specific aspects of human functioning (e.g., "afraid of the dark" or "can't fall asleep") as illustrated by the results of the factor analysis reported above and the empirical/conceptual classification illustrated by the clinical dimensions reported above has some utility as it directs attention toward aspects of human functioning effected by abuse. This would be greatly improved by a theoretical understanding of the nature and relationship among effects and how sexual abuse produces such effects.

Two preliminary theoretical statements have been offered in the form of Post-Traumatic Stress Disorder (PTSD) (see this volume) and the four traumagenic dynamics model presented by Browne and Finkelhor (1986). As unvalidated models, both should be approached with caution as their value and validity are currently unknown. Some problems are clear with both models. The PTSD model does not explain all effects of sexual abuse. For example, PTSD concepts do not explain why abused children are seen as more aggressive or antisocial than children who have not been abused. Components of the four traumagenic factor model confuse sources of trauma (stimulus events) with effects (response events). For example, isolation is viewed as a behavioral manifestation of stigmatization although it may equally be thought of as an aspect of abuse that produces effects.

While current theoretical work in this area is preliminary and needs further conceptual and empirical study, this kind of work is likely to be quite important, indeed, more important, than simple empirical descriptions of aspects of human functioning upon which abused and non-abused children differ.

Nonbehavioral Psychological Processes

Another limitation of research to date on the effects of abuse illustrated by the results above, is the emphasis on behavioral reactions of abused children. Although the behavioral specificity of items making up the dimensions and factors of functioning identified in this research vary considerably (e.g., daydreams excessively versus feels inferior), by and large the focus has been on behavior. Other kinds of psychological processes are also likely to be influenced by victimization. Indeed, these other psychological processes may be important because they serve as mediators between abuse and problems in living (effects). As mediating events these psychological processes may themselves become the targets of intervention and reduce or eliminate the risk for long-term consequences of victimization.

Research with adult survivors illustrates this interest. Briere (1984) and Meiselman (1979) indicate that sexual abuse survivors are more likely to have problems in interpersonal relationships (also with abusing alcohol or drugs, and with feelings of isolation) than are other clients. Further research will need to identify the mediators among abuse and such problems as relationship difficulties. For example, why are victims more likely to have relationship problems than other people needing help. Something may be altered by the abuse experience that subsequently results in an inability or difficulty in maintaining healthy relationships.

Clinical speculation can identify a number of potential mediating variables. Perhaps adults victimized as children do see themselves as unworthy or incapable of relationships with people they perceive as good or healthy. For some victims who have not recovered from the trauma of a destructive relationship, they may try to re-create it again and again in the hopes of gaining some mastery over it or having it end differently than in their childhood.

The field will benefit from the identification of nonbehavioral psychological processes altered by abuse. These are likely to include a wide range of emotional and cognitive aspects of human functioning. These include such aspects as feelings about one's self as a sexual being or as a person capable of caring for others; expectations about how relationships are likely to end; emotional needs to have events and relationships conform to beliefs about the world and one's self, or what kinds of sexual behavior one finds pleasing and congruent. This list illustrates the wide range of psychological processes that may be altered by abuse experiences and that may mediate between abuse and problems later in development (e.g., relationship difficulties). Further research will benefit from the identification and measurement of such processes. Future clinical work is likely to benefit as those processes found to result from abuse and found to mediate between abuse and subsequent problems are themselves targeted for change efforts.

NOTE

1. Tables presenting the control variables associated with each of the measures of child behavior are available from the first author at the University of Chicago, 969 East 60th Street, Chicago, IL 60637.

REFERENCES

Bender, L., & Grugett, A. (1952). A follow-up on children who had atypical sexual experiences. *American Journal of Orthopsychiatry, 22,* 825-837.

Briere, J. (1984). *The effects of childhood sexual abuse on later psychological functioning: Defining a post-sexual-abuse syndrome.*

Browne, A., & Finkelhor, D. (in press). Impact of child sexual abuse: A review of the research. *Psychological Bulletin.*

Browne, A., & Finkelhor, D. (1986). Initial and long-term effects: A conceptual framework. In D. Finkelhor (Ed.), *A sourcebook on child sexual abuse* (pp. 180-198). Beverly Hills, CA: Sage.

Burgess, A., Groth, N., & McCarslind, M. (1981). Child sex initiation rings. *American Journal of Psychiatry, 51,* 110-119.

Carroll, J., Schaffer, C., Spensley, J., & Abramovitz, S. (1980). Family experiences of self-mutilating patients. *American Journal of Psychiatry, 137,* 852-853.

Conte, J. (1985). The effects of sexual abuse on children: A critique and suggestions for future research. *Victimology: An International Journal, 10,* 110-130.

Conte, J., & Berliner, L. (in preparation). *What happens to sexually abused children after disclosure.* Available from the authors at the University of Chicago, 969 East 60th Street, Chicago, IL 60637.

Conte, J., Berliner, L., & Schuerman, J. (1986). *The impact of sexual abuse on children: Final report.* Available from the authors at the University of Chicago, 969 East 60th Street, Chicago, IL 60637.

Conte, J., & Schuerman, J. (1987). Factors associated with an increased impact of child sexual abuse. *Child Abuse and Neglect: The International Journal, 11,* 201-211.

Conte, J., Schuerman, J., & Berliner, L. (in preparation). *The effects of sexual abuse: A follow-up study.* Available from the authors at the University of Chicago, 969 East 60th Street, Chicago, IL 60637.

DeYoung, M. (1982). Self-injurious behavior in incest victims: A research note. *Child Welfare, 61,* 577-564.

Finkelhor, D. (1979). What's wrong with sex between adults and children? *American Journal of Orthopsychiatry, 49,* 692-697.

Friedrich, W., Urquiza, A., & Beilke, R. (1986). Behavior problems in sexually abused young children. *Journal of Pediatric Psychology, 11,* 47-57.

Goodwin, J., Simms, M., & Bergman, R. (1979). Hysterical seizures: A sequel to incest. *American Journal of Orthopsychiatry, 49,* 698-703.

Meiselman, K. C. (1979). *Incest.* San Francisco: Jossey-Bass.

Miller, L. (1981). *Louisville Behavior Checklist.* Los Angeles: Western Psychological Services.

Mrazek, P., & Mrazek, D. (1981). The effects of child abuse: Methodological considerations. In P. Mrazek & C. H. Kempe (Eds.), *Sexually abused children and their families.* New York: Pergamon.

Tufts New England Medical Center. (1984). *Sexually exploited children: Services and research project.* Boston: Author.

Weiss, J., Rogers, E., Darwin, M., & Dutton, C. (1955). A study of girl sex victims. *Psychiatric Quarterly, 29,* 1-27.

Yorukoglu, A., & Kemph, J. (1966). Children not severely damaged by incest with a parent. *Journal of American Academy of Child Psychiatry, 55,* 111-124.

10

Behavior Problems in Sexually Abused Children

An Adaptational Perspective

WILLIAM N. FRIEDRICH

Traditional perspectives on child psychopathology stipulate that a disease agent (stressor) activates an illness state (behavioral response), that is in direct relation to the severity of the stressor. This formulation has also been applied to child sexual abuse: The stressor is expected to result in a negative behavioral response that can persist into adulthood (Meiselman, 1978). However, retrospective research with adults (Tsai, Feldman-Summers, & Edgar, 1979) and recent research on children indicate that individuals vary widely in their response to sexual abuse (Finkelhor, 1984). This variability seems related to differences in the abuse and to differences among the victims.

Few published papers have systematically attempted to explain how children adapt to the trauma of sexual abuse (Gomes-Schwartz, Horowitz, & Sauzier, 1985). It is frequently ignored that the child actively adapts to the trauma of abuse, and is not a passive recipient as traditional psychopathology would state. It is difficult to link traumatic events directly

AUTHOR'S NOTE: I would like to acknowledge the contributions of the following individuals to the data collection, analysis, and conceptualization of this chapter: Anthony J. Urquiza, Robert L. Beilke, Alison J. Einbender, Carol Cole, and Lucy Berliner. Appreciation is also extended to the following agencies that assisted in subject recruitment: Sexual Assault Center, Children's Orthopedic Hospital, North Seattle Youth Services, Comprehensive Mental Health Center, Greater Lakes Mental Health Center, Luther Child Center, Pierce County Child Study and Guidance Center, Good Samaritan Mental Health Center, Parent Resource Center, and Child Development and Mental Retardation Center.

to specific and negative behavioral responses. First, sexual abuse is a heterogenous phenomenon, varying on the nature of the act, perpetrator, frequency, duration, and severity. Second, children may adapt differently depending upon their developmental level, coping style, and gender. Finally, the child is embedded in a number of social contexts. Sexual abuse will have an impact on the child, the child's family, and other social networks. Given that the majority of sexual abuse is committed by perpetrators who are either related to the child or are known to the child (Russell, 1984), the discovery of the abuse will affect the familial context in very basic ways.

When children are the subject of research, a developmental paradigm is basic (Kegan, 1982). For example, a younger child (concrete operations) will construe the abuse differently than an older child who utilizes formal operations. In addition, the family of the younger victim may respond differently than the family of the older victim. Finally, a preschool victim may have a longer period of time before adulthood to resolve the victimization than a victim who is older.

A second paradigm presented in this chapter pertains to the active adaptation that occurs in response to the abuse. A competence or coping-based model emphasizing the coping tasks and strategies involved in dealing with trauma has emerged in recent years as a cogent alternative to a model derived from psychopathology (Rutter, 1983). This does not diminish the very real and negative sequelae of sexual abuse but rather emphasizes again the active nature of the child and family's adaptation to this trauma. This adaptation process will vary from child-family to child-family, and it is those variables that contribute to nonadaptation that are of interest.

In addition, sexual abuse is a behavior that has complex cultural, social, legal, economic, and psychological implications (Finkelhor, 1982). Multiple systems are involved of a child's life and are related to the child's normal development. An extremely useful developmental perspective is derived from Bronfenbrenner (1979), who discussed development from an ecological perspective.

Using the language of Bronfenbrenner, the child's individual psychological competencies for coping with trauma (the Ontogenic system) are embedded in the style of family interaction in both the preabuse and postabuse discovery phases (the Microsystem). This family system is in turn embedded in the system involving the stability of the postdiscovery social environment and the social supports available to the family following the discovery of the sexual abuse (the Exosystem), which is embedded in the system that specifically involves cultural beliefs, attitudes, and values throughout sexuality and contemporary family life (the Macrosystem). The factors of each of these levels are interdependent and the nature of this interdependence changes with development (Kurdek, 1981).

This chapter discusses childhood sexual abuse from a perspective that includes developmental, coping, and ecological theories. A difficulty that always presents itself in a study of coping and adaptation is the selection of appropriate dependent variables. Coping is defined as the process whereby people respond to stressful events or situations. Lazarus and his colleagues (Folkman, Schaeffer, & Lazarus, 1979) write that coping serves the dual functions of problem solving and regulating emotional distress. Initially, it must be considered as a process that extends over time. Some coping processes increase the risk of maladaptation while others decrease it. Furthermore, there is not one, but rather multiple routes to both adaptive and maladaptive outcomes in response to stress.

It is possible to view the child's behavioral response to the sexual abuse as reflective of a coping style. The literature on classification of child psychopathology suggests two broad factors that subsume the majority of the behavior disorders in children (Achenbach & Edelbrock, 1983), internalizing and externalizing. Essentially, a child may respond to a traumatic event with regression and depression (internalizing). Another child may respond to trauma with an increase in aggressiveness (externalizing). On a very basic level, these behavioral responses reflect the child's style of adaptation to the traumatic event. Although overt behavior captures only one dimension of a child's response to traumatic events, it is one dimension that can be reliably measured and can generate greater understanding about children's adaptation to sexual abuse.

This chapter has been organized into four sections: (1) presentation of the methods used in the studies reported; (2) a discussion of the relationship between specific aspects of sexual abuse experience and the behavioral response in children; (3) data are presented that explicate children's behavioral responses, both immediately and over time, to sexual abuse; and (4) psychosocial variables that modulate and/or assist the child in coping with sexual trauma are discussed.

Research Methods

The sexually abused children involved in my research were not randomly selected. Rather, over the course of the past four years as a consultant to several social service and mental health agencies, as a supervisor of private child therapists, and in my own clinical practice I collected standardized behavioral assessment data on 155 sexually abused children between the ages of 3 and 12. The fact that these children were involved in assessment and/or treatment suggests that their responses may have been more pronounced than other sexually abused children.

For our purposes, sexual abuse was defined as sexual contact with a perpetrator at least 6 years older than the child, whether by force or consent. In addition, this abuse had been documented by at least two different sources, a state social service agency mandated with investigating sexual abuse and either a physician or mental health professional who was involved very closely with the child. In all cases, the sexual abuse had occurred within the previous 48 months (X = 11.2 months, S.D. = 7.3 months). The primary perpetrator was the father (54%), followed by other male relatives (23%), stepfather (12%), and smaller percentages of neighbor, family friend, and mother.

Three comparison groups were also studied. The first comparison group represented 67 children between the ages of 3 and 12 who were being seen for annual physicals and/or minor medical complaints at two local well-child clinics. These children had no history of mental health involvement. The remaining two groups were psychiatric outpatients, the first a sample of 23 4- to 7-year-old conduct disordered boys whose parents were being seen in a parent training study. The second outpatient psychiatric group included 58 children, ages 3 to 12, who were being seen in a child psychiatric outpatient facility for behavioral problems, including attention deficit disorder, conduct disorder, depression, phobias, and obsessive compulsive disorders.

The primary instrument utilized in these studies was the Revised Child Behavior Profile derived from the Child Behavior Checklist developed by Achenbach and Edelbrock (1983). It is a standardized checklist including 113 behaviors, scored on a three-point scale. Mothers or mother figures completed the CBCL in all cases.

Scores are derived for up to three dimensions of social competence, and ten measures of behavior problems, including sexual behavior problems. This latter score consists of the sum of the responses for six items of sexual behavior on the CBCL, for example, 5 "Behaves like the opposite sex"; and 59 "Plays with own sex parts in public."

In all cases a therapist/case worker familiar with the case provided the following information: the relationship of the child to the perpetrator, the type of sexual abuse, the duration of the abuse in months, the frequency of the abuse in times per month, number of perpetrators, and whether physical force accompanied the abuse. (See Friedrich, Urquiza, & Beilke, 1986, for more details.) For a subset of the children in this study (N = 53), the therapist/case worker also rated three dimensions of family functioning: the degree to which the child victim was supported by the family; the level of conflict in the family; and the degree to which the family was cohesive and not chaotic.

Again, this sample is not a random sample of sexually abused children. It is primarily a middle-class sample, in that 81% of the fathers or father figures and 58% of the mothers were in skilled trades or better. Slightly over one-third of the mothers were full-time housewives. Regarding ethnic distribution, 87% of the families were White.

When between-group comparisons were made, subsets of the sexually abused children were utilized that were most similar to the comparison group on dimensions such as family social class, age of children, and sex distribution of children.

Sexual Abuse: The Stressor

A stressful event is defined as *any change in the environment that typically induces a high degree of emotional tension and interferes with normal patterns of response.* The event activates individuals to modify or adapt to their situation, a process called coping. The properties of the stressful events must be examined in light of personal and family history, the social and physical contexts, and the individual's interpretation or cognitive appraisal of the event (Folkman et al., 1979). In this section, the specific act(s) of sexual abuse will be discussed as the stressor to the child.

However, this narrow definition of the stressor cannot consider such variables as premorbid functioning, concomitant neglect, individual differences in response to stress, and its multidimensional nature, for example, the intensity, familiarity, and predictability of the stressor.

It is currently recognized within psychosocial research that we need to adjust our perspective on stress and coping from a simple, individualistic view to a more complex, systemic view. Hetherington (1984) supports the need for an interactive view by pointing out that the transactional nature of stressful events can lead to an increase in the probability that a series of other stressors will follow the occurrence of the first stressor. This is called generativity and is a commonly seen clinical phenomenon. For example, with physical and sexual child abuse, many abused children grow up, become involved in abusive relationships, and have a child in turn who is abused (Browne & Finkelhor, 1986; Friedrich & Wheeler, 1982).

Despite the complex nature of the stressor of sexual abuse, it can be useful to determine what characteristics of the stressor of sexual abuse seemed most critical. A fundamental difficulty in the study of sexual abuse is that the range of phenomena covered by the term is enormously varied. In a recent paper (Finkelhor & Browne, 1985) a typology of the sources of trauma in child sexual abuse was posited. This typology is further explicated in this volume, and is not reviewed here. However, it provides a very useful framework to understand the specific impacts of various dimensions of the sexual abuse experience.

Research on Sexual Abuse and Its Behavioral Response

In the interest of understanding the stressor of sexual abuse more clearly, two studies were utilized. The first study examined the nature of the child's report. As researchers, we rely almost exclusively on the child's report of what occurred in the abusive relationship. This report, while presumably accurate in the primary details (Goodman, Reed, & Hepps, 1985), may not be as accurate with regards to such variables as use of force, frequency, duration, and severity of the sexual acts. I was struck by the importance of the child's account when beginning to develop a research study that has recently been published (Friedrich et al., 1986). Simultaneously, in developing this study, I became involved as the therapist to a child sexual abuse victim, who over the course of four months of therapy, gradually indicated more information about the abuse. This information included the presence of an additional offender, a duration and frequency that appeared to be twice that which she originally reported, and being involved in the making of a pornographic film, in addition to the forcible genital contact that she had originally reported. I was also able to obtain corroboration (the discovery of a film) for her expanded version. This clinical observation supports the contention by Berliner and Barbieri (1984, p. 127) that "many children who report being assaulted actually underreport the amount and type of abuse."

This led to the design of a study in which a total of 16 children from the original sample were followed for a period of time ranging from 4 months to 14 months. The children were chosen for this study solely because I could have continued access to them, and our discussing the nature of the sexual abuse appeared to be clinically warranted. Of these 16 children, 6 reported additional information during the course of my contact with them that was clearly indicative of a more stressful sexual abuse experience. The greatest variability pertained to duration and frequency, although additional types of abusive acts were also reported. For another 4 children, a gradual denial process ensued so that with additional contact, they reported less and less abuse having occurred, to the point of outright denial. Their denials could not be believed given that their behavioral symptomatology and/or the confession of the perpetrator, supported the fact that abuse had occurred. The remaining 6 children essentially recounted the same version as they had originally recounted when they came into contact with me. Thus research on the impact of the stressor of sexual abuse relies almost exclusively on a variable that is extremely difficult to quantify and operationalize, and any results that indicate one impact or another can be only as reliable and valid as the reporter.

Clinicians have long speculated on what types of abuse have the most serious impact on the child victim. Browne and Finkelhor (1986) found that empirical data were contradictory for the variable relating greater behavior problems to increased frequency/duration and earlier age at onset. Available empirical data were more conclusive about a greater likelihood of negative impact when the offender was the father (or a primary father figure), the molestation involved contact with the genitals, and the use of force accompanied the molestation.

A recent paper, utilizing the Child Behavior Checklist, found that frequency, sex of the child, perpetrator, and severity were significantly related to internalizing behavior (Friedrich et al., 1986). For externalizing behavior, duration, perpetrator, time elapsed since the last assault, and the sex of the child were significant predictors of externalizing behavior. Finally, for sexual behavior problems, frequency and the number of perpetrators were significantly related. This contribution stated that specific dimensions of the abuse appear to be related to behavioral sequelae. If one interprets these findings in terms of Finkelhor's (Finkelhor & Browne, 1985) typology of sexual abuse trauma, one can see that powerlessness and betrayal are two sources of trauma that are clearly supported.

The children in the previously mentioned study by Friedrich et al. (1986) are included in the larger sample described earlier in this chapter. Rather than repeating the analyses with a larger sample, I was interested in utilizing a technique called the classification tree technique (Breiman, Friedman, Olshen, & Stone, 1984). This process detects underlying interactions between the variables that are not readily identifiable simply by examining correlations. It does a recursive partitioning of the data to find homogenous subgroups in order to develop a detailed classification system in the form of a tree. Each branch of the "tree" represents small, homogenous groups. The technique uses cross-validation to "prune" this tree back to a simpler tree that holds up under scrutiny. A many-branched tree would indicate the presence of numerous, reliably detectable interactions.

The three dependent variables from the CBCL, Internalizing, Externalizing, and Sexual Problems were examined with this technique. Severity of the stressor was defined in this case by a severity score indicative of genital contact. A sample of 91 3- through 12-year-old children, all molested in the previous 18 months, were studied. These were children for whom we were confident that we knew as much about the abuse as possible, given our interviews, and who were as proximate as possible to the abuse. When turning to Figure 10.1, which pertains to Internalizing behavior problems, the first branch is on the variable of severity, divided into genital contact versus nongenital contact (50 and 41 in each group, respectively). For the less severe group, no consistent interactions could be identified with any of the other variables assessed, for example, force, duration, relationship to perpetrator. For the more severe group, a relationship with age existed, and also sex of the child. This indicates that greater Internalizing behavior problems can be reliably detected in younger victims of more severe abuse, with sex differences also evident, in that females exhibited more Internalizing behavior than males. Other abuse-specific variables are surprising by their absence. Even more surprising is the fact that no classification tree could be detected for either Externalizing or Sexual Problems, suggesting that these behavior problems do not appear to be consistently related to any child-specific, for example, age, sex, or abuse-specific, for example, force, duration, variables. At least for the single variable of presence or absence of genital contact, reliable interactions could not be detected. Possibly composite variables, for example, genital contact + duration + emotionally close perpetrator, could capture better the relationship between abuse-specific variables and behavior problems.

In summary, my clinical research on the stressor of sexual abuse leads to several conclusions: (1) defining the actual severity of abuse is a very difficult task at best, made all the more difficulty by our reliance on the victims for the particulars and extent of the abuse, and (2) the relationship between behavioral sequelae and abuse-specific variables does not appear to be very unitary or consistent. Child and ecological variables possibly contribute to the absence of a definite linear relationship.

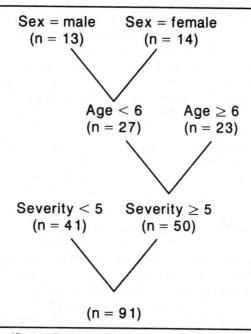

Figure 10.1   **Classification Tree Technique Illustrating Relationship of Internalizing Behavior with Severity of Abuse**

Sexualization

Stressors can have both a delayed as well as an immediate impact upon a child. Hetherington (1984) states that the point at which researchers assess the coping process of children and families will affect their view of the responses of parents and children to stress. She writes, "certain consequences emerge rapidly, some emerge over time and then abate, and still others show a delayed emergence . . . the research evidence suggests that most children can cope and adapt to the short-term crisis of divorce within a few years; however, if the crisis is compounded by multiple stresses and continued adversity, developmental disruptions may occur" (pp. 20-21). Rutter (1983) reports that early events may influence later outcome in at least three ways: (1) they may cause altered patterns of behavior that persist; (2) they may lead to changed family conditions that, in turn, predispose to later disorder; and (3) they may sensitize or harden the person to the effects of later stressors (e.g., becoming more or less vulnerable to later victimization). He states that the manner in which a child deals with stress is perhaps a more salient factor in his or her adjustment than is the number of stressors he or she encounters.

Understandably, some researchers have searched for an underlying behavioral response in sexually abused children, for example, "Post-Traumatic Stress Disorder" (Briere, 1984), an adult psychiatric diagnosis found in DSM-III (APA, 1980).

The most commonly identified behavioral sequelae of sexual abuse in children fits with a Post-Traumatic Stress Disorder conceptualization. Browne and Finkelhor (1986) have identified both initial and long-term effects in their review of clinical and empirical studies. The long-term consequences appear to be very similar to the initial consequences, particularly depression and problems with intimacy and sexuality.

Several researchers (Friedrich et al., 1986; Gomes-Schwartz, Horowitz, & Sauzier, 1985; Yates, 1982) have identified sexual behavior problems in sexually abused children. Our understanding of the role of sexualization in the child's adaptation to sexual abuse is made all the more difficult by the fact that we know very little about children's psychosexual development.

In a recent paper, Finkelhor and Browne (1985, p. 531) discussed the element of "traumatic sexualization." This refers to a "process in which a child's sexuality (including both sexual feelings and sexual attitudes) is shaped in a developmentally inappropriate and interpersonally dysfunctional fashion as the result of sexual abuse" (p. 531). The degree of sexualization will vary with the abuse experience and the child's level of development. The authors contend that a younger child, who understands less of the sexual implications for abuse, may be less sexualized. This also may partially explain how childhood sexual trauma may possibly result in the victim having a sexual interest in children (Russell, 1984).

In this section I want to discuss two additional studies performed in order to gain further understanding of the element of sexualization in the behavioral sequelae of childhood sexual abuse. In the first study, 20 sexually abused boys between the ages of 4 and 7 were contrasted with 23 boys who had a diagnosis of conduct disorder. This particular diagnosis is one in which the child's behavior is characterized by persistent aggressiveness and poor social relations. In fact, it is reported that some conduct disordered boys and girls will exhibit "precocious sexual activity" as part of their overall symptom pattern (APA, 1980, p. 46). Consequently, they appear to be an excellent comparison group against which to contrast sexually abused children. The two samples of boys did not significantly differ in terms of age (5.1 years, S.D. = 1.4, 5.5 years, S.D. = 1.3 for the abuse

TABLE 10.1
Mean Values of CBCL Variables for Sexually Abused
and Conduct Disordered Young Boys

Variable	SA		CD	
	M	S.D.	M	S.D.
Social Competence				
(Raw Scores)				
Activities*	8.4	1.8	6.4	2.5
Social	5.7	2.1	4.5	1.6
School	4.8	7.8	4.0	9.6
CBCL Subscales (Raw Scores)				
Somatic Complaints	4.5	4.5	3.8	3.0
Anxious-Obsessive	7.9	5.2	8.4	4.6
Depressed-Withdrawn	9.4	4.9	9.5	4.6
Hyperactive	6.0	3.2	8.2	4.5
Delinquent	3.8	4.2	4.7	2.5
Aggressive*	15.5	7.7	23.8	5.4
Sex Problems*	3.5	2.5	.9	1.3
Internalizing T Score	62.4	18.1	66.0	6.2
Externalizing T Score*	65.0	11.1	72.4	6.3
Total Behavior (Raw Score)	57.9	32.7	62.0	16.5

*$p < .01$.

and conduct disordered group, respectively) or parental social class. The results of the differences, determined by t-tests between the two groups of boys on the Child Behavior Checklist, are presented in Table 10.1.

It is apparent that very few differences existed between the conduct disordered and the sexually abused boys with the exception that the conduct disordered boys were true to their diagnosis and significantly more aggressive, and the sexually abused boys were significantly more sexualized. Thus, from this initial study, one suggestion is that the sexualization response to the trauma of sexual abuse that may be critical in delineating the behavioral response that exists for a proportion of abused children.

A second study was undertaken to determine the reliability of this finding. The sample of normal nonabused children (N = 67) and the second psychiatric outpatient group (N = 58), described earlier in this chapter, were contrasted with a matched sample of sexually abused children (N = 72) pulled from the sample of 155 children. These sexually abused children had all been molested within the previous two years. Females represented 65% in each of the three samples. Mean ages for the groups was approximately 7 years old, and did not differ between the groups. Parental SES was similar,

TABLE 10.2

Mean Values of CBCL Variables for Sexually Abused, Outpatient Psychiatric, and Normal Children

Subject Group	Sex Abuse (N = 72)		Outpatient (N = 58)		Normal N = 67)	
Behavior Problems	M	S.D.	M	S.D.	M	S.D.
Somatic Complaints	4.18	3.93	4.28	3.13	2.97	2.60
Anxious-Obsessive	9.19	6.03	8.64	4.71	4.09	3.89
Depressed-Withdrawn	10.32	6.83	11.43	7.08	4.70	3.89
Hyperactive*	6.97	4.67	9.26	4.19	3.82	3.19
Delinquent	3.56	4.00	4.98	4.36	1.78	2.62
Aggressive*	17.38	10.27	21.24	10.16	9.52	6.23
Sex Items*	2.67	2.74	.71	1.71	.18	.60
Externalizing*	65.74	12.86	69.07	14.03	55.30	9.48
Internalizing	65.09	15.36	67.90	9.32	56.28	11.29
Total Behavior Problem Score	61.04	34.91	67.62	28.66	31.4	21.03

*$p < .01$ (for SA vs. OP).

as measured by parental occupation level. The dependent variable was again the Child Behavior Checklist and the results of the comparisons, using ANOVA, are listed in Table 10.2.

Again, what is clear from this study is the fact that sexualization is again a critical discriminating variable. Both the outpatient and sex abuse groups differed significantly from the normal comparison group on all variables, but the outpatient group differed from the sex abuse group most clearly on the sex item variables. That was the only variable where the sexual abuse group was significantly elevated with respect to the outpatient sample.

Directly related to this finding of increased sexualization in sexually abused children is a recent paper on erotic orientation development (Storms, 1981). He writes that "erotic orientation results from an interaction between sex drive development and social development during early adolescence" (p. 346). Although the paper was written to explicate theories on the development of heterosexual/homosexual orientation, it is applicable to sexually abused children, whose sex development is accelerated, and whose social environment may be reinforcing of sexual behavior. Storms (1981) also states that earlier sex drive maturation appears to encourage homoerotic development, a finding that is supported in clinical research on latency age sexually aggressive children that is currently underway (Friedrich & Leucke, 1988).

As mentioned earlier, development over time must also be considered in the study of sexually abused children. Their behavioral response will vary from one time to the next, and in a recent paper by Friedrich and Reams (1987), data for up to 24 months was presented on 8 children to illustrate their symptom course over time. Several patterns were noted. For example, depression and somatic complaints would give way in some children to an increase in aggressiveness. Another pattern was for sexual problems to emerge and persist for some time in these children. Improvement in the children was never linear, with some children showing improvement followed by regression or improvement in some areas and not in others. Sexual abuse issues frequently emerged in the course of therapy with the children in the sample who were in therapy, and appeared to be resolved when the child was permitted to talk about these issues directly or indirectly. The CBCL proved to be a useful measure to document treatment course and outcome.

As a way of making more personal this discussion of sexually abused children, I would like to discuss an additional child, not included in the earlier paper, who was in therapy over a 13-month period under my supervision. His symptom course illustrates the importance of following these children over time, and the relative intractability of symptoms in a severely sexually abused child.

Jason was 8 years old at the time he was removed from his home and placed in a therapeutic foster care setting. He was the only boy of a family of 5 children, with 3 or 4 fathers responsible for the children. Jason's stepdad was abusive to all of the children and taught Jason to be sexually abusive with his sisters. In addition, Jason was raped numerous times over a several-year period by this man and was also physically abused. This came to light in November 1984 and Jason's father was jailed. He was having marked school and behavior problems, and was extremely sexualized with children and adults. In addition, he behaved sexually with his foster mother. Therapy began for Jason in February 1985 and continued until March 1986. Therapy was primarily group treatment although at least one individual session was held each month.

In Figure 10.2, a profile is presented that charts four different assessments of Jason over time, from the beginning of treatment in February 1985 to the end of treatment in March 1986.

At the time that Jason came into therapy, he was significantly elevated on the factors of anxiety, obsessive-compulsive, social withdrawal, hyperactive, aggressive, and delinquent. In addition, with regards to social

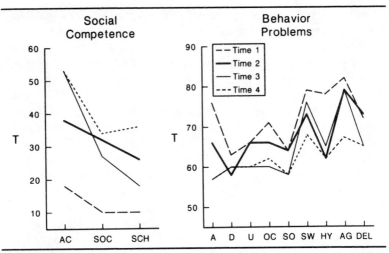

Figure 10.2   Course of Symptoms Over Time on the CBCL for a Sexually Abused Boy

competence, he was significantly below average with regards to activities, social relationships, and school performance. After seven months of weekly therapy, Jason was reevaluated (September 1985) and at that time showed significant elevations on the scales social withdrawal, aggressive, and cruel. This suggested that the anxious and obsessive behavior noticed earlier and that was probably related to his overactivity, had dropped off as significant behavior problems. In addition, considerable improvements were noticed in all areas of social competence, including activities, social relationships, and school performance. Yet a core of aggressive and sexualized behavior remained clearly evident, along with continued impairment in social relationships.

In December, further improvement was noted although Jason continued to be significantly elevated on the factors of social withdrawal and aggressiveness. This underscores how persistent socialization and aggressive disorders can be in children, despite improvements in the home environment and individual and group psychotherapy (Achenbach, 1982). A possible contributor to Jason's slow resolution of behavior problems was the fact that his living arrangements remained in flux, and it was not until January 1986 that the state was able to place him in long-term foster care, with the same foster parents, until the age of 18. In March 1986, an examination of the behavior profile indicates that Jason is within normal limits in all areas of social competence and all areas of behavior problems.

However, it must be underscored that his foster parents continued to report a greater than average level of sexual preoccupation by Jason. Despite the apparent resolution of behavioral symptoms, he persisted in his sexual preoccupation, although no further sexual aggression and generally appropriate peer and adult interaction was evident.

In summary, data from the two comparison group studies, and behavioral assessment of a sample of children over time, clearly indicate that sexualization is a persistent issue in these children. In addition, their symptom picture may vary depending on the time elapsed since the abuse and the amount and type of therapeutic intervention.

Familial Context

Using ecological terms, the Microsystem describes the interactive process operative in the pre- and postsexual abuse family system. This ecological context is extremely important, since families are "the central microsystem, the headquarters for human development" (Garbarino, 1982, p. 62). This fact is underscored by research on physically abused children. In a recent study, it was noted that physically abused children did not have significantly greater behavior problems than children from disrupted, but nonabusive, families (Wolfe & Mosk, 1983), supporting further that family discord is a very important and potentiating variable in child development.

As a framework for understanding family determinants of deviant behavior, Bahr's (1979) paper is very useful to consider. He presents an integrative model of those elements that research has found consistently related to deviant behavior in children. Parental support, consistent discipline, and the consensus in the family about values are related positively to the variables of self-esteem, attachment to parents, and moral commitment. These variables are, in turn, related negatively to the amount of deviant behavior seen in a child.

In a similar vein, Rudolph Moos (Moos & Moos, 1981) has discussed the concept of family social climate. He is interested in assessing those variables that make up the family environment and has developed a measure called the Family Environment Scale. This measure assesses numerous dimensions descriptive of the family context including presence of overt conflict, the moral-religious emphasis in the family, and the degree to which control is an organizing principle.

Some recent research by Moos and his colleagues (Holahan & Moos, 1981) has indicated that three dimensions in particular seem strongly related to the overall quality of family functioning and the relative functioning of individual members. These include the following variables: cohesion, or the degree of parental consistency, one's identification with a family unit, and nonchaotic family interaction; expressiveness, or the degree to which the various members of the family feel that they can speak freely on a wide range of topics and feelings; and conflict, or the presence of verbal and physical conflict and aggression in the family.

In trying to be sensitive to Bahr's (1979) discussion of critical variables and the research done by Moos, three variables were operationalized so that they could be rated by child protective case workers and/or mental health professionals involved with the sexually abused child. These variables were conflict, support of the child victim, and family cohesion. It was my belief that we can further illuminate the adaptation of the child to the trauma of a sexual abuse if we understood something about both the stressor of sexual abuse and the possible moderating variables provided by the family environment. In addition, I felt that it would be possible to begin to determine the relative contribution of abuse-specific and family-related variables to the behavioral sequelae of sexual abuse.

As mentioned earlier, we obtained case worker/therapist ratings on 53 children who had been sexually abused within the previous two years. These ratings were obtained in addition to the standard variables that were already assessed on the therapist/case worker rating sheet, including specific variables. Essentially, the therapist rated on a 3-point scale to the degree to which the family exhibited conflict, support of the child victim, and was an organized and cohesive family unit. These ratings are subjective and the results of the study are limited in that we were unable to obtain any measure of the reliability of these ratings. However, they do represent an initial attempt at examining those family variables that might contribute to the child's adaptation to sexual abuse.

Using stepwise multiple regression for each of the three dependent variables of Internalizing, Externalizing, and Sexual Problems, the three family variables and the abuse-specific variables of duration, frequency, severity, use of force, relationship of the child to the perpetrator, time elapsed since last abuse, and age and sex of the child were entered into the regression equation. See Table 10.3 for the results.

As can be seen from Table 10.3, the family variables appear to be of primary importance in both Internalizing and Externalizing behavior problems, and also seem to be related to the extent of sexual problems in these children. Both family conflict and family cohesion, in that order, were the primary independent variables for Internalizing and Externalizing,

TABLE 10.3
Regression Analyses of CBCL Factors

Dependent Variable	Variable Entered	Mult. R.	R^2	r	F	P
Internalizing	Family Conflict	.54	.29	.54		
	Family Cohesion	.61	.37	−.38		
	Time Elapsed	.66	.44	−.23	12.1	.001
Externalizing	Family Conflict	.58	.34	.58		
	Family Cohesion	.63	.40	−.41		
	Severity	.66	.44	.27	12.4	.001
Sexual Problems	Duration	.40	.16	.40		
	Support of Child Victim	.49	.24	−.32	7.7	.001

accounting for 37% and 40% of the variance, respectively. By way of contrast, similar regression analyses, which did not have therapist ratings for family variables, were examined in the Friedrich et al. (1986) paper. For Internalizing and Externalizing, child and abuse-specific variables accounted for 32% and 33% of the variance, respectively, whereas with these 53 cases, time elapsed since abuse adds an additional 7% for Internalizing and severity of abuse adds an additional 4% of variance for Externalizing. It would appear, from this brief series of analyses, with a limited sample size, that variables descriptive of the familial context of the sexually abused child are strongly related to the child's behavioral adaptation to sexual abuse.

Discussion

This chapter has presented a series of six related studies that have examined the following variables: (1) the reliability over time of the child's report of abuse-specific variables; (2) the relationship of abuse-specific variables to the dependent variables of Internalizing, Externalizing, and Sexual Problems; (3) behavioral differences between young sexually abused boys and conduct disordered boys; (4) differences among sexually abused children and children from an outpatient psychiatry sample and a normal, nonabused, and nonpsychiatric sample; (5) a brief description of developmental changes in sexually abused children as they are followed over time; and (6) an examination of the relationship between family variables and behavioral sequelae of sexual abuse and their relative contribution when compared to abuse-specific variables.

This research has underscored the importance of an adaptational perspective in the study of children who have been sexually traumatized. A linear relationship between severity of the stressor and degree of psycho-social sequelae is not apparent. Rather, there exists a variety of moderator variables that will alter the child's outcome over time. This chapter illustrates the importance of developmental and family variables in assessing sexual abuse outcome, but still has only begun to illumine the myriad of variables that facilitate or interrupt the child's adaptation.

As outlined in this chapter, research in the area of child response to sexual traumatization must satisfy several criteria. These include a developmental/transactional focus that is ecological in nature and framed within coping theory. The initial research in this area has followed the time-honored procedure of clinical case description and then contrasting small groups of target children with supposed normal children. Inevitably, this gives the reader a static and usually unreliable view of the impact of trauma on the child, since the tendency is to attribute the differences to the variables that define the groups. In addition, the variables assessed in these simple, though necessary, first studies are primarily individual in nature, and do not assess the larger context of the child. In addition, the comparison studies rely overly heavily on self-report or parent-report measures, which further narrows the focus.

Sexually abused children need to be studied developmentally. This means appreciating that younger children will differ from older children, and that the process of recovery from the trauma will extend over a time period. Recovery from rape, for example, measured in the victim's rebound from acute depression, is reported to take up to one year for the majority of victims (Atkeson, Calhoun, Resick, & Ellis, 1982). This clearly suggests the importance of more than one assessment of these children, and assessments that span the course of at least one year.

Sexually abused children need to be viewed as heterogenous, with the heterogeneity stemming from the age and sex of the child, characteristics of the abuse, the response of the family, and the response of the child. Consequently, a between-groups approach to studying the sexually abused and nonsexually abused children may still tell us very little about the heterogeneity of this group of children. Some children may exhibit few symptoms while others demonstrate primarily internalized behavior, others externalized behavior, some may be primarily sexualized, and certainly some children are both sexualized and externalized. A related area, and certainly one that is not as well developed with regards to instrumentation, is assessing the individual child's coping strategies. Clinicians would expect that problem-focused or emotion-focused coping would be more facilitative of the child's recovery than would be denial or avoidance types of coping.

Additionally, research may assess abuse-related stressors, including interviews the child has to experience with both friend and adversary alike, whether or not medical exams occurred, court testimony was required, the family was divided and faced a reduction in socioeconomic status, and therapy was initiated either with or against the child-family's wishes. The researcher must carefully assess the stressors, rate their valence, and determine the impact in the same manner life stress researchers assessed life events and related them to psychopathology (Cichetti & Rizley, 1981).

Clearly, the family needs careful assessment. There are data supporting the unique contribution of parental relationships, parent-child relationships, and entire family relationships to childhood outcome (Baldwin, Cole, & Baldwin, 1982). These data indicate that each of these areas should be assessed. This could include measures of marital satisfaction, family environment, and some rating of the quality of parent-child relations, ideally by an independent observer. In addition, coping styles of the family could be assessed, and might include both familywide and parental coping styles.

The integrity of the family unit will be affected by each parent's pathology, social networks, and other support systems. Assessing the parent's own experience with having been sexually abused would be directly related to this area, as well as an assessment of peer, job, and close friend social support. It is possible that positive treatment effects are related to the degree to which the parent is supported by the therapy process, and increases the overall density of their social networks. It would not be surprising, particularly given the literature on the isolation in incestuous families (Alexander, 1985), that unless parental isolation is reduced, and the family becomes more integrated into the larger social context, incest is likely to reoccur. The child in an isolated family is more than likely going to have greater difficulty with establishing a broad range of supportive relationships, again a variable with definite implications for how will this child cope with this trauma over the years.

One hopes the complexity of research findings in this area is evident, and research will attempt to delineate, more carefully, the potentiating and protective factors in a child-family's adaptation to sexual trauma.

REFERENCES

Achenbach, T. (1982). *Developmental psychopathology* (2nd ed.). New York: John Wiley.

Achenbach, T. M., & Edelbrock, C. (1983). *Manual for the child behavior checklist and revised child behavior profile.* Burlington: University of Vermont.

Alexander, P. C. (1985). A systems theory conceptualization of incest. *Family Process, 24,* 79-88.

American Psychiatric Association. (1980). *Diagnostic and statistical manual of mental disorders* (3rd ed.). Washington, DC: Author.

Atkeson, B. M., Calhoun, K. S., Resick, P. A., & Ellis, E. M. (1982). Victims of rape: Repeated assessment of depressive symptoms. *Journal of Consulting and Clinical Psychology, 50,* 96-102.

Bahr, S. J. (1979). Family determinants and effects of deviance. In W. R. Burr, R. Hill, F. I. Nye, & I. L. Reiss (Eds.), *Contemporary theories about the family: Research-based theories* (Vol. 1, pp. 615-643). New York: Free Press.

Baldwin, A. L., Cole, R. E., & Baldwin, C. P. (1982). Parental pathology, family interaction and the competence of the child in school. *Monographs of the Society for Research in Child Development, 47,*(5, Serial No. 197).

Berliner, L., & Barbieri, M. K. (1984). The testimony of child victims of sexual assault. *Journal of Social Issues, 40,* 125-137.

Breiman, L., Friedman, J. H., Olshen, R. A., & Stone, C. J. (1984). *Classification and regression trees.* Belmont, IL: Wadsworth.

Briere, J. (1984). *The long-term effects of childhood sexual abuse on late psychological functioning: Defining a post-sexual abuse syndrome.* Paper presented at the Third National Conference on Sexual Victimization of Children, Washington, DC.

Bronfenbrenner, U. (1979). *The ecology of human development.* Cambridge, MA: Harvard University Press.

Browne, A., & Finkelhor, D. (1986). The impact of child sexual abuse: A review of the research. *Psychological Bulletin, 99,* 66-77.

Cichetti, D., & Rizley, R. (1981). Developmental perspective on the etiology, inter-generational transmission, and sequelae of child maltreatment. *New Directions in Child Development, 11,* 31-55.

Finkelhor, D. (1982). Sexual abuse: A sociological perspective. *Child Abuse and Neglect, 6,* 95-102.

Finkelhor, D. (1984). *Child sexual abuse.* New York: Free Press.

Finkelhor, D., & Browne, A. (1985). The traumatic impact of child sexual abuse: A conceptualization. *American Journal of Orthopsychiatry, 55,* 530-541.

Folkman, S., Schaefer, C., & Lazarus, R. (1979). Cognitive processes as mediators of stress and coping. In V. Hamilton & D. W. Warburton (Eds.), *Human stress and cognition* (pp. 265-297). New York: John Wiley.

Friedrich, W. N., & Luecke, W. J. (1988). Young school-age sexually aggressive children. I. Assessment and Comparison. *Professional Psychology, 19,* 155-164.

Friedrich, W. N., & Reams, R. A. (1987). The course of psychological symptoms in sexually abused young children. *Psychotherapy: Theory, Research, and Practice, 24,* 160-170.

Friedrich, W. N., Urquiza, A. J., & Beilke, R. (1986). Behavior problems in sexually abused young children. *Journal of Pediatric Psychology, 11,* 47-57.

Friedrich, W. N., & Wheeler, K. K. (1982). The abusing parent revisited. *Journal of Nervous and Mental Disease, 170,* 577-588.

Garbarino, J. (1982). *Children and families in the social environment.* New York: Aldine.

Gomes-Schwartz, B., Horowitz, J. M., & Sauzier, M. (1985). Severity of emotional distress among sexually abused preschool, school-age, and adolescent children. *Hospital and Community Psychiatry, 36,* 503-508.

Goodman, G. S., Reed, R. S., & Hepps, D. (1985). *The child victim's testimony.* Paper presented at the 93rd Annual Convention of the American Psychological Association, Los Angeles.

Hetherington, E. M. (1984). Stress and coping in children and families. In A. Doyle, D. Gold, & D. S. Moskowitz (Eds.), *Children in families under stress.* San Francisco: Jossey-Bass.

Holahan, C. J., & Moos, R. H. (1981). Social support and psychological distress: A longitudinal analysis. *Journal of Abnormal Psychology, 90,* 365-370.

Kegan, R. (1982). *The evolving self: Problem and process in human development.* Cambridge, MA: Harvard University Press.

Kurdek, L. A. (1981). An integrative perspective on children's divorce adjustment. *American Psychologist, 36,* 856-866.

Meiselman, K. C. (1978). *Incest: A psychological study of causes and effects with treatment recommendations.* San Francisco: Jossey-Bass.

Moos, R. H., & Moos, B. (1981). *Revised family environment scale.* Palo Alto: Consulting Psychologist's Press.

Russell, D. (1984). *Sexual exploitation.* Beverly Hills, CA: Sage.

Rutter, M. (1983). Stress, coping, and development. In N. Garmezy & M. Rutter (Eds.), *Stress, coping, and development in children.* New York: McGraw-Hill.

Storms, M. D. (1981). A theory of erotic orientation development. *Psychological Review, 85,* 340-353.

Tsai, M., Feldman-Summers, & Edgar, M. (1979). Childhood molestation: Variables related to differential impacts on psychosexual functioning in adult women. *Journal of Abnormal Psychology, 88,* 407-417.

Wolfe, D. A., & Mosk, M. D. (1983). Behavioral comparisons of children from abusive and distressed families. *Journal of Consulting and Clinical Psychology, 51,* 702-208.

Yates, A. (1982). Children eroticized by incest. *American Journal of Psychiatry, 139,* 482-485.

11

The Effects of Child Sexual Abuse on Adolescent Sexual Offenders

JUDITH V. BECKER

The past two decades have seen an increase in public concern about sexual crimes. Researchers have focused on the incidence and prevalence of sexual crimes and the impact these crimes have on victims. Treatment outcome studies with adult victims are beginning to emerge; however, to date there have been no published treatment outcome studies on child sex abuse victims.

A body of literature has also developed on the assessment and treatment of adult sexual offenders. Two areas that have received little attention are male child victims of sexual abuse and adolescent sexual offenders.

This chapter will address both those issues and the increasing evidence that a relationship may exist between a history of sexual victimization and the development of a deviant sexual interest pattern.

A recent review of prevalence studies indicated that between 3% to 30% of males interviewed reported having been the victims of sexual abuse (Peters, Wyatt, & Finkelhor, 1986).

Some interesting data have emerged from interviews with adult sexual offenders. A recent study conducted by Abel and his colleagues (1987) found that of 153 adult male offenders who molested children unrelated to them, the frequency of molestation of male children was a mean of 281.7 deviant acts per offender compared to a mean of 19.8 victims for those men who molested female children. Male children are probably victimized in greater numbers than was previously suspected.

Differential Sex Disclosing
Patterns and Characteristics

Sexual abuse is underreported by both male and female children. However, male victims may be less likely to disclose sexual abuse than female victims. Rogers and Terry (1984) discuss the issues related to lack of disclosure in male victims; they include the following:

(1) Due to a cultural bias there is reluctance to identify the sexually molested boy as a victim.

(2) Since physical trauma appears less frequently in male victims as opposed to female victims, the tendency is for adults to deny that the boy was victimized.

(3) If a boy received money for the sex (either he was bribed or he prostituted himself), he is less likely to be identified as a victim.

(4) If a boy has a homosexual orientation and he is coerced into sex by an older adult male, the boy is often blamed for "the seduction" of the older male, instead of being acknowledged as the legitimate victim.

There are both similarities and differences in the patterns of sexual victimization of boys and girls. Rogers and Terry (1984), reporting on a sample of 401 child sex abuse cases, indicated that 81% of the male victims were younger than 12 years of age, compared to 70% of the female child victims. Both male and female victims were "engaged" in the sexual behavior by physical force (48% of males and 50% of females). A larger percentage of male victims (51%) were threatened with physical harm as compared to female victims (37%). Although both boys (43%) and girls (47%) are likely to be abused over time, boys (20%) had a higher incidence of multiple offenders than did the female victims (13%). Their data also indicate that female child victims (42%) are more likely to reside with the offender than are male child victims (21%). The authors noted that the most striking difference between male and female child victims are that female victims are more likely to be abused by a parent or parent surrogate (31%) than are male victims (8%). The male child victims were victimized by nonfamily members known to the victim or his family (63%) or by strangers (15%). Furthermore, 56% of the male child victims were abused by juveniles as compared to 28% of female child victims.

Impact of Sexual Abuse

Only a few studies have examined the impact of sexual abuse on male victims. Johnson and Shrier (1985) reported on a six-year experience in an adolescent medicine clinic in which all medical interviews of adolescent males included questions about sexual molestation. In total, 40 adolescent males who reported sexual victimization during their preadolescent years were compared with 40 randomly selected age-matched boys who had not been sexually victimized. Of the victimized males, 25% reported sexual dysfunctions compared to 5% of the nonvictimized males, and 60% stated that the sexual abuse had a significant impact on their lives.

Finkelhor (1981) reported that male children who had been victimized prior to age 13 by an older person were four times more likely to be currently homosexually active than those who had not experienced homosexual experience at all. Rogers and Terry (1984) report that male child victims exhibit behavioral changes that are unique and appear related to the "homoerotic" implications of the abuse: (1) confusion over sexual identity, (2) inappropriate attempts to reassert masculinity, and (3) recapitulation of their victimization, in which the boy attempts to deal with his own victimization and gain mastery by overidentifying with the offender and modeling his behavior. In summary, data available on male victims indicate that issues of sexual adjustment are of real concern.

A review of the literature did not reveal any therapy outcome studies involving treatment of sexually abused male child victims. Rogers and Terry (1984) offer guidelines for intervention with male victims beyond those "typically used with females." They include (1) working with both the boy and his parents since parents may blame the child for the victimization or have "unrealistic fears" about the impact of the abuse on the child; (2) enable the child to reestablish his masculine self-concept by helping him channel his feelings that are abuse related into socially acceptable outlets.

Porter (1986), in his book *Treating the Young Male Victim of Sexual Assault*, outlines both issues in working with this population as well as treatment strategies. He reports that group and family therapy are the strongest modalities in the treatment of male child victims.

The majority of male children who are sexually assaulted do not become sexual offenders. Furthermore, not all adolescent sexual offenders have been sexually abused. Longo (1982) reported that 47% of the adolescent sex offenders in his treatment program had been sexually abused. In total, 19% of adolescent sexual offenders seen at our clinic reported histories of sexual abuse.

The following section will describe a sample of sexually victimized boys who committed sexual crimes. A theory will be proposed to explain why some victims go on to commit sexual crimes and develop a deviant sexual interest pattern.

Characteristics of Juvenile Sex Offenders with a History of Prior Victimization

The Sexual Behavior Clinic at the New York State Psychiatric Institute provides evaluation and treatment to adolescents who have been accused of committing sexual crimes. Of 139 adolescent sexual offenders seen at the clinic, 27 (19%) indicated on initial interview that they were victims of sexual abuse. The mean age of the abused adolescents was 15 years and 6 months. Ages ranged from 12 to 19 years. In total, 56% were Black, 26% Hispanic, and 18% Caucasian. Clearly, for some of the adolescents (33%), the sexual crime was part of a pattern of delinquent behavior.

We consider our sample to be biased in that it overrepresents minorities. Minority adolescents are no more at risk than any other adolescents in the population.

Victimization Profile

Of the 27 adolescents who were sexually abused, 3 (11.1%) were abused by strangers and 24 (88.9%) by people they knew. These data are consistent with those reported by Rogers and Terry (1984) in that the majority of boys were abused by nonfamily members, but people known to the victim or his family.

Table 11.1 presents data on the relationships of the offenders to the victims. In total, 16 (59.2%) adolescents were sexually abused by nonrelative adults, most of whom were known to them. The second highest category was nonrelative juveniles (6 or 22% male and 1 or 4% female). It is of particular interest that 40.7% of the offenders were female. This finding may be related to how the adolescents were questioned as to abuse history. It has been our clinical experience that if adolescents are asked, "Were you sexually victimized?" they tend to answer in the negative. For many, that question is a direct threat to their masculinity. We have also observed that if the offender was a female, the adolescents are inclined to describe the

TABLE 11.1
Relationship of Offender to Victim, N = 27

Relationship	Percentage
Brother	3.7
Uncle	3.7
Other male relative	3.7
Other female relative	3.7
Nonrelative adult male	25.9
Nonrelative adult female	33.3
Nonrelative child/adolescent male	22.2
Nonrelative child/adolescent female	3.7

experience as "learning about sex" even though there was a considerable age difference and the juvenile experienced anxiety about the behavior.

Consequently, we ask the adolescent about every person he has had a sexual encounter with, the age and sex of the person, and whether the behavior was initiated or wanted by the adolescent. By posing the question in this manner one can obtain a much more accurate account of abusive behavior.

Our clinical experience has also indicated that a number of adolescents did not recall their own abuse until they were involved in our therapy. We will reinterview our sample when they complete therapy about sexual abuse history and we anticipate having a higher than 19% reported abuse history.

In total, 9 (33%) of the adolescents indicated that they were verbally coerced into engaging in the sexual behavior; 8 (29.6%) were physically coerced; 3 (11.1%) were the victims of excessive physical coercion (aggression beyond what was necessary to complete the sexual crime), and 7 (25.9%) indicated no coercion was used to gain compliance. Of the adolescents, 4% required medical attention for assault-related injuries.

Nondeviant Sexual Experiences

As part of history taking, adolescents are surveyed as to the age at which they first engaged in a nondeviant genital sexual experience. Nondeviant sex is defined as noncoercive sexual interaction with a peer. In total, 22% of the adolescents indicated that they had not had such a sexual experience. The mean age of those who did was 12 years (range 6 to 18 years). The

TABLE 11.2
Types of Deviant Genital Sexual Acts, N = 27

Sexual Act	Percentage
Vaginal penetration	5.4
Attempted vaginal penetration	5.4
Anal penetration	18.2
Attempted anal penetration	5.6
Oral sex	9.0
Fondling	25.5
Attempted fondling	7.3
Rubbing bodies	10.9

sample of adolescents had a total of 213 consensual female sexual partners and 3 male partners (mean = 8.2 partners; range 0 to 50 partners). None of the adolescents seen to date has reported any sexual dysfunctions in their consensual sexual relationships.

Using the Kinsey rating scale, 70% of the adolescents rated themselves exclusively heterosexual (Kinsey 0). The remainder self-rated as Kinsey 1-4. None of the adolescents rated as exclusively homosexual (Kinsey 5-6).

Deviant Sexual Behaviors

The sexual crimes of the 27 adolescents were divided into two categories: sexual acts that involved touching or penetration of genitals and sexual acts involving other types of sexually deviant behavior. Our sample of 27 adolescents had engaged in a total of 1,119 self-reported genital-contact deviant sexual acts, involving 55 victims (1 adolescent accounted for 994 of the deviant acts). Of their victims, 55% were male and 45% were female. In total, 9% of their victims were adults; 13% between the ages of 13 and 18; 32% were 9 to 12 years of age; and 46% younger than 8 years of age. Table 11.2 presents the types of deviant sexual acts these adolescents engaged in. There were 3 adolescents (12.5%) who reported that they had been falsely accused and did not engage in any deviant behavior.

Fondling was the most frequently occurring behavior the adolescents engaged in. The second most frequent offense was anal penetration.

Overall, 10 of the 27 youths engaged in a total of 564 other deviant sexual acts. The categories of offenses included voyeurism, exhibitionism, obscene phone calls, obscene letters, mooning (exposing buttocks), and frottage.

TABLE 11.3

Types of Nongenital Deviant Sexual Acts, N = 10

Sexual Acts	Percentage
Voyeurism	33.5
Frottage	21.1
Exhibitionism	17.7
Obscene calls	17.2
Mooning	10.3
Obscene letters	0.2

Frottage is included in this category because these cases did not involve rubbing or touching of the victim's genitals.

Table 11.3 presents the percentage of those 10 adolescents who engaged in nongenital deviant sexual behavior. These data indicate that the 27 adolescents who had been sexually victimized went on to commit a total of 1,683 sexual crimes ranging in behaviors from obscene letter writing to forced vaginal and anal penetration.

The following are two case studies of the type of adolescents we have evaluated who have a history of sexual victimization and have gone on to commit sexual crimes.

Case Study of M.

M. is a 16-year-old boy who was referred by his lawyer for placing his finger in the vagina of his 8-month-old half-sister. During the initial interview M. denied having done anything sexual with his half-sister but did reveal to the interviewer that since age 12 he had been having sexual intercourse with his three biological sisters. He reported that at age 12 he had intercourse with his sister (T.) who was 8 years old at the time. It was M.'s first sexual experience and he reported feeling bad about it because "we were raised together." At age 15, M. reported that he had intercourse with his 8-year-old sister (K.) on four separate occasions. M. then reported that two months later he had sexual intercourse with his 6-year-old sister (J.) on four separate occasions.

Relevant family and social history reveals that M. was raised by his grandparents until age 12. Following the death of his grandmother (M. was age 12), he went to live with his father (his parents were divorced shortly after his birth). During the time he was living with his father he would spend weekends with his mother who was remarried and had three daughters by her second husband. This is when the initial sexual conduct with his sisters began. Other history reveals that M. was sexually molested at age 10 by a 16-year-old female baby sitter. This occurred when he was living with his grandparents. He had no previous arrests nor a history of drug or alcohol abuse. M. did well in school and stated that his aspiration was to join the Air Force.

M.'s psychological testing indicated that he had a large number of distorted cognitions (irrational beliefs about the behavior) regarding appropriate sexual contacts. The Beck Depression Inventory (a self-report depression inventory) indicated that he was moderately depressed (score of 23); he admitted to being depressed because he knew what he did with his sisters was wrong, but he had never had sex before and stated that he was curious. The psychophysiologic evaluation (assessing arousal pattern using a penile plethysmagraph) indicated arousal consistent with the charges brought against him. He showed arousal to stimuli of female incest, forced sex with girls aged 13 to 18, exhibitionism, and to consensual sex with a female peer. He showed no arousal to males or to a neutral cue. The Sexual Interest Cardsort (a self-report of sexual behaviors) indicated that he self-reported arousal to exhibitionism, voyeurism, and consensual sex with a female peer.

Case Study of J.

J. is a 17-year-old Black male who was referred by his probation officer for anal intercourse with a 5-year-old boy. He had no prior arrests. During the evaluation, J. denied sexual involvement with the younger boy that he had been babysitting. The probation report indicated that he had forced the boy to have anal intercourse and had beaten him up. Witnesses had seen him in a park, place his hand over the boy's mouth, and drag him into the bushes. J. stated that he had pled guilty only because he had been threatened.

At the time, J. was living alone with his mother. He was isolated and didn't have many friends. He also had poor relationships with female peers.

Relevant social history revealed that he was sexually abused at the age of 8 repeatedly by a man in the neighborhood (this abuse was disclosed during the course of treatment). His older brother is currently in prison for murdering an elderly neighbor.

During the initial evaluation, J. was cooperative. His paper and pencil testing revealed that he had arousal to inappropriate sexual situations such as rape, sadism, and exhibitionism. They also revealed he had faulty cognitions about appropriate sexual behavior. For example, to the statement, "I know just how much sex between me and a child will hurt the child later on," he answered "true." The psychophysiologic assessment of J.'s sexual interest pattern indicated that he had significant arousal to assault and physical coercion against male children. He also was aroused to cues for consensual sex with a female peer.

Etiology of Deviant Sexual Behavior

There has been little success in defining specific etiologic factors that lead to the development of deviant sexual behaviors in adolescents. Abel, Mittelman, and Becker (1985) have postulated that inappropriate beliefs about sexual behavior, reinforcing inappropriate fantasies through masturbatory behavior, poor social assertive skills, and lack of sexual knowledge contribute to deviant sexual behavior.

Fehrenbach, Smith, Monastersky, and Deisher (1986) found poor academic achievement, school and behavior problems, social isolation, and a history of sexual or physical abuse common in the histories of the adolescent sexual offenders they evaluated. However, it is not clear to what extent these factors contribute to the development of a deviant sexual interest pattern.

Juvenile sexual offenders are not a homogeneous group. Some adolescents who commit sexual crimes may have a true paraphilia; that is, they have recurrent fantasies and urges to engage in deviant sexual behavior and may prefer the deviant activity over nondeviant sexual acts. Other adolescents who commit sexual crimes engage in the deviant sexual behavior as part of an overall pattern of delinquent or conduct-disordered behavior.

Social isolation may serve as a contributing factor. Adolescents who lack the requisite skills to interact with their peers may befriend younger children and then sexualize those relationships.

The above described characteristics are not meant to be all inclusive. There are often factors that may contribute to both the commission of sexual crimes and the development of a deviant sexual interest pattern.

The following hypothesized model that remains to be tested may assist us in explaining the commission of sexual crimes by juveniles. This model incorporates individual characteristics, family variables, and social environmental variables as possible precursors to the commission of the juvenile's first deviant sexual act. Individual characteristics might include an impulse control disorder, a conduct disorder, limited cognitive abilities, and a history of physical or sexual abuse. Family variables include (a) residing in a family where parents or parent surrogates engage in either coercive sexual or physical behavior toward each other, the children, or others; (b) residing in a family in which the belief system of one or both parents is supportive of coercive sexual behaviors; and (c) having parents who are lacking in empathy and in functional interpersonal skills experiencing emotional and/or physical neglect within the family. Social factors include a society that is supportive of coercive sexual behavior and the sexualization of children and/or bonding with a peer group that engages in antisocial behavior.

The above factors may interact with one another to contribute to the adolescent's committing a deviant sexual act. Following the commission of the first sexual offense, some adolescents will cease to engage in deviant sexual behaviors because of negative consequences to themselves. Others, however, go on to commit further sexual crimes and develop paraphilic arousal patterns. In a study in which 561 adult sexual offenders were accessed, 59% reported having had the onset of the paraphilic behavior during adolescence. The 561 adult offenders had committed a total of 291,737 deviant sexual acts over their lifetimes, involving a total of 195,407 victims. Those men who molested young boys had an incidence five times greater than the molestation of young girls. The mean number of paraphilias per offender was 2.2 (Abel et al., 1987).

Those adolescents who go on to reoffend are likely to be those who have (a) found the behavior to be very pleasurable, (b) experienced no or minimal negative consequences in relation to the commission of the sexual crime, (c) experienced reinforcement of the deviant sexual behavior through masturbation activity and fantasy, (d) were deficient in their ability to relate to age appropriate peers.

As mentioned previously, the majority of juveniles who are sexually abused do not go on to commit sexual crimes or develop paraphilia. There are protective factors within the individual, family, and environment that prohibit that behavior from occurring. Consider the following two examples:

A young boy is molested by an adult who is a friend of the family. The boy resides within a family where his parent(s) have served as good role models. He discloses the event to them, they are supportive of the disclosure and immediately act to protect the boy from any further contact with the offender. They inform the boy that it was the adult's responsibility in that adults should never be sexual with children and sex should never be forced on another person. They report the situation to the proper authorities and inform the boy that the man who abused him will suffer consequences for his behavior as well as receive help so that he will not behave in the same manner with other children.

The parent(s) obtain for the child appropriate medical and mental health assistance. The parent(s) seek guidance from the mental health worker as to what to anticipate and how to be of help to the child. The child has age appropriate peer relations that are functional. When the child reaches adolescence he fantasizes about consensual sex with peers. His belief system, which he learned from his parents and community, is supportive only of age appropriate consensual interactions. He does not attempt to recapitulate his own victimization.

In the second case a young boy is victimized by an adult known to the family. He does not disclose the abuse to anyone because he fears that he will not be believed and will be held responsible. The youngster has an impulse control disorder that his parent(s) have never sought treatment for. When anything has gone wrong, they have blamed him.

Because of his impulse control disorder and hyperactivity, prosocial peers do not associate with him. Consequently, he associates with younger children. He sexually abuses a younger child in an attempt to gain mastery over his own victimization and lack of empowerment. He finds the behavior to be pleasurable. The child does not disclose the abuse. He experiences no negative consequences and tells himself it was alright to engage in the behavior since it had happened to him. He masturbates to thoughts of abusing children and goes on to commit more sexual offenses.

There are numerous other factors that can combine and contribute to the development of deviant sexual interest patterns, however, since we cannot predict who will continue to commit sex crimes, we recommend that all adolescent offenders receive treatment.

Treatment to Reduce the Risk of Reoffending

Although there is a body of literature describing assessment and treatment methods for adult sexual offenders (Abel, Barlow, Blanchard, & Guild, 1977; Abel, Becker, Blanchard, & Flanagan, 1981; Abel, Blanchard, & Becker, 1976, 1977; Abel et al., 1985; Berlin & Meinecke, 1981; Marshall, 1979), there is a paucity of studies on adolescent sexual offenders.

Our treatment program for adolescent sexual offenders and pre-liminary data on treatment outcome has been described elsewhere

(Becker, Kaplan, & Kavoussi, in press; Becker & Kavoussi, n.d.). A cognitive behavioral treatment model is utilized to teach adolescents behaviors that are incompatible with reoffending. Adolescents are treated in groups (the same model can be utilized in individual therapy).

In working with adolescent sexual offenders it is imperative that parent(s) understand the nature and severity of their son's behavior. Parents will frequently deny or minimize that their son has a problem. Parental cooperation is necessary to ensure that the adolescent comes to the clinic for therapy as well as follow-up appointments.

Upon entering therapy the adolescents are informed that they have engaged in sexual behavior that our society prohibits because it harms the victim. The goals of therapy are outlined; they include (1) learning control over deviant sexual impulses, and (2) learning how to relate to people in a manner that is functional. There are seven components in the treatment: (1) satiation—a therapeutic technique that makes the deviant sexual fantasies boring; (2) covert sensitization teaches the adolescent the precursors to engaging in deviant sexual behavior and the consequences that will ensue if they continue to put themselves in "risk situations"; (3) cognitive restructuring that confronts the cognitive distortions and permission-giving statements that sex offenders use to support their behavior; in this segment of therapy, adolescents who have been sexually victimized are given the opportunity to discuss and deal with their own victimization; (4) through sex education and sexual values clarification, adolescent offenders are taught what our society considers appropriate sexual behaviors; (5) social skills training enables the adolescent to establish communication and relationships with peers; (6) anger control training enables the adolescent to express his feelings without resorting to verbal or physical aggression; and (7) relapse prevention—adolescents are taught how to identify stressful situations that may threaten their control and how to respond in an appropriate manner to those situations. Adolescents are seen for 18-months follow-up post completion of treatment.

Preliminary outcome data on the treatment approach with adolescents show a positive outcome (Becker, Kaplan, & Kavoussi, in press). Further research is needed to assess the effectiveness of other treatment modalities as well as controlled therapy outcome studies utilizing a cognitive behavioral strategy.

Conclusion

Research on male victims of sexual assault lags behind studies on female victims. In all probability this is related to cultural bias. Those few studies that have been reported demonstrate a range of sequela in male victims and stress particular concern about sexual adjustment and specifically victimized males being at risk to become offenders.

The field of mental health is lacking a widely accepted and empirically derived theory explaining the etiology of paraphilic behavior. A social learning theory model as described earlier in this chapter would appear to explain the phenomenon and is waiting validation.

Future research should focus on factors predisposing juveniles to commit sexual crimes. Controlled therapy outcome studies and follow-up studies are needed. Until such research is underway, children must be taught at a very early age that it is inappropriate to engage in coercive sexual acts. Children who have been victimized should be informed that there are resources available to support and provide them services.

Schools must take a more active role in educating the young about violence—both physical and sexual. The media must be made to be more responsible and take an active role in educating youth about the impact that coercive behavior has on others.

Pediatricians and adolescent medicine specialists should inquire during every annual checkup whether a child has been the recipient of unwanted sexual behavior or whether he or she has engaged in coercive sexual behavior or sexual behavior with age inappropriate peers. Appropriate referrals should be made when either behavior has occurred.

With an increasing divorce rate more children are being raised in single-parent households by a working parent and left in the care of babysitters or other child caregivers. Frequently, parent(s) do not have the money to provide adequate childcare. Our government needs to be more involved in funding rather than cutting services to women and children. On a national level, we need models of nonaggressive, caring, and empathic leaders who make our nation's children a priority if we are to ameliorate the problem of coercive behaviors in our society.

REFERENCES

Abel, G. G., Barlow, D. H., Blanchard, E. B., & Guild, D. (1977). The components of rapists' sexual arousal. *Archives of General Psychiatry, 34*, 895-903.

Abel, G. G., Becker, J. V., Blanchard, E. B., & Flanagan, B. (1981). The behavioral assessment of rapists. In J. R. Hays, T. K. Roberts, & K. Solway (Eds.), *Violence and the violent individual* (pp. 211-230). New York: Spectrum.

Abel, G. G., Becker, J. V., Mittelman, M., Cunningham-Rathner, J., Rouleau, J., & Murphy, W. (1987). Self-reported sex crimes of nonincarcerated paraphilias. *Journal of Interpersonal Violence, 2*(1), 3-25.

Abel, G. G., Blanchard, E. B., & Becker, J. V. (1976). Psychological treatment for rapists. In S. Bordsky & M. Walker (Eds.), *Sexual assault*. Lexington, MA: Lexington Books.

Abel, G. G., Blanchard, E. B., & Becker, J. V. (1977). An integrated treatment program for rapists. In R. Rada (Ed.), *Clinical aspects of rapists*. New York: Grune & Stratton.

Abel, G. G., Mittelman, M., & Becker, J. V. (1985). Sexual offenders: Results of assessment and recommendations for treatment. In H. Ben-Aron, S. Hucker, & C. D. Webster (Eds.), *Clinical criminology: Assessment and treatment of criminal behavior* (pp. 191-205). Toronto: M & M Graphics.

Becker, J. V., Kaplan, M., & Kavoussi, R. J. (in press). Measuring the effectiveness of treatment for the aggressive adolescent sexual offender. *Annals of the New York Academy of Science*.

Becker, J. V., & Kavoussi, R. J. (n.d.). *Diagnosis and treatment of juvenile sex offenders*. Manuscript submitted for publication.

Becker, J. V., Skinner, L., Abel, G. G., & Cichon, J. (1986). Level of post assault sexual functioning in rape and incest victims. *Archives of Sexual Behavior, 15*(1), 37-49.

Bender, L., & Grugett, N. (1952). A follow-up report on children who had atypical sexual experiences. *American Journal of Orthopsychiatry, 22*, 825-837.

Berlin, F. S. & Meinecke, C. (1981). Treatment of sex offenders with antiandrogenic medication: Conceptualization, review of treatment modalities and preliminary findings. *American Journal of Psychiatry, 138*, 601-607.

Corwin, D., Berliner, L., Goodman, G., Goodwin, J., & White, S. (1987). Child sexual abuse and custody disputes: No easy answers. *Journal of Interpersonal Violence, 2*(1), 91-105.

DeJong, A., Emmett, G., & Hervada, A. (1982). Epidemiologic factors in sexual abuse of boys. *American Journal of Disturbed Children, 136*, 990-993.

Fehrenbach, P. A., Smith, W., Monastersky, C., & Deisher, R. W. (1986). Adolescent sexual offenders: Offender and offense characteristics. *American Journal of Orthopsychiatry, 56*, 225-233.

Felice, M., Grant, J., Reynolds, B., Gold, S., Wyatt, M., & Heald, F. (1978). Follow-up observations of adolescent rape victims. *Clinical Pediatrics*, pp. 311-315.

Finkelhor, D. (1981). The sexual abuse of boys. *Victimization: An International Journal, 6*, 76-84.

Finkelhor, D. (1986). *A sourcebook on child sexual abuse*. Beverly Hills, CA: Sage.

Fritz, G. S., Stoll, K., & Wagner, N. N. (1981). A comparison of males and females who were sexually molested as children. *Journal of Sex and Marital Therapy, 1*(1), 54-59.

Johnson, R., & Shrier, D. (1985). Sexual victimization of boys: Experience at an adolescent medicine clinic. *Journal of Adolescent Health Care, 6*, 372-376.

Landis, J. T. (1956). Experiences of 500 children with adult sexual deviants. *Psychiatric Quarterly, 30*, 91-109.

Longo, R. E. (1982). Sexual learning and experiences among adolescent sexual offenders. *International Journal of Offender Therapy and Comparative Criminology, 26*, 235-241.

Mrazek, P., & Mrazek, D. (1981). The effects of abuse: Methodological considerations. In P. Mrazek & C. H. Kempe (Eds.), *Sexually abused children and their families*. New York: Pergamon.

Marshall, W. L. (1979). The modification of sexual fantasies: A combined treatment approach to the reduction of deviant sexual behavior. *Behavior Research and Therapy, 11*, 557-564.

McGuire, L., & Wagner, N. (1978). Sexual dysfunctions in women who were molested as children: On response pattern and suggestions for treatment. *Journal of Sex and Martial Therapy, 7*, 54-59.

Peters, S. D., Wyatt, G. E., & Finkelhor, D. (1986). Prevalence. In D. Finkelhor (Ed.), *A sourcebook on child sexual abuse* (pp. 15-59). Beverly Hills, CA: Sage.

Porter, E. (1986). *Treating the young male victim of sexual assault: Issues and intervention strategies*. Syracuse, NY: Safer Society Press.

Rogers, C. M., & Terry, T. (1984). Clinical interventions with boy victims of sexual abuse. In I. Stuart & J. Greer (Eds.), *Victims of sexual aggression* (pp. 91-104). New York: Van Nostrand Reinhold.

PART IV

Mediating Factors to Outcomes for Children

Not all victims of sexual abuse experience the same effects as children and later as adults. Indeed, some survivors develop coping strategies that mediate these traumatic experiences quite well, while others appear unable to develop effective methods of coping and remain at risk for revictimization and a host of other problems in life. This section will include factors that can mediate negative outcomes for children. Wyatt and Mickey examine the support of nonabusing parents and other adults and attributions toward victimization as mediators to later outcomes that may impair women's relationships in adulthood. This study, extracted from Wyatt's research on a range of women's voluntary and abusive sexual experiences, is one of the few multiethnic probability samples available on which to conduct multivariate analyses.

Psychotherapy is also widely used with victims and families in the evaluation and recovery process. Guidelines for establishing the therapeutic relationship, the process of disclosing abuse, cognitive restructuring of attributions to victimization, procedures to avoid revictimization, and developing effective coping strategies is reviewed by Wheeler and Berliner. Their chapter on the treatment of child victims is unique in that the dynamics that children present in therapy are discussed within the context of social learning and cognitive behavioral therapy. Techniques to empower and restructure children's self-perceptions, and to manage feelings when these experiences are recalled, are discussed to mitigate future behavioral and psychological problems.

The factors identified in these chapters deserve more attention in treatment outcome studies of recent child victims.

12

The Support by Parents and Others as It Mediates the Effects of Child Sexual Abuse

An Exploratory Study

GAIL ELIZABETH WYATT
M. RAY MICKEY

The growing awareness of the effects of child sexual abuse has emphasized the importance of the disclosure process. When children either fear disclosure, lack the ability to convince those who are told about the magnitude of the event, or are not believed, regardless of how convincingly the abuse is disclosed, feelings of powerlessness can be internalized and the overall adjustment to these experiences can be affected.

Since, for the most part, males tend to perpetuate sexual abuse toward female children (Finkelhor, 1979; Russell, 1983; Wyatt, 1985), one area of specific concern is women's heterosexual relationship difficulties and negative attitudes toward men years after abuse has occurred. Within the context of women's overall reactions to having

AUTHORS' NOTE: A modified version of this chapter was presented at the American Psychological Association Convention, Los Angeles, CA, 1985. We wish to thank the Women's Project Staff for data collection. This research was supported by the Center for Prevention and Control of Rape, NIMH (MH33603), and through a Research Scientist Career Development Award to the first author (MH269). Correspondence regarding this chapter should be addressed to the first author, UCLA, 760 Westwood Plaza, Los Angeles, CA 90024.

been abused in childhood, they may experience a lack of trust and avoidance of relationships where their ability to exert control over future sexual encounters may be at risk. Thus while sexual problems may appear to be strongly associated with childhood victimization, there may also be other problems in women's overall adult, heterosexual relationships that may be associated with earlier abuse experiences.

Aspects of the aftermath of sexual abuse have been described as mediating some of the lasting effects that influence women's adult lives. The response of adult caretakers to victimized children has been described as critical to children's perceptions of the experience (Adams-Tucker, 1982; DeFrancis, 1969; Fromuth, 1983). Having the opportunity to ventilate feelings about having been abused has been identified as an important aspect of the recovery process (Silver & Wortman, 1980). Apparently, the relationship to the victim of the nonabusing individual to whom the abuse is disclosed tends not to be as important as that individual's reaction to the disclosure.

A second component of the experience that may influence feelings of powerlessness are children's attributions and their evaluative interpretation of why they were victimized (Seidner & Calhoun, 1984). It has been suggested that attributions of control over past aversive events can lead to lessened long-term stress reactions to the events (Bulman & Wortman, 1977). The support of the victimized child by parents and other adults could be perceived as validation that a traumatic event has occurred, and this kind of recognition from supportive adults could minimize the victim's self-blame. However, at the other end of the continuum is nonsupport, including the victim being ignored or punished by parents or other adults to whom the incident is disclosed. Consequently, victims may tend to blame themselves because the incident occurred.

More information is needed about what happens if and when child sexual abuse comes to the attention of nonabusing parents and other adults (Finkelhor, 1984) in order to better understand what aspects of the aftermath of the experience may lessen lasting effects and facilitate children's and women's abilities to regain control of their lives.

This study examines the support of nonabusing parents and others as it mediated aspects of women's overall adjustment to their victimization and their resulting attitudes toward men. Attributions to victimization were also considered mediating factors to these lasting effects. Because most research on the prevalence of child sexual abuse has noted that those who are victimized may have had more than one abuse experience and that these experiences range in severity (Finkelhor, 1979; Russell, 1983; Wyatt, 1985), a rating of the severity of child abuse was used to take into consideration all sexual abuse experiences before age 18 and their effect upon women's overall and relationship-specific adjustment to abuse.

A variety of data collection procedures have been used in child abuse research. The use of retrospective data can help in understanding the recovery process from traumatic events in which control is lost and trust is violated. Although some reservations about the ability to recall events over time have been stated (Garobalo & Hindelang, 1977; Hunter, 1957; Klalzky, 1975; Loftus, 1980; Murdock, 1974), many of the supportive findings are based upon criminology and victimization literature, excluding those involving victims of sexual abuse. The salience of events may influence the process of recalling past experiences (Bradburn & Davis, 1983; Delameter & McKinney, 1982). To date, there are still unanswered questions as to the influence of salient events such as abuse upon memory performance. The use of retrospective data can be viewed from another perspective, however. It is a phenomenological approach to research on the antecedents, consequences, and mediators of child sexual abuse. Women's perceptions of abuse incidents are acknowledged to be, in some part, predictive of later functioning in adulthood (Ausubel et al., 1954; Goldin, 1969). Additionally, recent research has indicated that victims of child sexual abuse tend not to disclose the incident(s) until years later (Finkelhor, 1979; Russell, 1983; Wyatt, 1985). Thus retrospective reports of child sexual abuse may be more the rule than the exception until those to whom abuse is disclosed become more aware of the importance of the manner in which children are treated when they disclose abuse. Although attempts were made to assure the accuracy of responses, women's retrospective insights are considered to be important in their own right.

Method

Sample Selection

Multistage stratified probability sampling with quotas was used to recruit comparable samples of Afro-American and White American women 18 to 26 years of age in Los Angeles County. The age criteria excluded minors who could not participate without parental consent, but included women who had an opportunity to develop a number of adult, heterosexual relationships. The actual quotas used for the study were based upon the population of Afro-American women 18 to 26 years of age, with differing levels of education, marital status, and numbers of children. Afro-American and White American women were sought for the study and their inclusion in the sample was based upon their own ethnic identification (see Wyatt, 1985, for further discussion).

The subjects were located by the random-digit dialing of telephone prefixes in Los Angeles County combined with four randomly generated numbers. The specific procedures for recruiting the sample have been described (Wyatt, 1985). The first 248 women meeting the desired quotas were interviewed: 126 Afro-American women and 122 White American women and their demographic characteristics were found to be quite comparable across the control variables (see Wyatt, 1985).

The Procedure

Each participant was interviewed by a highly trained woman of the same ethnicity. Subjects were interviewed at the location of their choice, and were reimbursed $20.00 for their time and up to $2.50 for expenses. Interviews were usually conducted in two sessions and ranged in total from 3 to 8 hours. At the completion of the interview, referrals for mental health services were provided upon request.

Instrumentation

The Wyatt Sex History Questionnaire (WSHQ), a 478-item structured interview, was used to obtain both retrospective and current data regarding women's sexual histories from childhood to adulthood, including data on child sexual abuse. The reliability and validity of the measure are reported elsewhere (Wyatt, 1985).

At the end of an extended interview covering a range of sex-related topics, subjects were asked eight questions about whether they had experienced any of the types of sexual abuse most commonly reported before age 18. If a subject responded "yes" to any of these questions, she was asked a series of questions about that incident.

The Definition of Child Sexual Abuse

Although the specific definition of child sexual abuse has been described elsewhere (Wyatt, 1985), sexual abuse required contact of a sexual nature occurring prior to age 18 by a perpetrator of any age or relationship to the subject. If the perpetrator was five years or older than the subject, the incident was considered to be sexual abuse. If the age difference was less than five years, only situations that were not wanted by the subject and that involved some degree of coercion were included. Experiences were considered as abuse if the subject was 12 years or younger, even if she consented to participate with an adult perpetrator since children cannot distinguish between the sexual behaviors in which they should engage and do not have the freedom not to participate (Finkelhor, 1984).

In this study the term *sexual abuse* was restricted to incidents involving body contact, because information regarding the lasting effects of sexual abuse was available only for these experiences. These contact abuse incidents included fondling and attempted or completed vaginal and/or oral intercourse. They ranged in severity considering the total number of abuse incidents per victim, the duration of the abuse, the frequency of abuse, and a rating of the overall severity of each subject's abuse experiences. The inclusion of a variety of indices of the intensity and severity of sexual abuse made it possible to examine the cumulative impact of the total number of sexual abuse incidents involving body contact and factors that mediated their lasting effects. Of the 154 women who reported at least one incident of child sexual abuse, 112 reported experiencing contact sexual abuse before age 18. However, some of these women also experienced noncontact abuse (i.e., exhibitionists and masturbators). In this study, only the 61 subjects, 25 Afro-American and 36 White American women, who reported experiencing contact abuse exclusively before age 18, were included. These women's demographic characteristics of age, education, marital status, income, and the presence of children were representative of the larger sample.

Scoring of Variables

The overall severity of each subject's sexual abuse incident was rated by the interviewer on a scale of 1 to 10 taking into consideration the circumstances, the age and relationship of perpetrator and victim, and the use of coercion. For example, a severity rating of 1 might have been assigned to one incident of breast fondling while the victim was clothed. A rating of 10 might be assigned to two incidents of repeated rape by several perpetrators, with threats of death or the use of a weapon to coerce the subject into participation. For purposes of analysis, the ten-point rating scale of the interviewer's ratings of the severity of sexual abuse was collapsed into 3 points: less severe (1-3), moderate (4-6), and severe abuse (7-10).

The support by parents and others was assessed for all abuse incidents and was categorized into four possible responses: subjects receiving "support" (39%); a "mixed" response of support and non-support (34%); and "nonsupport" (10%). One additional category "told no one" (10%) was included.

Women who experienced contact abuse were asked to recall what may have contributed to their having been victimized (termed attribution). The categories were "self-attribution" (33%), "mixed" attribution (11%), and "external" attribution (56%).

Women were asked questions regarding the effects of the abuse on their attitudes toward men (attitudes) and the lasting effects on their lives in general (effect). The effects of abuse on women's attitudes toward men as a result of having experienced childhood abuse were categorized as "none" (36%), "minimal" (20%), "moderate" (24%), or "severe" (20%).

The lasting effects of each abuse experience were categorized as "positive" (5%), "negative" (28%), "cognitive" (23%), or "none at all" (44%).

Data Analysis

Because so little is known about the disclosure of abuse, mediating variables (such as attributions regarding its occurrence, the level of support offered), and the effects upon women's overall adjustment and heterosexual relationships it is possible that the constructs described for this study may not have been clearly measured by the items selected. Consequently, two separate analyses were carried out. The primary analysis used methods for categorical data based on log linear models. In these models the logarithms of the expected cell sizes are expressed as linear combinations of parameters representing effects and interactions. Since data from 61 women were concerned with 576 combinations of levels of 5 variables, most cells were empty and linear models considered were limited to parameters representing the interaction of at most pairs of variables. Computations were carried out using computer program BMDP4F (Dixon et al., 1983). A second analysis was based on logistic scoring[1] of the ordered categorical variables. Product-moment correlations of the scored variables were calculated and analyzed by factor analysis, using computer program BMDP4M (Dixon et al., 1983). Principal component analysis and varimax rotation were the options used. The correlation analysis was summarized by a path diagram. The paths were chosen to conform to temporal sequence and to provide close approximations to the numerical values of the correlations.

Results

The prevalence of child sexual abuse did not differ significantly between ethnic groups. In total, 41% of Afro-American women and 59% of White American women reported at least one incident of sexual abuse involving body contact before age 18. An ethnic difference was found on one item regarding women's attitudes toward men. Overall, Afro-American women were significantly more cautious and less trusting of men as a result of their abuse experience(s): χ^2 (4, n = 177) = 10.23, $p < .05$. Since no data regarding attitudes toward men were available prior to the abuse incident(s), it cannot be concluded the sexual abuse alone influenced negative attitudes toward men.

About one-quarter (23%) of women reported more than one abuse incident per person. Three in four women (73%) reported being abused only once by a given perpetrator before age 18. The remaining 27% were abused so often that they could not recall the number of occurrences.

Sexual contact between the perpetrator and the victim occurred less than once a month for 30% of women, two to four times monthly for 21%, and more than once weekly to daily contact with the perpetrator for several years for 49%. Thus those who reported repeated incidents experienced sexual abuse that differed greatly in intensity and frequency.

Interviewers rated about 27% of incidents as less severe abuse, 49% as moderate, and 26% as severe incidents.

Table 12.1 illustrates the frequencies of women's responses for the intervening and outcome variables. About one-third of the women received at least some support from parents and others. About one-third attributed their victimization to themselves. Overall, 20% reported severely negative attitudes toward men as a result of their abuse. In total, 28% described negative overall effects of child sexual abuse. Thus there was appreciable variability in the intensity and severity of sexual abuse in the victims' responses to the experience and in the support received from parents and others.

This exploratory study suggests that the long-term consequences of abuse are related to severity of abuse in ways that depend upon intervening factors. If the effect of abuse is defined in terms of "attitudes toward men," and the intervening variable considered is the level of "support" by parents and others, then the outcome is not related to the severity of abuse if "support" by parents and others is held constant. There is an overall association between the severity of abuse and attitudes toward men, but the association is accounted for by the association between severity of abuse (as measured by interviewer's ratings) and level of "support" and the association between level of "support" and "attitudes toward men." The result is derived by first forming Table 12.1a, which illustrates for each attitude the chance that a woman who experienced sexual abuse in childhood would develop that attitude if she received the support level indicated by the row of the table. For example, Table 12.1a indicates that 55% of abused women who received positive family support had no negative lasting effect on their attitudes toward men, 21% had minimal effects, 12% had modest effects, and 12% had severe effects. Table 12.1b illustrates the numbers of abused women classified by "severity of abuse" and level of "support." Given Tables 12.1a and 12.1b, one can synthesize a cross-tabulation of severity of abuse and attitude. Consider as an example a less severe level of abuse and no lasting effect on "attitudes toward men." Of the 7 women who reported less severe abuse and positive support, (7) (.55) = 3.85 would be "expected" to have no negative effect on "attitudes toward men"; of the 7 women reporting less severe abuse who did not disclose to anyone (level 2 of family support), (7) (.33) = 2.31 would be "expected" to have no negative effect. Similar calculations for level 3 (mixed support) and level 4 (nonsupport) were (1) (.17) = .17 and (2) (.10) = .20. Thus the total "expected" number of women with mild abuse and no effect was the sum of 3.835 + 2.31 + .17 + .20 = 6.53. This value closely approximates the observed value of 7 women in this cell of the cross classification of level of abuse, by later "attitudes toward men." The synthetic "expected" table and the observed table were displayed as Table 12.1c. The high level of agreement between "observed" and "expected" in Table 12.1c indicates that the attitudes toward men at the time of the interview were accounted for by the level of support received following the abuse incident.

A more formal analysis was carried out using log linear models relating the five factors "severity of abuse," level of family "support," "attribution to victimization," "attitudes toward men," and "overall

TABLE 12.1
The Relationship Between Severity of Abuse and Attitude Toward
Men as Accounted for Through Relations of Each to Level of Support

(1a) Conditional distribution (i.e. fraction of row total) of "Attitudes toward mem" given
"Support" by parents and others.

| Support Categories | Attitudes toward Men | | | | |
	None	Minimal	Moderate	Severe	n
positive	.55	.21	.12	.12	24
not tell	.33	.24	.29	.14	21
mixed	.17	.17	.33	.33	6
nonsupport	.10	.10	.40	.40	10

(1b) Cross tabulation of "Support" by parents and others and "Severity of Abuse."

Support by Parents	Mild	Moderate	Severe	Total
support	7	13	4	24
not tell	7	11	3	21
mixed	1	1	4	6
nonsupport	2	4	4	10
	17	29	15	61

(1c) "Expected" and Observed cross tabulation of "Attitudes toward men" by "Severity of
Abuse."

| Severity | Attitudes | | | | | | | |
| | None | | Minimal | | Moderate | | Severe | |
	Obs.	Exp.	Obs.	Exp.	Obs.	Exp.	Obs.	Exp.
Less Severe	7	6.5	5	3.5	3	4.0	2	3.0
Moderate	12	11.3	5	5.9	8	6.7	4	5.1
Severe	3	4.2	2	2.6	4	4.3	6	3.9

lasting effects." These models can be thought of as simultaneously
fitting all two-way marginal tables. The rejection of the hypothesis that
all two-factor interactions are zero χ^2 (252, n = 61) = 445, p < .001
indicates that at least some two-factor interactions are present. The
strongest partial associations were for "attitudes toward men" and
"support" by parents and others (maximum ratio of estimated parameter
to standard error = 2.51) and for "attitudes toward men" and "overall
lasting effects" of abuse (maximum ratio of estimated parameter to
standard error = 2.88). There were also indications of a relationship
between "severity of abuse" and "attribution" (women having had

severe abuse tended not to report external attributions; ratio of estimate to standard error = 2.45), "attribution" and "support" by parents and others (women who had not talked about their abuse experiences tended to report self-attribution; ratio of estimate to standard error = 2.46), and "attribution" and "overall lasting effects" (women reporting external attribution tended to have the most severe long-term effects; ratio of estimate to standard error = 2.05). The further consideration of models analyzing "severity," "support," and "attitudes toward men" led to the findings summarized in Table 12.1. The model based on all three pairs of factors fitted the data well (goodness-of-fit) χ^2 (18, n = 61) = 19.5, p = .36. However, the model based on only the two pairs, "severity-support" and "support-attitude" fitted the data just as well χ^2 (24, n = 61) = 23.3, p = .50. This demonstrated that the relation between "severity of abuse" and "attitudes toward men" was accounted for by the interrelation of each with support from parents and others, as was indicated by the less formal analysis of Table 12.1. Similar sets of models were fit with "overall lasting effects" replacing "attitudes." The best-fitting model, as indicated by the chi-square test, was with the two pairs of factors "severity-support" and "support-overall lasting effects" (p = .63). The relationship between "support" and "overall lasting effects" was weaker than that between "support" and "attitudes," although in neither case could the relationship be considered very strong.

An alternative analysis was conducted by applying methods of correlation analysis to scores constructed for each of the five variables by logistic scoring of the ordered categories. Two analyses of the correlations were made: (a) factor analysis and (b) a summary of correlations in terms of a path analysis diagram.

Two eigenvalues of the correlation matrix, 1.74 and 1.19, were greater than 1.0 and factors 1 and 2 were rotated. Loadings for factor 1 were "severity" .63, "support" .73, "attitudes" .76, "attribution" –.26, and "overall effects" .31. Loadings for factor 2 were complementary: .75 for "attribution," .75 for "lasting effects," and –.01 for "severity," –.13 for "support," and .36 for "attitudes." The two factors accounted for 59% of the variance.

A path diagram summary, including path coefficients, which illustrate the correlations, is shown as Figure 12.1. Correlations are approximated as sums of the products of factors along paths joining factors. For example, the correlation between "severity" and "attitude" were approximated from the product along the upper path (.20) (.39) = .078, plus the product along the middle path (.25) (.72) = .187 to give (.078) + (.187) =

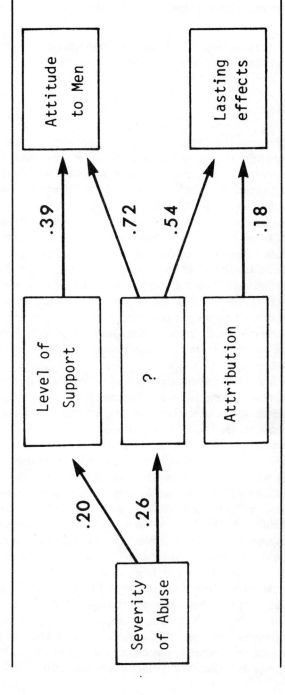

Figure 12.1 Descriptive Path Diagram Summarizing the Correlations Between Study Factors Related to Effects of Abuse

.26. In this representation, "attribution to victimization" was correlated only with "attitudes toward men."

Discussion

While these results provide insights into aspects of the aftermath of abuse experiences that may mediate lasting effects, they are of a tentative nature. The number of abused women (61), while large in the sense of their experiencing at least one incident of contact abuse before age 18, was small in terms of log linear analyses of categorical data. The summarizing categories used, while appropriate to this study, were not the product of refinement by several investigators based upon independent studies. Research in this area is still in its infancy. Despite possible limitations, however, it was considered desirable to begin the process of understanding the factors that occur routinely in the aftermath of abuse and that might lessen the lasting effects. The importance of gaining insight into the variety of social, sexual, and psychological problems that emerge as a consequence of child abuse and how abused women learn to cope place the limitations of this exploratory research into perspective.

Both the log linear and correlation analysis indicated that the items "severity of abuse," level of family "support," and "attitudes toward men" separated out as interrelated factors. The findings from the log linear analysis that the level of family support "uncoupled" abuse from lasting effects (as assessed by these variables) were encouraging in that some of the harmful effects of abuse might be nullified by the support of nonabusing parents and others. One would have expected that the finding would be reflected in the scores by a lack of partial correlation between "severity" and "attitudes," given "support." The computed partial correlation (.21) was similar in magnitude to the direct correlation (.26). Although neither value was well-established statistically, the indication was that the correlation analysis was insensitive to some of the features represented in the categorical analysis.

The correlation analysis was summarized by the rather speculative path diagram. The diagram was appropriately based on the temporal sequence: abuse during childhood, subsequent processing, and long-term consequences. The unidentified block is less satisfactory and was included to account for the correlation between "attitudes toward men" and "lasting effects" along with the lack of correlation between "level of support" and "lasting effects." The diagram does not conform to the finding from the categorical analysis, in that the diagram indicates a pathway from "severity of abuse" to "attitudes toward men" that is alternate to the path through "level of support." Although the categorical appears to be the more appropriate analysis, we have not entirely dismissed the correlation analysis as invalid and have included the path diagram as an indication that future research might investigate possible concepts for the unidentified link.

It might be useful in future research to distinguish between appropriate ("I was shy and alone") and inappropriate attributions to victimization ("My breasts developed early"), as perceived by the victims. We did not make this distinction in our interviews. It may not be possible to obtain even moderately reliable data on the appropriateness of attributions in the course of a broad retrospective study such as this one. However, more specific information regarding the influence of self versus external attributions might help in understanding their role in the recovery process.

Clinicians and researchers often assume that severe child sexual abuse, involving higher levels of coercion or the more serious types of sexual behaviors, should generate lasting consequences that might be reflected in women's adult lives. It was surprising to note that overall lasting effects of abuse and severity of abuse were not correlated. The observed fact was that several women had a comparatively less severe abuse experience but also attributed serious long-term effects to that abuse. One interpretation might be that the perceived lasting effects were largely determined by other characteristics, for example, dimensions of personality, that were not assessed in this research. Therefore, it is important to obtain not only specific information from victims about the circumstances of the incident and their reaction, but also to assess dimensions of personality that may influence lasting effects (Briere & Runtz, this volume). Such a conclusion was supported by the correlation between "attribution" and "lasting effects." However, the interrelations are most likely too complex to be reflected completely in the summary analysis.

Attribution is possibly a more important consideration than indicated by these analyses. It was found that while self-attributions were associated with aspects of the experience, the severity of abuse, and nondisclosure, whereas external attributions were associated with the lasting effects of child sexual abuse. Among the responses included with those defined as "external" were descriptions of the perpetrator, his method of involving the victim in the incident, or "bad luck"—being in the wrong place at the wrong time. These responses suggest that some victims become aware of their inability to fend off powerful perpetrators or their inability to control chance events. Consequently, many women may continue to perceive of themselves as powerless to control the world, some of the people in it, and events that take place (Finkelhor, 1987).

It might be argued that attributions to victimization should be perceived as a lasting consequence. However, consistent with other reviews of research examining reactions to traumatic events (Thompson, 1981), it was more appropriate to consider attribution as an intervening variable than as an outcome variable. These analyses also supported "attitudes toward men" and "lasting effects of child sexual abuse" as sufficiently different aspects of the experience to be distinguished separately. Because patterns of correlation with the other three variables were distinctly different, the "lasting effects" and "attitudes toward men" were not combined into a single score. This finding suggests that, although the overall effects of child abuse and resulting attitudes toward men may appear to affect women's adjustment and future relationships where sex may be involved, they may be separate entities. The overall effects of child abuse may be more specifically related to what the victim learns about their vulnerability to abuse and women's attitudes toward men may be more specifically related to relationship difficulties.

Implications of Findings for
Victims of Child Sexual Abuse

This study emphasized the importance of parents and other adults in providing some level of support for and validation of child sexual abuse victims' disclosure of their experience(s) and confirms findings in other research. It is sad that, of the incidents that were disclosed, only five resulted in the perpetrator being caught and jailed or referred for therapy. The legal process requires a great deal of information about the perpetrator, a strong supportive family willing to endure countless questions, and a great deal of patience and money to persevere until the process is complete. Even with all of this, there is no guarantee that the perpetrator will be convicted of sexual abuse.

Still, helping victims regain control over their lives is critical to the recovery process. While the involvement of parents and other adults appears to mediate some of the lasting effects, there are those remaining women who were unwilling to disclose their abuse to anyone at the time that the abuse occurred (in this sample, 34%). Thus the recovery process might occur if victimized children or women who were victims during childhood seek therapeutic help or if, through careful history taking, their victimization is uncovered by a clinician.

The most valuable aspect of discussing these past aversive events is that the therapist can offer support, which sexually abused women and children did not receive either because of nondisclosure or because responsible adults did not provide it. The delayed process of recognition and validation that the incident was traumatic can finally take place in therapy. This is especially important, because attribution to victimization can also be redirected in the appropriate direction—in therapy, if necessary.

Unfortunately, only 13% of women in this study reported that they received medical or therapeutic help for their child abuse victimization, per se. If these findings indicate the likelihood that few health-related professionals may have the opportunity to facilitate the regaining of control in abuse victims' lives, nonabusing family members, friends, and other loved ones may continue to be the most sought after persons to whom abuse is disclosed, even though this support may be requested years after the incident occurred. And yet, with the current educational information available to the public about the effects of child sexual abuse and the consequence of disclosure, significant persons, like many professionals, are often still confused as to their role in facilitating the disclosure of abuse and what to do with the information that is revealed. Thus victims are frequently at risk for yet another type of victimization. With continued research and educational efforts aimed at describing child sexual abuse and the factors that mediate its lasting effects, the public and professional groups must be made more knowledgeable about helping children and women to disclose their victimization, and in so doing begin the process of regaining control of their lives.

REFERENCES

Adams-Tucker, C. (1982). Proximate effects of sexual abuse in childhood: A report on 28 children. *American Journal of Psychiatry, 139*, 1252-1256.

Ausubel, D. P., Balthazar, E. E., Rosenthal, I., Blackman, L. S., Schpoont, S. H., & Welkowitz, J. (1954). Perceived parent attitudes as determinants of children's ego structure. *Child Development, 25*, 173-184.

Bradburn, N. M., & Davis, C. (1983). Potential contributions of cognitive sciences to survey questionnaire design. In J. Tanur (Ed.), *Cognitive aspects of survey methodology* (pp. 15-25).

Bulman, R. J., & Wortman, C. B. (1977). Attributions of blame and coping in the "real world": Severe accident victims react to their lot. *Journal of Personality and Social Psychology, 35*, 351-363.

DeFrancis, V. (1969). *Protecting the child victim of sex crimes committed by adults.* Denver: American Humane Association.

Delameter, J., & McKinney, K. (1982). Response effects of question content. In W. Dijkstra & J. Van der Zouwen (Eds.), *Response behavior in the survey-interview.* London: Academic Press.

Dixon, W. J., Brown, M. B., Englemen, L., Frame, J. W., Hill, M. A., Jennrich, R. J., & Toporek, D. J. (1983). *BMDP statistical software.* Berkeley: University of California Press.

Finkelhor, D. (1979). *Sexually victimized children.* New York: Free Press.

Finkelhor, D. (1984). Child sexual abuse in a sample of Boston families. In D. Finkelhor (Ed.), *Child sexual abuse: New theory and research.* New York: Free Press.

Finkelhor, D. (1987). *The trauma of child sexual abuse: Two models.* Newbury Park, CA: Sage.

Fromuth, M. E. (1983). *The long term psychological impact of childhood sexual abuse.* Unpublished doctoral dissertation, Auburn University.

Garobalo, J., & Hindelang, M. (1977). *An introduction to the National Crime Survey.* Washington, DC: U.S. Department of Justice.

Goldin, P. G. (1969). A review of children's reports of parent behaviors. *Psychological Bulletin, 71*, 222-236.

Hunter, I.M.L. (1957). *Memory.* Middlesex, England: Penguin.

Klalzky, R. L. (1975). *Human memory: Structures and process.* San Francisco: W. H. Freeman.

Loftus, E. F. (1980). *Memory.* Reading, MA: Addison-Wesley.

Murdock, B. B. (1974). *Human memory: Theory and data.* Potomac, MD: Lawrence Erlbaum.

Russell, D. (1983). The incidence and prevalence of intrafamilial and extra-familial sexual abuse of female children. *Child Abuse and Neglect, 7*, 133-146.

Seidner, A. L., & Calhoun, K. S. (1984, August). *Childhood sexual abuse: Factors related to differential adjustment.* Paper presented at Second Annual National Family Violence Research Conference.

Silver, R. L., & Wortman, C. B. (1980). Coping with undesirable life event. In J. Garber & M.E.P. Seligman (Eds.), *Human helplessness: Theory and applications.* New York: Academic Press.

Thompson, S. C. (1981). Will it hurt less if I can control it? A complex answer to a simple question. *Psychological Bulletin, 90*, 89-101.

Tsai, M., Feldman-Summers, S., & Edgar, M. (1978). Childhood molestation: Variables related to differential impacts on psychosexual functioning in adult women. *Journal of Abnormal Psychology, 88*, 407-417.

Wyatt, G. E. (1982). The sexual experience of Afro-American women: A middle income sample. In M. Kilpatrick (Ed.), *Women's sexual experience: Explorations of the dark continent.* New York: Plenum.

Wyatt, G. E. (1985). The sexual abuse of Afro-American and White-American women in childhood. *Child Abuse and Neglect, 9*, 507-519.

13

Treating the Effects of Sexual Abuse on Children

J. ROBERT WHEELER
LUCY BERLINER

It is now widely recognized that there are multiple adverse effects of child sexual abuse (CSA) (Briere, 1984; Browne & Finkelhor, 1986) but there has been little attention in the literature to formulating the psychological effects of CSA in terms of explicit theoretical constructs that can in turn be correlated with recognized therapeutic interventions or provide the basis for their development. Consequently, there has been little formal knowledge to guide practitioners working with abused clients. Much of the available clinical literature focuses on describing client characteristics and psychological dynamics. Proposed treatment approaches tend to be generic. For example, a conventional therapeutic modality, such as individual or family psychotherapy, is modified for application to this population by incorporating an emphasis on abuse-related themes (James & Nasjleti, 1983; Rogers & Terry, 1984). Furthermore, there has been no systematic outcome evaluation of any set of treatment procedures with this population. The purpose of this chapter is to integrate existing research, emerging diagnostic conceptualizations of the effects of CSA, and bootstrapped clinical interventions within an existing body of psychological theory. These are tentative efforts intended to provide some direction for continued attempts to develop, refine, and empirically evaluate systematic interventions.

The general position taken here is that the effects of CSA can be understood as a combination of classically conditioned responses to traumatic stress and socially learned behavioral and cognitive responses to the abuse experience. This analysis differs from but is not incompatible with the recent conceptualization by Finkelhor and Browne (1985). The current formulation is based on assumptions about hypothesized causal processes rather than on a categorization of observed effects in terms of rationally derived categories of psychodynamics. Both initial and long-term effects, as well as the extensive heterogeneity of effects, are accounted for by classical and social learning theory.

The discussion of the treatment of the effects of CSA is organized around two main themes: affective responses characterized by anxiety that are the result of classical conditioning, and cognitions and behavior patterns that are the result of social learning processes. Although different mechanisms of acquisition are implied by these two types of learning, the adverse effects each produces are considered to have originated as attempts to cope with traumatic stress. It is hypothesized that treatments that are directed at altering the conditioned and socially acquired responses to the victimization will alleviate initial symptoms and will reduce the likelihood of long-term or more serious disruptions in development.

Theoretical Perspectives on Child Sexual Abuse

Child Sexual Abuse and Anxiety

Much of the initial symptomatology reported in abused children is consistent with the diagnostic criteria for Post-Traumatic Stress Disorder, which is a subset of the category of anxiety disorders (APA, 1980). Children's responses to a variety of traumatic events (Terr, 1983, 1985), of which sexual abuse is one type (Goodwin, 1985), include the two basic dimensions of posttraumatic reactions: repetition of the trauma and attempts to deny the trauma (Brett & Ostroff, 1985). Studies of clinical and nonclinical populations of children and adults confirm that there are multiple affective, cognitive, and behavioral effects of CSA and that in many cases these effects persist over long periods of time (Bagley & Ramsey, 1985; Briere, 1984; Conte & Berliner, 1987; Friedrich, 1986; Gomes-Schwartz, Horowitz, & Sauzier, 1985). Initial effects are predominated by responses characterized by fear and anxiety (Browne & Finkelhor, 1986), and frequently include such specific symptoms as fear of being harmed, nightmares, phobias, regressive behavior, and somatic complaints. Aggressive behavior, anger, guilt and shame, sleep and eating disturbances, running away, truancy, and inappropriate sexual behavior also occur with varying degrees of frequency (Browne & Finkelhor, 1986). These symptoms can be thought of as attempts to master or cope with the anxiety produced by traumatic stress, either through approach strategies or through avoidance and denial (Roth & Cohen, 1986).

Anxiety is a theoretical construct that is used to describe a complex set of responses characterized by autonomic arousal, including increased heart rate, sweating, dryness of the mouth, dizziness, hyperventilation, and feelings of muscular weakness; subjectively experienced feelings of apprehension, tension, worry, and dread; and behaviors characterized by attempts to avoid or master the stimuli that elicit these intensely unpleasant feelings (Spielberger, Pollans, & Worden, 1984). The distinction between fear and anxiety is not a sharp one but is based on an individual's appraisal of the extent to which there is actual, external danger to him or her in a given situation. Insofar as it elicits autonomic arousal that prepares the individual to cope with the danger or avoid it, fear is adaptive. To the extent that similar responses are elicited by situations or stimuli that pose no external danger or threat of harm and interfere with adaptive behavior, they are likely to be labeled as anxious. Because anxiety is experienced as an intensely unpleasant state, the anxious individual is motivated to engage in responses to reduce or eliminate the anxiety. These coping responses may be behavioral; for example, by avoiding situations or persons associated with anxious feelings. Or they may be cognitive; for example, by attempting to reinterpret anxiety-producing cues in such a way as to render them inert.

Causal explanations of anxiety have been dominated by psychoanalytic and learning theories (Spielberger et al., 1984). The psychoanalytic view dates from Freud's danger signal theory, in which anxiety was described as an internal warning system that alerts the individual to the presence of danger. Freud distinguished between "objective" anxiety, which is synonymous with simple fear, and "neurotic" anxiety arising from an individual's own unsuccessful attempts to cope with conflictual impulses. Consider the case of a child who has been sexually abused by a father for whom she has feelings of affection and upon whom she is dependent, and whose sexual abuse, in addition to its aversive features, at times produces pleasurable physical feelings. The feelings of anger and aggressive impulses that the child is likely to feel toward her father conflict with her fear of loss of affection or punishment she would incur if her anger were expressed directly. It is this conflict that produces initial feelings of anxiety. Because anxiety is intensely unpleasant, the child engages in coping behaviors to alleviate the aversive feelings. Psychoanalytic theory suggests that the child learns to cope by repressing from her awareness feelings of anger in order to resolve temporarily the conflict between her aggressive feelings, on the one hand, and the fear of losing the affection of or incurring punishment were she to express those feelings directly. In the long run, however, the inevitable failure of repression results in "neurotic anxiety," and the production of associated symptoms.

Traditional learning theory postulates that anxiety essentially results from the pairing of an unconditioned stimulus (fear) with previously neutral or even reinforcing stimuli (e.g., the offender) (Wolpe, 1958). In the example just given, the child would be presumed to associate the fear she experiences during or as a direct consequence of sexual abuse with her father. She would be expected subsequently to experience feelings of fear and anxiety in his presence, particularly in situations most similar to the one(s) in which the abuse occurred (e.g., when alone together). Over time her fear could, through generalization, produce anxiety in the presence of persons (e.g., other males) or other stimuli (physical surroundings, sights, sounds, smells, or other associations) similar to those associated with the abuse. Similarly, through higher-order conditioning, these more recently conditioned cues for anxiety could themselves become paired with other, previously neutral stimuli, producing still more cues for anxiety. As the processes of generalization and/or higher-order conditioning proceed, the child might experience anxiety in the presence of persons or situations far removed from the initial abusive experiences. While the anxiety might have been adaptive initially, in the sense that it alerted the child to the dangers posed by her father or even of the potential dangers of, for instance, being alone with men, in the long run as the process of generalization and higher-order conditioning evolve and the child's developmental level and needs change, the anxiety could become maladaptive and even debilitating.

Extension of these basic theories of anxiety have tended to focus more attention on the mediating role played by cognitions in anxiety (Bandura, 1977; Goldfried, 1971, 1973) or have attempted to integrate the psychodynamic and behavioral theoretical perspectives (Wachtel, 1973). While a detailed consideration of these elaborations is beyond the scope of this chapter, Wachtel (1973) provides an especially illuminating analysis and integration of the behavioral and psychoanalytic perspectives in his thoughtful analysis of the classic work of Dollard and Miller (1950). Wachtel makes several points about repression and its consequences which are particularly relevant to the current discussion. First, Wachtel argues that repression can be understood as a learned process of avoiding thoughts or events associated with anxiety. Discomfort is minimized and avoidant behaviors or thoughts are reinforced as the individual learns to redirect attention from the cues or signals associated with fear. As the individual learns to anticipate the anxiety-related cues or signals, very small decrements in discomfort or tension reinforce further avoidance. In effect, repression is conceptualized in terms of avoidance learning. Repression has two important harmful consequences. First, by teaching the child to avoid what he or she fears, he or she never learns at what point, if ever, his or her fears are no longer justified or adaptive. Second, because it interferes with higher cognitive processes, repression inhibits the use of language to help to understand, distinguish, and sort out the stimuli that are producing or maintaining anxiety, and thereby interferes with the acquisition of effective coping strategies and skills.

Approach strategies for coping with stress and counterproductive anxiety "allow for appropriate action and/or the possibility for noticing and taking advantage of changes in a situation that might make it more controllable. Approach strategies also allow for ventilation of affect" (Roth & Cohen, 1986, p. 813). In contrast, "avoidant strategies seem useful in that they may reduce stress and prevent anxiety from becoming crippling" (p. 813). Approach strategies tend to be more effective in situations in which the stressful situation is controllable, whereas avoidant strategies have more utility in situations beyond the individual's control. Given this perspective on the relative utility of approach and avoidant coping strategies, and based on the foregoing analysis of anxiety, treatment interventions proposed in the remainder of this chapter are most often directed toward active but gradual "mastering" of anxiety through strategies that gradually foster engagement and coping with the anxiety and fears and minimize counterproductive denial and avoidance. This assumes, of course, that sexual victimization of the child has terminated. Treatments characteristically include gradual direct exposure to the feared stimulus or symbolic representations of it (graduated exposure, participant modeling); altering perceived self-efficacy in coping with the anxiety-producing events or situations (cognitive restructuring, assertiveness training); rendering autonomic stimuli associated with anxiety inert by producing incompatible autonomic responses (desensitization, coping skills instruction, stress inoculation); or extinction through abreaction (provided that the feared stimuli are no longer present). However, it should also be explicitly recognized that avoidant strategies may be therapeutic given certain conditions. If they allow for a gradual recognition of threat and prevent the individual from feeling overwhelmed, "partial, tentative or minimal use of avoidance can lead to increased hope and courage, particularly over a long period of time. One can also achieve a sense of mastery over unpleasant emotions associated with the threatening material" (Roth & Cohen, 1986, p. 817). Thus we will repeatedly stress the need for sensitive clinical judgment as well as the importance of assessing the child's current developmental and psychological status in formulating interventions.

CSA and Social Learning

The second major pathway to postabuse maladjustment is through the maladaptive social behaviors, beliefs, and attitudes that children learn from sexual abuse and the adaptive ones they fail to learn. From their abuse children learn certain patterns of behavior that are harmful to themselves or to others or that restrict their development and prevent them from attaining adequate functioning. They acquire inaccurate or harmful ideas about major dimensions of human experience. Finkelhor and Browne (1985) have incorporated many of these effects within their four categories of "traumagenic dynamics" and they are reviewed in Finkelhor's chapter. The following is a brief review and reconceptualization of some of the major effects from a social learning perspective. The purpose of reframing these effects in explicit social learning terms is to link them directly to a substantial body of psychological theory that can provide the basis for deriving therapeutic interventions.

The position taken here is that much of what a child learns from sexual abuse is mediated through social learning processes (Bandura, 1969, 1977). The offender's behavior most often can be conceptualized as a form of instrumental aggression that produces sexual gratification (Malamuth, Feshbach, & Jaffe, 1977). Through the offenders' modeling, instruction, direction or differential reinforcement, and punishment or threat of punishment abused children acquire a repertoire of sexual behaviors and experiences before they have the necessary emotional cognitive or social capabilities to regulate their own sexuality. They learn a set of subtle discriminations based on the unique circumstances of their abuse about how sexual behaviors are used to obtain reinforcement or avoid punishment. Interventions aimed at modifying, ameliorating, or correcting the socially learned responses to victimization must at a minimum alter the conditions under which the behaviors and cognitions were acquired, including the contingencies of reinforcement of inappropriate behavior.

Additionally, social learning theory predicts that the autonomic arousal associated with the abuse may itself have a direct facilitative effect on the acquisition of sexual behaviors. This premature sexualization can disinhibit the child's expression of sexual behaviors in circumstances that will lead to social ostracism and stigmatization, additional sexual abuse of the child, victimization of other children, and potentially to long-term sexual dysfunction. Finkelhor and Browne (1985) have described in greater detail many of these effects as examples of "traumatic sexualization" and "stigmatization." Interventions intended to ameliorate these effects must alter the child's cognitions about sexual behavior and restore or instate effective self-regulatory controls through appropriate cognitive-behavioral and contingency management strategies. The specific strategies selected will obviously be determined by the child's age and developmental status as well as by the specific history of sexual abuse.

In addition to overt behavioral effects, children's beliefs, values, and attitudes are influenced and shaped by CSA. In her analysis of the responses of adults, Janoff-Bulman (Janoff-Bulman & Frieze, 1983) contends that victimization shatters three basic assumptions about the world: a belief in personal invulnerability, a perception of the world as meaningful and predictable, and a positive self-concept. While children may not have such well-formed assumptions about the world, sexual abuse affects their ideas about themselves, about others, and about relationships that mediate their behavior and future development. For example, the child abused by a male teacher may conclude from the experience that all men or trusted adults are exploitive, or may develop distorted perceptions, unjustified apprehensions, and a loss of confidence in his or her judgment, which results in avoidance of relationships. What begins as an experience with one individual becomes the basis for overgeneralized responses to many. Finkelhor and Browne (1985) describe this learning as "betrayal." Interventions designed to counter maladaptive tendencies to respond in an overgeneralized fashion will require that the child acquire the ability to make finer discriminations without undermining the adaptive aspects of the mistrust he or she has learned. Often these interventions will need to be blended with appropriate anxiety-reduction treatment as well.

Also implicit in the sexual coercion of the offender is a disregard of the child's legitimate wishes and a usurpation of his or her control over something as fundamental to one's sense of self as his or her body. From this experience the child can be expected to experience diminished expectations of self-efficacy (Bandura, 1977), the expectation that one can produce desirable outcomes or avoid undesirable ones. Finkelhor and Browne (1985) refer to the outcome of this process as a sense of "powerlessness." Interventions targeted at countering these effects will focus on instating or restoring a sense of self-efficacy through acquisition of coping responses, including assertiveness, problem-solving, and communication skills.

Strategies for Treating the Effects of Child Sexual Abuse

The treatment methods that follow from the preceding theoretical analysis focus more specifically on the victim than is the case with alternative treatment approaches that view the child's reactions to the sexual abuse primarily as a function of parental responses (Freud & Burlingham, and Solomon, cited in Benedeck, 1985) or disturbed family interactions (Alexander, 1985). The therapeutic interventions proposed here do not imply that the responses of parents and other adults are unimportant but they are predicated on the basic premise that the abuse itself is traumatic and that the child's victimization is the essential focus of treatment. They also assume that not all adverse effects of the abuse will be apparent immediately. As a result, attention is paid to prevention of potential adverse effects.

Because the child's experience is the immediate focus of therapy, individual or group therapy are the primary modalities recommended. Intervention with parents is also necessary to educate them about the effects on their child and to instruct them in helping support the child's coping efforts or to assist them in managing problematic behaviors. Many parents want assistance with their own reactions to the victimization of their child as well as with other possible disruptions to their lives that may be directly or indirectly associated with the abuse. Individual, family, or group therapy, or participation in support groups, are therefore often important adjuncts to child-focused treatment.

The child's age and developmental status determine the mixture of verbal and nonverbal interventions. Play therapy is often considered the treatment of choice for the very young child. School age children may respond best to a combination of talking, activities, therapeutic exercises or games, art therapy, and play acting. Again, a time-limited approach may be most appropriate developmentally. Adolescent victims are generally more assertive about the types of therapeutic endeavors they will engage in and the length of their participation.

Initial Intervention and Assessment

The initial intervention following disclosure is focused upon managing the immediate consequences of disclosure. Sgroi (1982) has outlined the steps in this process. The more structured treatment of effects is neither the priority nor feasible until the immediate crisis has been stabilized.

Formal assessment subsequent to stabilization of the initial crisis provides the basis for treatment interventions; a baseline from which to measure recovery or decline in adjustment; a point of reference should the child require treatment in the future for problems which did not arise until a certain developmental stage was reached; and evidence that may be required for subsequent legal actions. Thorough documentation of the child's status may be part of the basis for dispositional recommendations in juvenile or adult court or as supportive evidence in a civil damage suit. Despite great variability in the presence or severity of symptoms, assessment and some intervention is warranted in all cases.

Although no psychological measures currently assess the specific impact of CSA, a complete psychological evaluation may be useful in assessing the existence or extent of impairment in the child's functioning or the amount of distress the child is experiencing. At a minimum the symptoms described by the child, the caretaker and noted by the evaluator should be systematically recorded. Eliciting the children's beliefs and attitudes about the abuse is as important for directing interventions as description of the abuse itself and observations of symptomatic behavior. What children believe about the sexual abuse and their role in its occurrence, their attitudes about themselves, and their expectations of others are significant foci of treatment.

Anxiety-Reduction Strategies

Treatment of fear and anxiety involves reducing the arousal to fear-producing cues and teaching management strategies for neutralizing the subjective feelings of anxiousness. Since anxiety reduction generally requires exposure to aversive stimuli, an important function of therapeutic intervention is to provide the children with an environment where this can take place. Children may be very resistant to these efforts because it is common for trauma victims to develop anticipatory avoidance behaviors. Therapy should assist the children in overcoming these behaviors when they hinder ultimate resolution of the trauma.

While not conceptualizing their treatment from an explicit social learning framework, Reams and Friedrich (1985) propose a form of play therapy that allows the very young child to master fear and anxiety by incorporating elements of desensitization, graduated exposure, modeling, and assertiveness training into the treatment. Therapeutic content is structured through the use of puppets or dolls, and the process is facilitated by gently encouraging and directing reenactment and discussion about various aspects of the abuse experience. As the therapy proceeds, appropriate responses are modeled by the therapist, and successive approximations of effective coping responses by the child are reinforced. Nondirective therapy is not recommended since the child may very well avoid abuse-related activities, which reduces opportunities for mastering symptoms of anxiety.

With older children a more direct approach combines elements of graduated exposure and abreaction by encouraging children to talk about the abuse in situations that are safe and supportive. Although children complain when they are repeatedly interviewed about the facts of the case, they frequently are quite willing to describe their thoughts and feelings to a therapist or to other children in a group. Through a process of talking about abuse-related material in a regular matter-of-fact way, the memories eventually lose the capacity to elicit arousal. Sensitivity and clinical judgment are required in determining at what rate to proceed in eliciting this material. Children should not be forced prematurely to recall or talk about the abuse because the therapist and the therapeutic environment may become simply an aversive reminder of the abuse.

Ventilation of affect. Appropriate expression of affect may, over time, reduce the power of abuse cues to elicit arousal and discomfort. Feelings of anger and grief are common. They share similar qualities but require a different resolution (Pynoos & Eth, 1985). Children may not feel free to express anger or may lack the verbal skills to do so. Adults are not always comfortable with children's anger and may overtly or covertly discourage its expression or induce guilt in the child who expresses it. Grief in a sexual abuse situation can result from the loss of an important relationship (e.g., big brother, babysitter) or from a legally mandated separation from the abuser (e.g., grandparent). Further, there may be an irrevocable change in the view of the person or role (e.g., "It's like I don't really have a dad").

Therapy provides children with a safe environment in which to express anger, grief, and other emotions and teaches constructive strategies for handling them. Therapeutic process can range from verbal statements to reenactment in play therapy. Children can be encouraged to put feelings into words in poems, stories, and songs or into pictures and drawings. They can learn to recognize and describe emotions (e.g., "When I get mad I am tense; I clench my fists, and I want to yell at someone"). Management strategies that are age appropriate and situation specific can be devised. The 4-year-old scribbles her "mad" red marker on a piece of paper and then crumples it up and throws it away. The 10-year-old counts to ten while holding his breath, then breathes out deeply three times as soon as he first gets the feeling; and the teen goes in the bathroom, turns on the shower, and says what she feels out loud.

Angry feelings toward the offender are common. They can be expressed through direct discussion in group or individual therapy sessions, composition of a letter that may or may not be actually mailed, or stated to a picture, drawing, doll, or other stand-in for the person. The criminal justice system can afford a legitimate outlet for the anger. Even young school-age children can write a letter to the judge at the time of sentencing.

The resolution of grief can also be facilitated by the therapist. First the child learns that the sad feelings are acceptable and do not reduce the seriousness or wrongfulness of the abuse. A ritual ceremony or funeral can be conducted where memories are shared. The various stages of mourning are explained and systems for being aware of and accepting different feelings are devised. The child might make a plan to spend a designated period of time just feeling sad or crying and thinking about the loss. The normal process of mourning considered necessary for recovery also includes positive reminiscing.

Specific anxiety-reduction strategies. With older children a combination of relaxation training and problem-solving training (Goldfried & Davison, 1976) may be helpful in acquiring skills to cope with the discomfort of feeling anxious and afraid, and can be applied to everyday life. All children can be taught strategies to anticipate and manage the situations where they become afraid by making symptom-specific plans or strategies to carry out.

Systematic desensitization or related procedures (Goldfried & Davison, 1976) can be more or less useful depending on the imaginal and attentional abilities of the child. In general, the child is gradually desensitized to the arousal by imagining anxiety-producing cues while in a state of relaxation or mild trance induction. Identifying the sources of the child's anxiety usually requires eliciting specific information from the child about the contents of their intrusive memories, dreams, or nightmares or identifying the cues that evoke anxiety responses. Children may be asked to draw pictures of the worst part of the abuse experience, of the fear itself, or of the content of the bad dream. The children can be instructed to "make a list of reminders of the abuse" or "tell all the situations when you get scared." These procedures may be best reserved for use with older children or adolescents and where the child is able to visualize the various situations and have the attention span necessary to participate effectively in the process.

One of the most common posttraumatic complaints relates to fears that have to do with going to bed at night. Children may refuse to sleep in their own bed, make excuses to get up or stay up, or wake often in the night. Creating a ritual for ensuring a sense of safety preceding bedtime may decrease this anxiety. It can be a tour of the house to check doors and windows, in closets, and under beds. Safety procedures can be reviewed, a relaxing and soothing experience can assist the child in falling asleep (e.g., taking a hot bath, listening to music, having a warm drink, getting a back rub). The parent may identify a special story or song that is particularly reassuring or familiar. Initially it may be quite appropriate for children to be allowed exceptions or regressions such as sleeping with the parent. Gradual but steady return to the usual expectations is a part of recovery. In therapy sessions the therapist, parent, and child plan the gradual steps toward a return to ordinary, age-appropriate behavior.

Nightmares, often in the form of reenactments of the assault or other frightening scenes, are frequently reported. A useful anxiety-mastery technique is to transform the content of the dreams with the child and to create a scenario in which the child vanquishes the offender or slays the monsters. This can be done with drawings or in discussion. Another method is to have the child make up a competing pleasant scene to rehearse just before falling asleep.

Dealing with the fears, phobic reactions, or regressive behaviors that may appear in the children often requires extensive parental involvement. The idea is to expose the child gradually to the feared situation. For example, the child who clings to the mother and will not leave her side needs to be progressively accustomed to being away from her. Perhaps she can begin by being in a different room for short periods of time. Periods of play outside or in the immediate vicinity may then be encouraged as long as the child does not react fearfully. Next, brief trips to the store with another adult can be planned. Finally, the parents may be able to leave the child with a babysitter for an evening. Persistence and patience are usually necessary to accomplish the desired goal, especially when the behavior is well established. A key concept is gradually to expose the child to anxiety-producing situations or circumstances without requiring him or her to proceed at a rate that exceeds what he or she can tolerate. Gauging the appropriate rate of exposure is obviously a delicate task requiring sensitive clinical judgment.

Reports of intrusive thoughts or an inability to concentrate are also common. Specific strategies to interrupt intrusive memories include using some type of thought stopping (e.g., visualizing a stop sign), making a self-statement (e.g., "Wait a minute, I don't want to think about this"), or having a prepared alternative to substitute (e.g., reciting a poem, memorizing a speech). To interrupt daydreaming, the child must learn to recognize or become aware of the state. Teachers, friends, and parents can be enlisted to help in alerting the child by using a certain phrase or contact (e.g., "There you go again, spacing out" or gentle tapping on the shoulder).

**Strategies for Treating
Socially Learned Responses**

Altering attributions of responsibility. It is important to provide sexually abused children with a straightforward explanation of what has happened and assurances that they are not culpable for their abuse. This is not as easy as it sounds because there is not universal agreement among professionals about the causes of sexual abuse, the relative contribution of different factors in it, or the motivations of the actors. To take the position that children should not be told at all (Lamb, 1986), however, may leave them at risk subsequently for developing feelings of guilt or confusion about their role in the abuse. In addition, developmental capabilities dictate different levels and elaborations of explanation.

In current practice, children are often assured repeatedly in therapeutic settings that the abuse was not their fault. Although it is both morally and legally correct to convey to children that adults are always responsible for their abuse regardless of the children's behavior, there is some evidence that recovery is enhanced in victims of traumatic experiences when there is some degree of self-blame (Janoff-Bulman, 1986). A distinction is made between characterological self-blame, which may be maladaptive, and behavioral self-blame, which may represent an adaptive coping response. Children can be provided explanation about why adults are assumed more responsible (e.g., they know more, they are more mature, they have more options, they are bigger, they control resources). The concept of consent can be explained (e.g., when people are afraid or don't think they can say no or don't know what they are agreeing to, then it isn't a fair agreement). Within this framework the choices and the reasons for the choices can be explored. By identifying the children's perceptions of behaviors that they believe make them responsible, the therapist can ameliorate characterological attributions of blame while facilitating choices and behaviors that decrease their risk of future victimization. For example, the child who believes he or she caused his or her molestation by asking his or her father where babies come from requires reassurance that his literal demonstration was a result of his disturbed thinking and behavior and that the child's conduct was completely normal. On the other hand, the child who has repeatedly returned to the neighbor's home knowing of the possibility of molestation or who has sought extra privileges in exchange for compliance with abuse can be gently helped to acknowledge that a choice was made and learn to understand why at the time it seemed the better or only alternative.

The degree to which the child became a participant or accommodated (Summit, 1983) to the abuse may influence how long it takes and how hard it is for the child to recognize how he or she behaved. Children abused for a long time by significant adults almost invariably have secrets they dread sharing: for example, that they were sexually aroused; that sometimes they actually initiated the sexual contact; or that they imagined marrying their father. Or, with hindsight, they see that there were many opportunities to avoid or escape or simply to disclose their abuse, yet they chose not to. An important therapeutic objective is to elicit this information and the accompanying beliefs so they can be reframed and new behaviors learned in order to prevent repetition of these patterns.

Explaining the offender's behavior. Several lines of evidence suggest that victims of trauma adjust better when they have a causal explanation (Silver, Boon, & Stones, 1983), even if inaccurate (Taylor, 1983), of their experience. An explanation of the offender's behavior can be provided that is consistent with current conceptualizations (Araji & Finkelhor, 1986) and empirical evidence (Quinsey, 1986). Such an explanation involves telling children, in effect, that, "He has a problem; he wants to be sexual with children, something that most grownups don't want. And he tells himself it's okay to do it even though he knows it is wrong." This is preferable to the explanation that, "He's sick." The concept of sickness is associated with not being responsible for one's actions and tends to diminish the intentionality of the conduct. Presenting the offender in this fashion may cause the child to feel sorry for him or guilty for having strong negative feelings toward him. Similarly, explanations of the abuse in terms of confusion or misguided love may simply confuse the child or be inconsistent with the child's experience.

There may be other distorted beliefs held by the child that hamper resolution. For example, if the offender has told the child or the child independently assumes that the reason the abuse occurred was because his or her mother did not fulfill her role as a sexual partner, there may be unwarranted resentment toward the nonoffending parent. Children are more negatively affected when they believe others knew of the abuse but took no action to protect the child (Conte, 1986).

Restoring expectations of self-efficacy. Restoring or enhancing children's sense of competency and assisting them in acquiring skills to cope with the effects of abuse takes varied forms depending on the developmental status of the children and the specific nature of the effects themselves. Young children may be engaged in play reenactments in which coping responses are modeled and shaped. In the therapeutic setting the therapist can gradually redirect or restructure the content and expression so that the child becomes powerful, avoids abuse, or conquers the offender. Older children can educate themselves about abuse by reading pamphlets or books, or doing a paper for school and interviewing the counselor and other professionals. They may reach out to another child in their group or to a friend and try to help him or her solve a problem; plan how they might react if confided in by a friend; or plan how they will be different as an adult or a parent. Even participation in the criminal justice system or juvenile proceeding may be a means of enhancing the child's sense of self-efficacy.

An important aspect of coping with an abuse experience is reducing the sense of vulnerability to subsequent abuse. There is evidence that victims are at increased risk for future victimization (Russell, 1984). One strategy to reduce vulnerability is to teach children to become knowledgeable about preabuse warning signs. Children can recall the specific events or behaviors that preceded actual abuse (e.g., he always wanted to be alone; he treated me too old for my age; he wanted me to give him back rubs; he told me things about his sex life). If these indications are recognized earlier on in the process, an incident of abuse may be averted. Formal review of prevention knowledge and strategies can include any of the numerous educational materials that are widely available. Every child should at least know how to recognize abuse; that it is wrong; who to notify in the event of an attempted assault; and how to cope with a potentially threatening situation.

The therapeutic relationship itself can counter the exploitation of an abusive relationship and serve as one reliable, safe, and predictable model of a reciprocal relationship. For some children, therapeutic relationships may provide the only adults who are genuinely interested in their welfare. In therapy children can learn to improve relationships with concerned adults in their life (e.g., parent, relative) and to seek out relationships with helping adults (e.g., school counselor, coach) that compete with negative expectations caused by the sexual abuse experience or other forms of abuse and neglect.

Teaching skills enable children to evaluate situations and meet needs more effectively. Acquisition or strengthening of problem solving, assertiveness, communication, and social skills can reduce feelings of powerlessness or isolation. A positive self-image is enhanced and opportunities for positive interactions with others are increased; family and peer conflict is reduced. These can be incorporated into the therapy sessions through discussion and role play or through more structured rehearsals and videotaping.

Traumatic sexualization and sexual behavior problems. Sexual abuse is by definition sexual and is at least partially sexually motivated. It also may be experienced by children as sexually arousing and for some may result in orgasm. There is no generally shared set of values about normal and acceptable sexuality for adults or children. Among both children and adults, there are vastly different levels of knowledge, experience, and beliefs about sex and sexuality. These factors complicate both the assessment of the effects sexual abuse has on sexuality and the tasks of assisting a child in understanding and coping with the abuse. Although not all children have sexual behavior problems following sexual assault it should be assumed that the abuse will have a potentially damaging effect on their ideas about sexuality or will facilitate engaging in sexual behavior that is potentially harmful. Berliner, Manaois, and Moastersky (1986) have described three categories of such sexual behaviors: (1) sexually inappropriate behavior (e.g., persistent, public, or painful masturbation); (2) developmentally precocious sexual behavior (e.g., attempted or completed intercourse by prepubertal child with another); and (3) coercive sexual behavior (e.g. aggressive or socially coerced sexual contact with another child). The goals of treating traumatic sexualization are to correct the child's thinking about sexual behavior, increase internal inhibitions and external controls against unacceptable sexual behavior, and ensure that the child has the skills to control behavior and meet sexual needs in culturally acceptable ways.

Because children are strongly influenced by family beliefs, and may be punished when they express attitudes or engage in behaviors that are not acceptable to their family, therapists should elicit the parents' views and, to the extent possible, structure interventions to be respectful of and consistent with the family values, regardless of the therapists' opinions. Informing parents in advance about the general content of sessions will prepare them for the change in language or kind of questions that their child may exhibit and protect against shock occasioned by the unanticipated and graphic public comment about some sexual matter.

Age-appropriate basic sexual knowledge should be reviewed and/or taught. Children should know about reproduction and body parts, learn and/or use correct terminology, and be aware of different sexual activities. There are numerous publications (e.g., books, pamphlets, videos for children, adults, or families) available in libraries, bookstores, and through community agencies such as Planned Parenthood. Values clarification and awareness of different social attitudes about sexuality accompany the provision of information about sexuality. Understanding the concepts of consent and mutuality, defining readiness to be sexually active, knowing the reasons why people are sexual, and assisting in the formulation of a personal set of beliefs assist in placing the abuse experience in perspective. Since they have already had an abnormal experience, probably have not had competing appropriate sexual experiences, and may not yet be ready to be sexually active, specific instruction and discussion of these issues is necessary even though for other children it might be premature.

Since the children's awareness of physical boundaries may have been compromised by the abuse and they may have learned to meet other needs through relating sexually, the parent-child and the therapeutic relationships become vehicles for modeling appropriate conduct. Abused children may show their confusion by being physically intrusive in the office: moving objects on the desk, getting into drawers, climbing on furniture, or touching or sitting on the therapist. Children should be gently instructed or confronted or firmly disentangled from the therapist. This does not mean that some affectionate physical contact (e.g., a quick hug, pat on the head, arm across a shoulder) is not appropriate with some children under some circumstances. Parents may need assistance in setting limits on certain behaviors and in increasing appropriate affectional contact.

With older children behavior management strategies can be learned and rehearsed in therapeutic settings to manage sexually inappropriate behavior. A relapse prevention approach (Pithers, Marques, Gibat, & Marlatt, 1983) can be adapted for use with children. Using this model, children identify the sequence of events and the accompanying affective states and cognitions that precede the conduct. They learn to recognize points where decisions can be made to avoid actually repeating the behavior. Then a set of strategies is developed to challenge cognitions that facilitate the progression (e.g., verbalizing a prohibition out loud such as "I get in trouble when I do that; my mom will be mad at me"). Alternative behaviors are identified and rehearsed (e.g., remove self from situation, engage in relaxation exercise or a physical activity, seek help by making contact with a supportive adult).

Parents can be taught behavior management skills so they may work with the child through systematic and consistent reward or punishment to deal with behavior that is persistent and has not responded to verbal confrontation. Parents should increase supervision to protect this child and others from having the opportunity to misbehave sexually. Parents are also assisted in developing and/or communicating clear family rules about privacy and acceptable sexuality.

Conclusion

To date, no clinical outcome studies have demonstrated the efficacy of any treatments of the effects of sexual abuse on children, much less their differential efficacy or which treatments are effective for what problems. Clearly it is premature to advocate for any theoretical orientation or intervention to the exclusion of alternatives. Furthermore, the multiplicity and complexity of the effects suggest that multiple interventions are likely to be necessary. The theoretical orientation and strategies derived from it described in this chapter are offered in an effort to pull together the diverse strands of an emerging field and to interpret them in the context of an existing body of theory and knowledge. The interventions await more rigorous evaluation.

REFERENCES

Alexander, P. (1985). A systems theory conceptualization of incest. *Family Process, 24*, 79-88.

American Psychiatric Association. (1980). *Diagnostic and statistical manual of mental disorders* (3rd ed.). Washington, DC: Author.

Araji, S., & Finkelhor, D. (1986). Abusers: A review of the research. In D. Finkelhor (Ed.), *A sourcebook on child sexual abuse* (pp. 89-119). Beverly Hills, CA: Sage.

Bagley, C., & Ramsey, R. (1985). *Disputed childhood and vulnerability to sexual assault: Long-term sequels with implications of counseling.* Paper presented at Conference on Counseling the Sexual Abuse Survivor, Winnipeg, Canada.

Bandura, A. (1969). *Principles of behavior modification.* New York: Holt, Reinhard & Winston.

Bandura, A. (1977). *Social learning theory.* Englewood Cliffs, NJ: Prentice-Hall.

Benedeck, E. (1985). Children and psychic trauma: A brief review of contemporary thinking. In R. Pynoos & S. Eth (Eds.), *Post-traumatic stress disorders in children* (pp. 3-15). Washington, DC: American Psychiatric Press.

Berliner, L., Manaois, O., & Monastersky, C. (1986). *Child sexual behavior disturbance: An assessment and treatment model.* Unpublished manuscript, Seattle, WA.

Brett, E. A., & Ostroff, R. (1985). Imagery and post-traumatic stress disorder: An overview. *American Journal of Psychiatry, 142*(4), 417-424.

Briere, J. (1984). *The long-term effects of childhood sexual abuse on late psychological functioning: Defining a post-sexual abuse syndrome.* Paper presented at the Third National Conference on Sexual Victimization of Children, Washington, DC.

Browne, A., & Finkelhor, D. (1986). Impact of child sexual abuse: A review of the research. *Psychological Bulletin, 99*, 16-77.

Conte, J. R., & Berliner, L. (1987). The impact of sexual abuse on children: Empirical findings. In L. Walker (Ed.), *Handbook on sexual abuse of children: Assessment and treatment issues.* New York: Springer.

Dollard, J., & Miller, N. E. (1950). *Personality and psychotherapy.* New York: McGraw-Hill.

Finkelhor, D., & Browne, A. (1985). The traumatic impact of child sexual abuse: A conceptualization. *American Journal of Orthopsychiatry, 55,* 530-541.

Freidrich, W. (1986). Behavior problems in sexually abused young children. *Journal of Pediatric Psychology, 11,* 47-57.

Gelinas, D. (1983). The persisting negative effects of incest. *Psychiatry, 46,* 312-332.

Goldfried, M. R. (1971). Systematic desensitization as training in self-control. *Journal of Consulting and Clinical Psychology, 37,* 228-234.

Goldfried, M. R. (1973). Reduction of generalized anxiety through a variant of systematic desensitization. In M. R. Goldfried & M. Merbaum (Eds.), *Behavior change through self-control.* New York: Holt, Rinehart & Winston.

Goldfried, M. R., & Davison, G. C. (1976). *Clinical behavior therapy.* New York: Holt, Rinehart & Winston.

Gomes-Schwartz, B., Horowitz, J. M., & Sauzier, M. (1985). Severity of emotional distress among sexually abused preschool, school-age and adolescent children. *Hospital and Community Psychiatry, 35,* 503-508.

Goodwin, J. (1985). Post-traumatic symptoms in incest. In R. Pynoos & S. Eth (Eds.), *Post-traumatic stress disorder in children* (pp. 157-186). Washington, DC: American Psychiatric Press.

James, B., & Nasjleti, M. (1983). *Treating sexually abused children and their families.* Palo Alto, CA: Consulting Psychologists Press.

Janoff-Bulman, R. (1986). The aftermath of victimization: Rebuilding shattered assumptions. In C. Figley (Ed.), *Trauma and its wake: Study and treatment of post-traumatic stress disorder* (pp. 15-36). New York: Brunner/Mazel.

Janoff-Bulman, R., & Freize, I. H. (1983). A theoretical perspective for understanding reactions to victimization. *Journal of Social issues, 39,* 1-17.

Lamb, F. (1986). Treating sexually abused children: Issues of blame and responsibility. *American Journal of Orthopsychiatry, 56,* 303-307.

Malamuth, N. M., Feshbach, S., & Jaffe. (1977). Sexual arousal and aggression: Recent experiments and theoretical issues. *Journal of Social Issues, 33,* 110-131.

Pithers, W. D., Marques, J. K., Gibat, C. C., & Marlatt, A. A. (1983). Relapse prevention with sexual aggressives: A self-control model of treatment and maintenance of change. In J. Greer & I. Stuart (Eds.), *The sexual aggressor: Current perspectives on treatment* (pp. 214-239). New York: Van Nostrand Reinhold.

Pynoos, R., & Eth, S. (Eds.). (1985). *Post-traumatic stress disorders in children.* Washington, DC: American Psychiatric Press.

Quinsey, V. (1986). Men who have sex with children. In D. Weisstub (Ed.) *Law and mental health: International perspectives.* New York: Pergamon.

Reams, R., & Friedrich, W. (1985). *A manual for time-limited play therapy with abused/neglected children.* Unpublished manuscript, University of Washington, Seattle.

Rogers, C. M., & Terry, T. (1984). Clinical intervention with victims of sexual abuse. In I. Stewart & J. Greer (Eds.), *Victims of sexual aggression.* (pp. 1-104). New York: Van Nostrand Reinhold.

Roth, S. R., & Cohen, L. J. (1986). Approach, avoidance, and coping with stress. *American Psychologist, 41,* 813-819.

Russell, D. (1984). *Sexual exploitation: Child sexual abuse, rape and workplace harassment*. Beverly Hills, CA: Sage.

Sgroi, S. (1982). *Handbook of clinical intervention in child sexual abuse*. Lexington, MA: D. C. Heath.

Silver, R., Boon, C., & Stones, M. (1983). Searching for meaning in misfortune: Making sense of incest. *Journal of Social Issues, 39*(2), 81-102.

Spielberger, C. D., Pollans, C. H., & Worden, T. J. (1984). Anxiety disorders. In S. M. Turney & M. Hersen (Eds.), *Adult psychopathology and diagnosis* (pp. 263-303). New York: John Wiley.

Summit, R. (1983). The child sexual abuse accommodation syndrome. *Child Abuse and Neglect, 7*, 177-193.

Taylor, S. E. (1983). Adjustment to life threatening events: A theory of cognitive adaptation. *American Psychologist*, pp. 1161-1173.

Terr, L. (1983). Chowchilla revisited: The effects of psychic trauma: A clinical study of ten adults and twenty children. *American Journal of Orthopsychiatry, 53*(2), 244-261.

Terr, L. C. (1985). Psychic trauma in children and adolescents. *Symposium on Child Psychiatry, 8*(4), 815-835.

Wachtel, P. L. (1973). *Psychoanalysis and behavior therapy: Toward an integration*. New York: Basic Books.

Wolpe, J. (1958). *Reciprocal inhibition therapy*. Stanford, CA: Stanford University Press.

PART V

Conclusions and Issues for Research, Treatment, and Social Policy

The final chapters by two outstanding child advocates provide future directions for the field of child sexual abuse and its professional constituency. Social policy is sorely needed to acknowledge the complexities of the diagnosis and treatment of victims and their families and to improve the training of professionals involved in educational, therapeutic, social welfare, and legal service delivery. David L. Corwin describes the tedious processes involved in establishing the first national conferences and organizations for professionals and in proposing the Sexually Abused Child's Syndrome as a diagnostic category. The progress made in establishing this structure in the area of child sexual abuse cannot be fully appreciated without knowledge of the political atmosphere in which advocates for children operate.

Gloria Johnson Powell's chapter on clinical issues and future research directions identifies areas that are seldom discussed or yet to be explored. She addresses the following difficult questions: When should treatment of victims begin? For whom is it most appropriate and how long should victims or survivors be in therapy? Dr. Powell suggests that because sexually victimized children and adults molested as children often experience other traumatic life experiences that the therapist should develop a treatment plan to address all traumas. Certainly research also will need to identify the cumulative impact of negative life experiences upon victims of sexual abuse in order to understand fully the extent of trauma upon the victim. There are still many challenges to face. These chapters give us an appreciation of the progress made and will, one hopes, motivate those in the field to continue their work.

14

Early Diagnosis of Child Sexual Abuse

Diminishing the Lasting Effects

DAVID L. CORWIN

Child sexual abuse is a frequent and injurious phenomenon. As described in Roland Summit's chapter in this volume, the sexual victimization of children evokes so much denial and repression that even though it surfaced into professional awareness three previous times during the past 130 years it was resuppressed each time by the formidable denial and backlash it illicited.

Many well-designed scientific studies conducted during the last decade by researchers such as David Finkelhor, Ph.D. (1979), Diana Russell, Ph.D. (1983), and Gail Wyatt, Ph.D. (1985) have irrefutably proven that the sexual victimization of children is common. Hence, instead of attempting to dispute the prevalence of child sexual abuse, the current backlash focuses on the technical aspects of its identification, evaluation, and legal handling. The current counterattack has shifted from denial of the "bad tidings," the fact that child sexual abuse is widespread among all social classes, religions, and races of people, to the "messengers" bearing these "bad tidings" (Summit, 1986). That is, the professionals and specialized techniques that overcome the usual

AUTHOR'S NOTE: I would like to acknowledge the following people for their significant contribution to the development of the National Summit Conference on Diagnosing Child Sexual Abuse, the "Sexually Abused Child's Disorder" drafts, the two subsequent consensus meetings, and/or this chapter: Lucy Berliner, MSW, Dennis Cantwell, MD, David Chadwick, MD, David Finkelhor, Ph.D., Kenneth Freeman, JD, Moira Garvey, Michael Grogan, LCSW, Lois Haight Herrington, JD, Beverly James, LCSW, Gloria Powell, MD, Kay Ryan, Theresa Shuman, Ph.D., Roland Summit, MD, Michael Wald, JD, and Gail E. Wyatt, Ph.D., and many others.

avoidance and denial of child victims. Without this recently developed knowledge and methodology or the professionals working in this field, today's awareness of child sexual abuse would once again be resuppressed leaving unchallenged those who sexually abuse children and the child victims once again unseen, unprotected, and untreated.

To meet this challenge effectively, professionals who wish to assist sexually abused children must increase the precision and scientific validation of their work. This chapter presents draft criteria for diagnosing sexually victimized children and describes the development of the interdisciplinary field of study and professional practice focused on child sexual abuse. Research diagnostic criteria, such as those presented here would facilitate professional education and help focus ongoing refinement of evaluation methodology and professional decision making regarding child sexual abuse. Short of preventing the sexual victimization of children, early identification, protection, and treatment offer the greatest hope for diminishing its lasting effects.

The National Summit Conference on Diagnosing Child Sexual Abuse and the "Sexually Abused Child's Disorder"

In August of 1985, discussions began between several colleagues and myself on the advisability and feasibility of developing a psychosocial diagnostic category for sexually abused children. One of those consulted was Dennis P. Cantwell, the Joseph Campbell Professor of Child Psychiatry and Director of the fellowship program in Child Psychiatry at UCLA. Dr. Cantwell had been involved in the development of the child diagnostic categories in the third edition of the Diagnostic and Statistical Manual of the American Psychiatric Association, DSM-III, and, at the time, was working on its revision. He encouraged the effort to proceed as fast as possible so that it could be submitted to the revision of DSM-III that was scheduled for completion in December of 1985. Dr. Cantwell also assisted in editing early drafts of the "Sexually Abused Child's Disorder."

With the support of many experts in the field of child sexual abuse identification, intervention, treatment, and prevention, plans were begun for an interdisciplinary "Summit Conference" on diagnosing child sexual abuse. Ultimately, nearly one hundred professionals, including many of this country's foremost experts on child sexual abuse from the disciplines of medicine, nursing, psychiatry, psychology, social work, investigation, and law, assembled in Los Angeles, California, in October 1985.

The goals of the "National Summit Conference on Diagnosing Child Sexual Abuse" were to delineate the consensus among these experts on child sexual abuse. The participants were asked to review and to discuss the third draft of the "Sexually Abused Child's Disorder," which was advanced as a possible remedy for the lack of an adequate diagnostic category for sexually abused children in DSM-III. One of the potential benefits from including such a category and diagnostic guidelines for identifying sexually victimized children is that it could reduce the risk of mental health professionals failing to recognize and correctly diagnose sexually abused children. Failure to identify such children precludes their protection and provision of appropriate treatment.

It has been well established that many sexually abused children demonstrate few of the most typical symptoms associated with sexual victimization (Conte, Berliner, & Schuerman, 1987), and that many refuse to acknowledge having been sexually abused (Russell, 1983). Hence if a diagnostic category for sexually victimized children is to be based on objectively verifiable signs and symptoms, it cannot encompass all sexually abused children. Delineating such a disorder, however, could assist in focusing future research on the identification of most children who have been sexually abused. And, in some cases, the "Sexually Abused Child's Disorder" might also be useful in protecting sexually abused children who are too young or for some other reason unable to testify convincingly. Such usage would be similar to the current use of the "Battered Child's Syndrome" in legal proceedings.

The "Child Sexual Abuse Accommodation Syndrome" (Summit, 1983) is becoming well-known, but it is not a diagnostic formulation. It is an empirically derived description of common, yet often misconstrued, tendencies of sexually abused children to make delayed, inconsistent, and unconvincing disclosures of their abuse and frequently to recant. The primary purpose of Summit's Accommodation Syndrome is to educate clinical and legal decision makers that the presence of these features does not reliably invalidate a case of alleged sexual abuse. Nor is the presence of such features alone sufficient proof that sexual abuse has occurred. This is so because theoretically there may be false allegations of child sexual abuse that have these same characteristics. Summit advises that decision makers must look beyond the Accommodation Syndrome and weigh the other evidence that supports or detracts from the apparent validity of a particular case of alleged sexual abuse.

The Sexually Abused Child's Disorder is, on the other hand, an attempt to describe the specific signs and symptoms that are specific enough that together they constitute compelling clinical substantiation that a particular child has been sexually victimized. The clinical determination of child sexual abuse is an important prerequisite to instituting the most specific and effective treatment for sexually abused children. Such a clinical determination is often important in protecting sexually victimized children and in maintaining their ongoing protection against revictimization and coercion to recant.

The format of DSM-III facilitates the recognition of alternative etiologies that may create similar clinical findings as they are listed in differential diagnostic sections. This increases the likelihood that other possible etiologies will be considered prior to clinical substantiation of sexual abuse.

The Sexually Abused Child's Disorder was initially drafted in 1985 and, with the review and critique of many experienced and recognized authorities on child sexual abuse, it was redrafted prior to presentation at the National Summit Conference on Diagnosing Child Sexual Abuse that same year. The version presented here incorporates input from the "Summit Conference" plus two subsequent consensus meetings held in 1986, one on the clinical signs and symptoms of child sexual victimization and the other on false allegations. This draft also reflects additional clinical experience and recent research findings. It is presented here to generate further discussion and research on its validity and reliability.

Sexually Abused Child's Disorder: Fourth Draft, November 1987

The primary feature of the Sexually Abused Child's Disorder is an age-inappropriate increased awareness and altered emotional reaction to neutral inquiry about genital anatomy or exposure to differentiated sexual experiences, such as exhibitionism, sexualized kissing, fondling, vaginal or anal penetration, child pornography, and oral copulation. There is a normal range of age-appropriate, sexually naive responses to such questions. While school-aged children may show more normal discomfort or embarrassment than preschoolers, both usually demon-

strate a lack of recognition and occasional incredulity when asked about such experiences (Goodman, Aman, & Hirschman, 1987). Indicators of likely age-inappropriate, differentiated, sexual experience include anxiety, fearfulness, excitement, overdetermined denial and/or avoidance in response to such questions, for example, a 4-year-old boy who denies ever having seen a penis. *This altered emotional reaction plus a child's ability to show or to describe differentiated sexual practices are the core clinical findings of the Sexually Abused Child's Disorder. These findings combined with additional similarities to known cases of child sexual victimization constitute the criteria for the disorder.*

Sexually abused children often feel that if they disclose their victimization they will be seen as bad and punished accordingly. This may be especially true in the majority of such cases that involve victimization by someone close to or in a position of authority over the child. Along with their reluctance to rekindle the emotional reactions that accompanied their sexual victimization through recollection and recounting, this fear frequently contributes to delayed and conflicted disclosures of sexual abuse, and a tendency to minimize the extent of victimization initially. Another prominent tendency of sexually abused children is to deny or to recant previous disclosures, particularly when met with disbelief, adverse consequences, and various pressures conducive to denial and recantation. This includes being directly asked or told to recant. Such directives are sometimes accompanied by threats, which may include a loss of special privileges, attention, possessions, and the prediction of dire consequences to the child, the child's family, or other important objects of love, nuturance, protection, and security. Children are sometimes offered rewards for recanting, and, in some cases, the recantations are precipitated by the emotional distress that accompanies recollecting and recounting the abuse. In general, both the treated and the untreated sexually abused children will increasingly suppress or repress their memory of the abuse as time passes. False recantations and other factual distortions may also occur in the context of prolonged, intimidating, and or redundant questioning.

The validity of a child's disclosure of sexual abuse is most accurately determined by thoroughly reviewing all relevant factors including their communication content, tone, facial expressions, gestures, mannerisms, and occasional unconscious behavioral partial reenactments of the abuse experiences that are precipitated by specific inquiry, as well as any behavioral or emotional changes. When a child's convincing account of sexual victimization is combined with a history, signs, and symptomatology similar to known cases of child sexual victimization, then it is probably valid.

Children who are 4 to 5 years old can often show with dolls and 2- to 3-year-olds on themselves what has occurred more easily than they can verbally describe such occurrences (Goodman et al., 1987). Such young children usually have difficulty placing their experiences in time, remembering quantities, and in keeping multiple experiences separate. However, even very young children are often capable of describing or showing what occurred and where and identifying who did it.

The developmental limitations of very young children frequently results in minor apparent inconsistencies from one telling to the next. These should not be misconstrued as sufficient to discredit the major facts that they consistently describe or invalidate other affirmative evidence of sexual victimization (Saywitz, in press). Sexually abused children may display fluctuating recall from one interview to the next.

If many months or years have passed since the sexual abuse occurred, there may be additional difficulties in consistent recall. Actual forgetting of details may further complicate the effects of psychological denial and repression.

Physical findings and history indicative of sexual abuse may occur without the diagnostic criteria for the Sexually Abused Child's Disorder being met. In such cases, the physical findings should be listed on Axis III. Because of this possibility and the fact that not all children who are sexually abused will develop or demonstrate during evaluation the signs and symptoms of the Sexually Abused Child's Disorder, it is not valid to argue that a child has not been sexually abused simply because he or she does not meet the diagnostic criteria for the Sexually Abused Child's Disorder. However, if a child does meet these criteria, it is very likely that they have been sexually abused.

Associated features. Although some sexually abused children will show no observable signs or symptoms, many problems have been noted to occur among such children. Some are less specific indicators of stress and developmental regression such as the development of bed wetting or fecal soiling. Fecal soiling, however, can also be a result of stretching or tearing accompanying anal penetration. Other common yet less specific indicators include refusal to sleep alone, undifferentiated nightmares, night terrors, clinging, separation problems, and other regressions to less mature forms of behavior and affect (AMA, 1985).

There are, however, several reactions that are more specific to the circumstances and emotional impact of sexual abuse. Premature eroticization (Friedrich, this volume), overdetermined denial, and avoidance of genital anatomy, or exposure to nudity, person- or gender-specific fearfulness or aggressiveness are such indicators. Severe nightmares precipitated by reexposure to particular persons, places, or objects and those nightmares that include physical movements or vocalizations that are consistent with sexually abusive experiences are more discriminating for actual sexual victimization than less differentiated sleep disturbances.

Although most sexually abused children deal with such experiences by denial and avoidance, some children are unable to suppress the resultant thoughts and behavioral impulses. They display the most specific primary reactions to sexual abuse such as repetitive sexually aggressive behavior or preoccupation with sexual anatomy and feelings. Other more specific indicators include the depiction of genitals in human figure drawings, masturbatory behavior that is excessive and unusual when compared to peers, sometimes including penetration with objects or repeated attempts to engage others in sexual behaviors.

Some sexually abused children will meet the diagnostic criteria for other psychiatric disorders, they should be listed along with the Sexually Abused Child's Disorder. Most frequently associated with child sexual abuse are the depressive, dissociative, and Post-Traumatic Stress Disorders (Briere & Runtz, this volume). Anxiety and conduct disorders also occur (Sansonnet-Hayden, Haley, Marriage, & Fine, 1987). If precocious sexual behavior is believed to be the result of sexual abuse and the child meets the diagnostic criteria for the Sexually Abused Child's Disorder, then conduct disorder should not be diagnosed on the basis of the sexual misconduct alone.

Differential Diagnosis

The following are aspects of children's behavior that should be examined before a diagnosis is made.

Consensual peer sex play. Noncoercive sexual experimentation among children is common, it may occasionally result in precocious sexualization that may be misinterpreted as a sign of sexual abuse. This can usually be discriminated during interview by questioning about this possibility. Consensual sex play should be differentiated from reenactment behavior initiated by a sexually victimized child.

Misinterpreted physical contact. This may occur in the context of bathing, dressing, or toileting of children, and may be more a product of parental naivete or inexperience than intent to sexually abuse. These children show little conflict about or preoccupation with genital anatomy and sexual behavior.

Observed sexual acts. With the proliferation of X-rated movie channels and video cassettes, children's potential for exposure to sexually explicit behavior is increased. Viewing of such material may increase a child's awareness of differentiated sexual behavior.

Fabrications or misperceptions. Most studies have found these to be less than 10% of the total number of suspected cases reviewed (Cantwell, 1981; Goodwin, 1982; Jones & McGraw, 1987; Peters, 1976). Allegations between separated parents present the most difficult challenge for assessment. The stresses, dynamics, and circumstances of a family break-up are both conducive to the occurrence of actual sexual abuse or disclosure of previous abuse and to the making of misperceived or fabricated allegations (Corwin, Berliner, Goodman, & White, 1987). Most validated cases of fabrication originate with an adult who is believed to have coached or otherwise indoctrinated the alleged child victim. In a small number of cases, however, it has been reported that children have initiated false reports themselves. A history of prior victimization has been noted in some of these children (Jones & McGraw, 1987). Once these and other issues are examined, the diagnosis for child sexual abuse victimization can be made.

Diagnostic Criteria for the Sexually Abused Child's Disorder

(A) Displays an increased awareness of differentiated sexual behaviors as demonstrated by specific knowledge, or by emotional and behavioral reactions to direct questions about parts of the body and inquiries about actual exposure to:
   (1) provocative exhibition of genitals
   (2) sexualized kissing
   (3) sexual fondling
   (4) vaginal or anal stimulation or penetration
   (5) mock intercourse
   (6) oral copulation
   (7) child pornography: being shown or photographed
(B) Can describe or demonstrate being subjected to any of the above sexual experiences by an adult or child at least 3 years older than the reporting child, or of any age differential when force or coercion is described.

(C) One or more of the following:
  (1) During initial disclosures, tried to resist, minimize, deny, or to avoid recalling the sexually abusive experiences. This may be followed by intermittent denial and recantation.
  (2) History of repeated attempts to engage others in sexual behavior.
  (3) Age-excessive preoccupation with genital anatomy or related terms, or differentiated sexual behavior (A. 1-7 above), for example, excessive talking about or drawing of genitals and/or repeated sexualized play with dolls.
  (4) Overdetermined or anxious avoidance of genital anatomy or related terms.
  (5) Excessive masturbation that is significantly different from peers.
  (6) Nightmares triggered by person, place, or object or including physical movements or vocalizations that are consistent with sexually abusive experiences.
  (7) Dissociation.
  (8) Unexplained person, place, or object avoidance and/or fearfulness.
  (9) Medical findings indicative of sexual victimization.
(D) Onset before the age of 10.
(E) Not due to consensual peer sex play, misinterpreted physical contact, observed sexual acts, fabrication or indoctrination.

Outcome of the "Summit Conference"

The "Summit Conference" participants agreed upon the need for a new psychosocial diagnostic category that more accurately encompassed the typical emotional and behavioral problems of sexually abused children than those currently included in DSM-III. They were, however, in the brief time available, unable to decide under which of the various divisions of psychiatric disorders such a category should be placed or what it should be called. Although there was little objection to the validity of the Sexually Abused Child's Disorder, as presented in its third draft, only about one-third of the participants supported it as the most desirable approach. Another third favored a subcategory for sexually abused children under Post-Traumatic Stress Disorder while the remaining third proposed the inclusion of a new category under psychosexual disorders that would focus on premature erotization and would not presume the prior occurrence of sexual victimization.

The group accepted Dr. Cantwell's suggestion that it should request the American Psychiatric Association to include in the Appendix of

DSM-III-R a section designed to assist mental health practitioners in identifying child sexual abuse victims. In December of 1985, this recommendation was presented to the APA committee overseeing the revision of DSM-III. The chairman of the workgroup to revise DSM-III expressed his opinion that there was no such thing as a Sexually Abused Child's Disorder and the topic of child sexual abuse and psychiatric diagnosis was referred to committee for further study. DSM-III-R, published in the summer of 1987, contains "Appendix A" entitled, "Proposed Diagnostic Categories Needing Further Study." In this section are "Late Luteal Phase Dysphoric Disorder," "Sadistic Personality Disorder," and "Self-Defeating Personality Disorder." One hopes the clinical recognition and differential diagnosis of sexually abused children will be addressed in the development of DSM-IV.

Several other consensuses and disagreements among the experts who attended the "Summit Conference" are worth noting. There was unanimous agreement that the polygraph was unreliable in evaluating and investigating suspected cases of child sexual abuse. Many of the participants knew of cases with strong evidence and even subsequent confessions where the responsible adults were able to pass polygraphs supposedly demonstrating truthful denials. A recent review of the available data on the reliability of polygraphs entitled, "Predictive Power of the Polygraph: Can the 'Lie Detector' Really Detect Liars?" (Brett, Phillips, & Beary, 1986) discusses why this may be so. As reviewed in the December 1986 Harvard Medical School Mental Health Letter, the authors are cited as stating that in situations where the prevalence of lying is high, using 90% as an example, "the number of false negatives is also high; nearly 70 percent of subjects who register as truth tellers will be liars."

One area of disagreement at the "Summit" was whether children who are allegedly molested by a parent in the context of parental separation should be routinely interviewed with the accused parent. The group was sharply divided with those favoring such a practice, citing it as a usual and necessary part of a thorough and unbiased evaluation. Those opposing the routine use of this procedure questioned the validity of inferences drawn from such interviews. They cautioned that such a procedure might well precipitate false recantations, and mislead naive evaluators who erroneously believe that incestuously abused children will react predictably with fear or overt sexualized statements or behaviors in the presence of a parent who has molested them. The observation that incestuously molested children often display warm and affectionate relationships with their molesting parents is well-known to clinicians experienced in treating incestuous families. Those objecting to this procedure were also concerned that it could be quite stressful to the child who may have been threatened or told by the abusing parent not to disclose. They further cautioned that these interviews might be injurious to such victimized children, further decreasing their trust in adults and making them less likely to disclose again. Since abused children are often very reluctant to disclose threats or other coercion they have experienced (Finkelhor, 1979; Russell, 1983; Wyatt, 1985), it is likely that evaluators will seldom know in advance whether a particular allegedly molested child has been subjected to such manipulations or not. A recent study (Starr, 1987) found that neither professionals skilled in working with abusive families nor university students could discriminate between known abusive parent-child dyads and matched control parent-child dyads by watching videotapes of their free play interactions.

Perhaps the most significant consensus at the Summit Conference was that there was a pressing need for a new interdisciplinary professional society that would focus its attention and efforts on refining and supporting professional efforts to cope with child sexual abuse. Following that mandate and with the support of many leaders in the field of child abuse prevention and intervention, the California (CAPSAC) and the American (APSAC) Professional Societies on the Abuse of Children were founded during 1986. Among the goals of these new professional societies is the promotion of increased professional education on child abuse.

Finding the Consensus on Diagnosing Child Sexual Abuse

The possibility of intervening on behalf of sexually victimized children is limited by the degree to which health care, legal, and social-welfare systems acknowledge the problem. Several recent California appellate court rulings have limited the admission of certain types of evidence into legal proceedings that are frequently used in the assessment of suspected child sexual abuse. This evidence, including children's interactions with anatomically detailed dolls and the use of syndromes for diagnosing child sexual abuse, is now precluded in California unless it can be shown, in a separate hearing, that such a "new scientific proof

... has been generally accepted as reliable in the scientific community in which it was developed." This legal requirement, known in California as the "Kelly-Frye" rule (*People v. Kelly* [1976] 17 Cal. 3d 24; *Frye v. United States* [D.C. Cir 1923, 293 F. 1013]) raises a question. What is the scientific community from which procedures for assessment and validation of child sexual victimization derive? A review of the professional literature and development underlying our current understanding of child sexual abuse provides the answer. The appropriate scientific community to which new scientific methods of proof of child sexual abuse should be referenced is not any single existing professional discipline such as law enforcement, medicine, psychiatry, psychology, or social work. It is the interdisciplinary field that has grown to address all forms of child abuse and neglect and most specifically that segment of this larger group that has focused its most intense study and practice on the problem of child sexual victimization. The following section describes the development of this scientific community.

Development of the Interdisciplinary
Subspecialty Field on Child Sexual Abuse

During the ten years between the early 1970s and the early 1980s, several major groups converged in their concern and exploration of the child sexual abuse problem. A review of these developments and the literature of this period clearly demonstrates the interdisciplinary foundations of the professional subspecialty field addressing the sexual victimization of children.

Psychotherapists and legal professionals concerned with intrafamilial child sexual abuse and the community treatment of incestuous families constituted one of these major groups. The Child Sexual Abuse Treatment Program (CSATP), in Santa Clara County, California, one of the earliest and most influential of such programs, was developed by therapists Henry Giarretto and Anna Giarretto during the early 1970s. CSATP combined professional oversight and treatment with a self-help component that became known as Parents United.

Another important group extended the professional concern for rape victims and perpetrators to sexually abused children and their abusers. One of the earliest and most influential books on child sexual abuse, *Sexual Assault of Children and Adolescents* (Burgess, Groth, Holmstrom, & Sgroi, 1978), reflects this development. The professional disciplines of these pioneering authors included nursing, psychology, sociology, and medicine, respectively. Seattle's Harborview Sexual Assault Center, directed by social worker Dorris Stevens, in collaboration with pediatrician Shirley Anderson and social worker Lucy Berliner, was one of the earliest and most influential of hospital-based programs exemplifying a similar evolution.

A third major group consisted of those professionals who pioneered in the area of physical child abuse and neglect. Pediatrician C. Henry Kempe, along with radiologist Frederic N. Silverman, psychiatrist Brandt F. Steele, and pediatricians William Droegemueller and Henry K. Silver helped bring the plight of physically abused children into professional awareness by publishing "The Battered Child Syndrome" in the July 7, 1962, issue of the *Journal of the American Medical Association*. In 1976, Kempe collaborated with others in founding the "International Society for the Prevention of Child Abuse and Neglect." This international, interdisciplinary professional society with its journal, *Child Abuse and Neglect*, helped to focus public and professional attention on child sexual abuse. The International Society and its journal remain today the primary international forums for the general field of child abuse and neglect.

Although beyond the scope of this brief review, other groups and individuals made major contributions toward bringing the problem of childhood sexual victimization into professional and public awareness. Included among these are educators, filmmakers, newspeople, and writers, as well as many other professionals and nonprofessionals.

Within the United States, the First National Conference on the Sexual Victimization of Children was held in 1979. Over the next seven years, Joyce Thomas, a nurse with public health and pediatric nursing degrees and Carl Rogers, a research psychologist of the Children's National Medical Center, initiated this and three additional National Conferences at two-year intervals on the Sexual Victimization of Children. In 1979, Thomas and Rogers explored the possibility of developing a national specialty organization focused on child sexual abuse but received insufficient support. The fourth of their conferences, held in 1986, was attended by over 2,000 professionals from the United States and Canada. During her keynote address at this meeting, conference director Thomas asked the conference attendees if they felt there was now a need for a new multidisciplinary professional society that would work to refine the knowledge and practice of professionals who work on the problem of child sexual abuse. The consensus was clear as nearly all those in attendance were in support. The actual process of developing such a society had begun at the National Summit Conference on Diagnosing Child Sexual Abuse in late 1985. The "Summit Conference," which I initiated and chaired, concluded with a strong mandate from the nearly 100 professionals in attendance that such a society was needed.

Many significant developments occurred within the field of child sexual abuse identification, intervention, treatment, and prevention between 1979 and 1986, creating the need and desire for such a professional society within this country. As the problem of child sexual abuse and its complexities exploded into public and professional awareness, the difficulties and obstacles that prevented or discouraged earlier professional attention became more clear.

As legislatures and jurists attempted to make the courts more accessible to children, the courts increasingly turned to medical and mental health professionals for assistance in coping with the various medical and mental health questions surrounding sexually abused children, their families, and perpetrators. Accompanying this trend, there have been various challenges and critiques of the techniques used in evaluating allegedly molested children.

To assist medical practitioners in the identification and treatment of child abuse, the American Medical Association published its "Diagnostic and Treatment Guidelines Concerning Child Abuse and Neglect" in the *Journal of the American Medical Association* (1985). Earlier that year, the California Medical Association, as part of its ongoing effort to improve professional recognition and approaches to child abuse, sponsored an invitational forum that promoted the concept of interdisciplinary brainstorming and problem solving within California. The vitality and promise of that process inspired the form and procedural template for the National Summit Conference on Diagnosing Child Sexual Abuse.

Improved Lists of Emotional and Behavioral Indicators for Identifying Sexually Abused Children and Adolescents

Continuing work started at the "Summit Conference." A group of experienced professionals from the western United States met in early

1986 to develop a consensually agreed upon list of emotional and behavioral indicators of child sexual victimization that acknowledged that such findings change from one developmental period to another and that they vary in their degree of specificity for discriminating sexual abuse as opposed to other forms of childhood stress and trauma. Summaries 1 through 3 are the products of that effort. They have also been incorporated into the diagnostic criteria for the "Sexually Abused Child's Disorder, draft four." As with the disorder, they are presented here to stimulate further critique and study.

Possible Emotional and Behavioral Indicators of Child Sexual Abuse (CSA)

Summary 1

Preschooler (0-4 Years)

(A) Most Specific to CSA
    (1) Nightmares triggered by place, person, objects related or including physical movements or vocalizations that are consistent with sexually abusive experiences
    (2) Premature Eroticization
        (a) preoccupation with genitals
        (b) repetitive seeking to engage others in differentiated sexual behavior
        (c) excessive and indiscriminate masturbation or masturbation with objects
        (d) precocious, apparently seductive behavior
        (e) depiction of differentiated sexual acts in doll play
    (3) Fearfulness
        (a) overdetermined denial of genital anatomy and exposure to normal nudity
        (b) avoidance and anxiety in response to specific questions about differentiated sexual behavior
        (c) unexplained person, gender, place, or object avoidance or fearfulness
    (4) Child's Age-Appropriate and Circumstantially Congruent Description of Being Sexually Abused
    (5) Dissociative Phenomenon

(B) Less Specific than Category A but More Specific than Category C
  (1) Somatic Complaints
  (2) Sleep Disorders
  (3) Aggressive Behavior Versus Overly Inhibited Aggression
  (4) Impaired Trust
  (5) Enuresis and Encopresis
  (6) Increased Physical Concerns
(C) May Be Related to CSA but Least Specific
  (1) Heightened Anxiety
  (2) Unexplained Guilt
  (3) Socially Withdrawn—inhibited play (apathy)
  (4) Emotional/Behavior Regression
  (5) Hyperactivity
  (6) Lying
  (7) Increased Separation Anxiety

Summary 2

School Aged Children (6-11 Years)

(A) Most Specific to CSA
  (1) Nightmares (see Summary 1-A1 for explanation)
  (2) Premature Eroticization (see Summary 1-A2 for explanation)
  (3) Fearfulness (see Summary 1-A3 for explanation)
  (4) School Aged Children's Age-Appropriate and Circumstantially Congruent Description of Being Sexually Abused
  (5) Sexual Aggression and Coercion Toward Other Children
  (6) Dissociative Phenomenon
  (7) Cross Dressing
  (8) Prostitution
(B) Less Specific than Category A but More Specific than Category C
  (1) Somatic Complaints
  (2) Sleep Disorders
  (3) Aggressive Behavior
  (4) Impaired Trust
  (5) Enuresis and Encopresis
  (6) Unexplained Change in School Behavior (social, peer, academic)
  (7) School Phobias
  (8) Hostility and Cruelty
  (9) Overly Compliant Behavior
  (10) Destructive Behavior
  (11) Running Away

    (12) Substance Abuse

    (13) Age-Inappropriate Fears Related to Threats

(C) May Be Related to CSA but Least Specific

    (1) Heightened Anxiety

    (2) Unexplained Guilt

    (3) Social Withdrawal

    (4) Emotional/Behavioral Regression

    (5) Hyperactivity

    (6) Lying

    (7) Chronic Unexplained School Difficulties

    (8) Unexplained Unhappiness or Misery

    (9) Pseudo-Maturity

    (10) Delinquency

Adolescents (12-18 Years)

(A) Most Specific to CSA

    (1) Nightmares (see Summary 1-A1 for explanation)

    (2) Premature Eroticization (see Summary 1-A2 for explanation)

    (3) Fearfulness (see Summary 1-A3 for explanation)

    (4) Adolescent's Age-Appropriate and Circumstantially Congruent Description of Being Sexually Abused

    (5) Sexual Aggression and Coercion Toward Other Children

    (6) Dissociative Phenomenon

    (7) Cross Dressing

    (8) Prostitution

    (9) Extreme Sexual Inhibition

(B) Less Specific than Category A but More Specific than Category C

    (1) Somatic Complaints

    (2) Sleep Disorder

    (3) Aggressive Disorder

    (4) Impaired Trust

    (5) Enuresis and Encopresis

    (6) Unexplained Change in School Behavior (social, peer, academic)

    (7) School Phobias

    (8) Hostility and Cruelty

    (9) Overly Compliant Behavior

    (10) Destructive Behavior

    (11) Running Away

    (12) Substance Abuse

    (13) Self-Mutilation

    (14) Refusal to Disclose Paternity

(C) May Be Related to CSA but Least Specific
  (1) Heightened Anxiety
  (2) Unexplained Guilt
  (3) Social Withdrawal
  (4) Emotional/Behavior Regression
  (5) Hyperactivity
  (6) Lying
  (7) Chronic, Unexplained School Difficulties
  (8) Unexplained Unhappiness or Misery
  (9) Pseudo-Maturity
  (10) Delinquency
  (11) Eating Disorders
  (12) Major Psychiatric and Identity Disorders

Conclusions and Future Directions

The problem of child sexual abuse is being addressed today by increasing numbers of professionals from many different disciplines. Significant amounts of work and study are being focused on this form of child maltreatment and there is ongoing refinement of procedures and criteria for the early diagnosis of sexually abused children.

The Sexually Abused Child's Disorder and the consensus lists of emotional and behavioral indicators presented in this chapter may be useful to clinicians, researchers, and legal decision makers. Without legal affirmation, sexually victimized children often receive little protection or assistance and those who sexually victimize children continue unopposed.

The professional interdisciplinary field focused on child sexual abuse is growing more knowledgeable and skillful. However, there is the need for additional epidemeological studies to establish a diagnostic category for sexually abused children.

As with most significant social advances, there is an influential countervailing force. This backlash, while making it more difficult to intervene in many cases of child sexual abuse, is constructive in discouraging the prosecution of questionable cases thus diminishing the risk to innocent persons.

With the continued commitment from society as a whole, additional research and professional education for all those who confront this problem, our ability to identify accurately and successfully intervene on behalf of sexually victimized children will continue to improve and the lasting effects of child sexual abuse will be diminished.

REFERENCES

American Medical Association. (1985). AMA diagnostic and treatment guidelines concerning child abuse and neglect. *Journal of the American Medical Association, 6,* 796-800.

Brett, A. S., Phillips, M., & Beary, J. F. (1986). Predictive power of the polygraph: Can the "lie detector" really detect liars? *Lancet,* pp. 544-547.

Burgess, A. W., Groth, A. N., Holmstrom, L. L., & Sgroi, S. M. (1978). *Sexual assault of children and adolescents.* Lexington, MA: Lexington Books.

Cantwell, H. (1981). Sexual abuse of children in Denver, 1979: Reviewed with implications for pediatric intervention and possible prevention. *Child Abuse and Neglect, 5,* 75-85.

Conte, J., Berliner, L., & Schuerman, J. (1986). *The impact of sexual abuse on children.* Executive summary, available from first author at 969 East 60th St., Chicago, IL 60637.

Corwin, D., Berliner, L., Goodman, G., & White, S. (1987). Child sexual abuse and custody disputes. *Journal of Interpersonal Violence, 2*(1), 91-105.

Finkelhor, D. (1979). *Sexually victimized children.* New York: Free Press.

Goodman, G. S., Aman, C., & Hirschman, J. (1987). Child sexual and physical abuse: Children's testimony. In S. J. Ceci, M. P. Toglia, & D. F. Ross (Eds.), *Children's eyewitness memory.* New York: Springer-Verlag.

Goodwin, J. (1982). *Sexual abuse: Incest victims and their families.* Boston: Wright/PSG.

Jones, D.P.H., & McGraw, J. M. (1987). Reliable and fictitious accounts of sexual abuse to children. *Journal of Interpersonal Violence, 2(1),* 27-45.

Peters, J. (1976). Children who are victims of sexual assault and the psychology of offenders. *American Journal of Psychotherapy, 30,* 398-421.

Russell, D.E.H. (1983). The incidence and prevalence of intrafamilial and extrafamilial sexual abuse of female children. *Child Abuse and Neglect, 7,* 133-146.

Russell, D.E.H. (1984). *Sexual exploitation: Rape, child sexual abuse, and workplace harassment.* Beverly Hills, CA: Sage.

Sansonnet-Hayden, H., Haley, G., Marriage, K., & Fine, S. (1987). Sexual abuse and psychopathology in hospitalized adolescents. *Journal of the American Academy of Child and Adolescent Psychiatry, 26*(5), 753-757.

Saywitz, K. (in press). The child witness: Experimental and clinical considerations. In A. M. La Grecca (Ed.), *Childhood assessment: Through the eyes of the child.* New York: Allyn & Bacon.

Starr, R. H. (1987). Clinical judgment of abuse-proneness based on parent-child interactions. *Child Abuse and Neglect, 11,* 87-92.

Summit, R. C. (1983). The child sexual abuse accommodation syndrome. *Child Abuse and Neglect, 7,* 177-193.

Summit, R. C. (1986, February 5). No one invented McMartin "secret": Techniques were right ones to get at facts, help victims. *Los Angeles Times.*

Wyatt, G. (1985). The sexual abuse of afro-american and white-american women in childhood. *Child Abuse and Neglect, 9,* 507-519.

15

Child Sexual Abuse Research

The Implications
for Clinical Practice

GLORIA JOHNSON POWELL

Recent research on child sexual abuse, particularly the long-term effects, offender treatment, prevention, and legal decisions has demonstrated that child victimization is a multifaceted social psychological problem that is endemic to our society. Thus the way in which society responds to this issue has many ramifications in terms of further research, clinical practice, prevention, and social policy.

New directions are being explored in the field: the study of adolescent perpetrators, with a particular interest in former victims; the problems of family unification, important because of the difficult issue of where and when to place children out of the home; and the effects of the court and the legal process on child victims (Runyan et al., 1986).

In this chapter, some of the ramifications of the findings about child sexual abuse that have emerged as a result of the empirical research that has been conducted will be discussed. However, in doing so it is recognized that clinical practice extends to prevention and both are influenced by social policy and vice versa. Thus this chapter will also discuss some areas of prevention and social policy that are affected by current research.

271

The Implications
for Clinical Practice

During the 1970s, many adults molested as children emerged as rapidly as child victims. The result was an upsurge in the research of adult victims, which added to the credibility of child victims. However, the research on child victims lagged behind for many reasons, the greatest of which is the fact that the subjects are children and not miniature adults. Any research on children needs to be designed within a developmental context. The interplay between the temperament of the child and the stress and coping styles are also important (Garmezy & Rutter, 1983; Thomas & Chess, 1977; Werner & Smith, 1982). Finally, most children live in families and families are complex social institutions. Research on child victims becomes even more complex because children are involved in a wide variety of sexual activities—for example, child pornography, sex rings, intrafamilial and extrafamilial abuse, and by many different kinds of perpetrators.

A review of the research offers an extensive list of problems that child sexual abuse victims present. However, clinicians are looking for those symptoms that are unique to sexual abuse and not a potpourri of complaints that are similar to symptoms of other children with different problems. Indeed, the differential impact of sexual abuse on children has been noticed by many researchers (Conte, 1985; Seidner & Calhoun, 1984) and various theories have been supported. Friedrich (this volume) has found that sexually inappropriate behavior, aggression, and sexual aggression can most frequently be identified in sexually abused children, but not all sexually abused children present those symptoms. Hence the search goes on for a standardized scale that is suitable to sexually abused children—that captures "the experience."

Clinicians wonder why some victims are more affected than others. Are there sleeper effects that appear later? Should all sexual abuse victims be treated whether they have symptoms or not?

An understanding of the coping and stress paradigm is helpful in understanding differential effects. Temperament or innate differences in children cannot be ignored in attempting to understand the complexity of the behavioral repertoire children present. Most important, boys often differ from girls in their reactions to sexual victimization and other stressful events (Friedrich, this volume; Powell, 1987a). Finally, children are in the developmental process, which may determine their differential response to child sexual abuse. They may have either initial effects and then no symptoms for an extended period of time, experience both short-term and long-term effects, or report neither.

The confusion among the practitioners about the effects of child sexual abuse and its long-term consequences has a great deal to do with the assessment process. Friedrich (this volume) and Powell (in press) have found the Child Behavior Checklist (CBCL) very helpful in establishing behavioral manifestations on a standardized scale for boys and girls of different ages (Achenback & Edelbrock, 1983). There are two CBCL forms that are generally used, parent and teacher, but there is also a Youth Self-Report. I have found that an item analysis of the CBCL along with other standardized measures and data from a semi-structured interview is useful in obtaining a more comprehensive view of the victimization experience and what that experience means to the child. Measures of self-concept, depression, and social competency are all useful in eliciting various consequences of the abuse experience. More recently, the Child Assessment Schedule (Hodges, Kline, Stern, Catyrn, & McKew, 1982) is being used in a national study of child victims and will provide some data regarding behavioral patterns that are most frequently seen among sexually abused children (Runyan et al., 1986).

In spite of the most sophisticated measures of child psychopathology, there are a number of sleeper effects that will not be evident until years later. An example of such a pattern is illustrated in the case of Mrs. K.

Mrs. K., age 36, was hospitalized in 1965 because of three serious attempts at suicide—that is, an overdose of medication, the ingestion of lye, and knife stabs to her liver and spleen.

After the birth of her third child, her husband noted that she became moody and irritable. She finally confided that she wanted to see her younger sister, the third child in her family whom she had not seen for twenty years.

Her husband, a wealthy businessman, hired detectives, and after a lengthy search her sister was found in San Francisco, a drug addict and a prostitute. A lengthy rescue process ensued, during which time Mrs. K.'s sister came to live with her, entered a drug treatment program, and was given a job in Mr. K.'s business. Eventually, however, Mrs. K.'s sister ran off with a drug dealer and returned to prostitution. Six months later, she was found dead from an overdose of drugs.

Mrs. K. buried her sister and seemed to adjust to her sister's death rather well. However, two months later, on the birthday of her third child, she made her first suicide attempt. The second attempt occurred on her sister's birthday, and the third on the anniversary of her mother's death.

During the lengthy psychiatric hospitalization that ensued, she was on suicidal observation for four months because of her obsession with killing herself. E.C.T. and antidepressants did not break the morbid ideation about punitive self-destruction. As the anniversary of her sister's death approached, she finally disclosed for the first time in her life the sexual molestation by her father since the age of 4. At age 13, she decided to tell her mother and arranged to be alone with her. Her mother then told her that she was dying of cancer and wanted Mrs. K. to promise to help her father raise the younger children—three brothers and a sister. After her mother's death, she stayed at home until she was 15 and could no longer tolerate the daily molestation by her father. When she found her sister, Mrs. K. discovered that after she ran away her father began to molest the sister.

In reviewing this case, it seems obvious now that if the symptoms most frequently associated with a history of sexual abuse were known, maybe the disclosure would have come sooner. However, since adult victims often go undetected for long periods of time, the assessment process for adults needs to be reconsidered. In Mrs. K.'s case, treatment after the disclosure did deal with the molestation—the guilt, the shame, the depression, the betrayal, and the many losses, but only after five months of an expensive hospitalization.

However, even in today's times many clinicians do not know how to obtain a sex history and a history of sexual assault. Such information may be crucial to the treatment process. If there is a history of abuse, the clinician needs to know: (1) the initial effects; (2) the aftermath of the disclosure and its impact; (3) an assessment of the client's symptoms as sequalae of the abuse or other stressful events; and (4) the history of sexually transmitted diseases. With this information, the clinician can develop a treatment plan with short-term and long-term goals.

The effects of child sexual abuse on sexuality has been further illuminated by more recent research that indicates an earlier onset of sexual partners, and briefer sexual relationships in adolescence (Wyatt, 1987). In addition, results from a community sample of adult women found that women who are sexually abused before age 18 had significantly more unplanned pregnancies and abortions than their nonabused peers (Wyatt, 1986). Such findings are extremely important during this period of history marked by the advent of AIDS because sexually abused children may be at higher risk for AIDS.

Indeed, the issue of sexuality during childhood (excluding abusive situations) is an area that needs more attention in research. What was considered the standard norm of information and discussion of sexuality among children twenty years ago may not be the same in today's world. Latency age children date and go to parties, the media bombards the young child with sexualized ads and even daytime soap operas have bedroom scenes. Video cassettes present a variety of subjects, some appropriate and some inappropriate for children. An example of the precocious latency age child raised in a peer-centered society is brought to mind by this particular case.

> A 6-year-old girl, the daughter of a judge, left a note in her lunch pail which said: "Dear David—I'm glad you like me as much as you like Susie. I hope you'll do it to me the way you do it to Susie soon." When asked what she meant by the note, she replied that she wanted to have sex with him. None of the three children had been sexually abused.

The "copy cat" behavior of latency age children in terms of early dating and talking about sexuality expanded into a sex ring in one elementary school, where ten children were found to have gonorrhea. When an 11-year-old's sex ring, consisting primarily of adolescents and an older male, disbanded, he began a sex ring at his elementary school. Some of the sexual activity occurring at school was noticed by school officials, and was finally investigated. While the extent of such activity is not widespread, the fact that it does exist suggests that childhood sexuality is changing.

A good sexual history should be included for every child, not only because of changing norms regarding sexuality among children but also because a youngster may not volunteer a history of sexual victimization unless asked. I have seen many children who only disclose sexual molestation retrospectively. They described the ways in which they tried to make a disclosure earlier during therapy, but were afraid or ashamed to do so because of fears of retribution by the perpetrator or a lack of trust in the therapist to protect them from abusing parents (Powell, in press).

As the evaluation of child sexual abuse becomes more complex, whenever possible a team approach seems the most feasible and efficacious way to proceed. Such a team should include a mental health professional, a pediatrician, a nurse, a Department of Children's Services (DCS) worker, a developmental psychologist, and a legal adviser. The complex array of decisions that have to be made can be best achieved in such a consultative process.

Finally, the question remains as to whether or not children should receive treatment if they are not showing any effects. The better part of wisdom would seem to indicate that treatment should be given. However, the length and kind of treatment for the victim and family can only be determined after an empirical assessment.

Directions for Future Research

It should be noted that most research primarily includes girls and never mentions ethnic or cultural differences on the effects of child sexual abuse. Although the ratio of females who are at risk for child sexual abuse is reportedly 2.5 for every male, male sexual abuse tends to be underreported. Indeed, the ratio between the sexes may be smaller than the data suggest. Some research suggests that more boy than girl victims exhibit acting out behaviors (Friedrich, this volume). Becker (this volume) has reported on the effects of child sexual abuse on adolescent sex offenders, all of whom were males. Friedrich (this volume) has noted the continued sexual aggression in boy victims of sexual abuse, and Finkelhor (1981) has noted the increased incidence of homosexuality among male victims. Future research needs to consider male and female victims as well as victims from various socioeconomic backgrounds and ethnic/cultural groups.

Although there is no consistent difference in the prevalence of sexual abuse among ethnic groups, there is some indication that the impact may be more severe or negative for some ethnic groups (Russell et al., this volume; Stein et al., this volume). Many more minority group children may be in the DCS system because the poor and minorities have no other recourse. Lindholm and Willey (1983) found that in Los Angeles County, child abuse cases overall were underreported with respect to their representation in the population, but Afro-Americans were overrepresented in that group. With regard to sexual abuse in particular, Afro-American children (16.6%) were less likely to have been sexually abused than were Anglo (26.8%) or Hispanic (28.2%) children. There was a significant difference between ethnicity and type of sexual abuse: (1) fondling occurred half as often among Afro-Americans than it did among Hispanics and Anglos; (2) there were fewer ethnic differences with respect to boys; (3) fewer Anglo females had to participate in sexual intercourse than Hispanic or Afro-Americans; and (4) oral copulation occurred more frequently with Anglo children than it did with Afro-American and Hispanic children.

In terms of the impact of sexual abuse on minority group children, if the four traumagenic dynamics of child sexual abuse described by Browne and Finkelhor (1986) are considered, it becomes apparent that the traumagenic effects of racism are very similar. Afro-Americans, for instance, have been victims of traumatic sexualization since their arrival in this country during slavery. Stigmatization has affected all minority groups who could "not pass" as Whites. The betrayal of human and civil rights has been experienced by most minority group people, and there has been a longstanding battle to combat the powerlessness that many minority group people feel (Wyatt, 1987).

It has been my experience that the disclosure of sexual abuse in a minority group family is often the "straw that breaks the camel's back." They are more fearful and distrustful of the social service and legal systems, with good reason.

Wyatt and Mickey (this volume) describe some methods that victims use to overcome the trauma of sexual assault and demonstrate how parental support mediates the lasting effects of child sexual abuse. Indeed, more studies regarding the disclosure and its aftermath would be helpful in the prevention of the long-term effects of sexual abuse.

The Implications for Prevention

As service providers find themselves overworked with cases and with few resources, the ultimate questions will continue to be—what effective preventive measures can be mounted? Within the past five years prevention programs have proliferated and public awareness has increased. However, prevention must be targeted at the major etiologic factors in order to be most effective.

Understanding the causes of perpetration and providing effective treatment, at an earlier age or after the first offense, becomes crucial to the elimination and curtailment of sexual victimization. More recently, there has been increased interest in research on adolescent perpetration (Becker, this volume). In a follow-up study of 143 sexually abused children (Powell, in press) more than 10% became adolescent perpetrators. Although a linear relationship between abuse and perpetration cannot always be established, there may be some aspects of the sexual socialization process of the abuse that leads to a sexual identity process that incorporates the self-precept of a victim to that of a perpetrator.

There are, however, some troublesome aspects. First of all, most of the perpetrators studied are incarcerated or within the criminal justice system, with a preponderance of lower socioeconomic and/or minority group subjects. Second, studies of treatment outcome are not methodologically stringent enough to know what really works and why. Third, there are no definitive guidelines to determine when reunification should occur. Most decisions are made primarily on the basis of expediency. Last but not least is the problem that there is a growing tendency within the legal system to think that to believe the child is to discount the rights of the perpetrator and child advocates are viewed as misguided professionals who must have been sexually abused as children and are trying to work through their own victimization (Greene, 1987).

Thus many judges in the name of human rights assume the stance that the allegations are false until proven true and the burden of proof rests with the child whose human rights are considered secondary to those of the adult. This "child backlash" also denies the offender the right to rehabilitation. More often, they are released without any treatment or follow-up. The research on children as witnesses (Goodman, 1984) may help diffuse such a dichotomy in the legal perspective and decrease the trauma of the aftermath of disclosure.

Implications for Social Policy

Seldom is social policy planned. Usually it evolves over an extensive period of time, fraught with trial and error. Sometimes society backs into it—a series of decisions are made in rapid succession with which most people agree and these decisions become the accepted *modus operandi*. The field of child sexual abuse forced society to make some decisions that were implemented for better or worse. One of the most controversial issues is when or if a child should be removed from the home once sexual abuse is reported. One would hope that each decision is made based on four factors: (1) the individual situation; (2) the status and development of the child; (3) the preservation of sibling relationships; and (4) the removal of the perpetrator in cases of intrafamilial abuse. However, it is difficult to prioritize complex issues when one has a very heavy caseload and limited resources.

As clinicians became more aware of the special needs of child victims, the demand for services has increased. A health care delivery system for sexually abused children has been put in place in many states. However, as the number of cases increases, as public revenues remain static, as the needs of the homeless, the mentally ill, and the elderly demand their share of the tax revenue, services to children may dwindle and particularly for those who have been abused. This country does not have a history of a strong commitment to children's rights. Children don't vote. This was a major theme in the Report of the Joint Committee on Mental Health of Children (1970) reiterated in the President's Commission on Mental Illness (1970), and in the 1987 NIMH report.

Consequently, social policy should set research priorities to pursue those areas of child sexual victimization that we understand the least so that a health care delivery system can be created that is specific to the needs of the sexually abused child and one that is cost effective. Preference should be given for prospective studies on the differential impact and long-term consequences on children as well as prospective studies on adolescent perpetrators.

Another critical area of social policy development is professional training. Most states have a law that requires mental health professionals, with the exception of psychiatrists, to take an eight hour relicensure course in child abuse. This requirement should be expanded to include psychiatrists. In addition, child abuse should be part of (1) every pediatric/child psychiatry rotation in medical school; and (2) an integral part of pediatric, psychiatry, emergency medicine, and family practice residencies. Health practitioners should be well versed in human sexuality, and know how to take a sex history that includes sexually transmitted diseases and sexual assault.

Ultimately, social policy will need to address issues of standards of practice, quality assurance, treatment planning, and the requirements for a subspecialization in child abuse.

Conclusion

Within the past decade, major strides have been made in the identification, treatment, prevention research, and social policy in this difficult field of child sexual abuse. There have been many pioneers and they are to be commended. There needs to be continued efforts in the field that in many ways have forged new trails in legal procedures, treatment, and research. However, there are still critical life threatening problems to be resolved. It is interesting to note that the first case of AIDS and the required systematic reporting of child sexual abuse arrived about the same time. It seems like a coincidence of history that the controversy and rediscovery of child sexual abuse should surface with the discovery of this fatal disease. For those who would like to deny the existence of child sexual abuse and place it in the closet again, AIDS is a reminder that we must protect our children by understanding childhood sexuality, child sexual victimization, and current sexual practices. It is hoped that the child abuse/AIDS connection (Powell, 1987b) will remain contained, but there can be no assurance unless there is a continual effort to understand the causes of sexual victimization and concentrated, coordinated efforts to curtail it.

REFERENCES

Achenback, T. M., & Edelbrock, C. S. (1983). *Manual for the Child Behavior Checklist.* Burlington: University of Vermont.

Browne, A., & Finkelhor, D. (1986). Impact of child sexual abuse: A review of the research. *Psychological Bulletin, 99,* 16-77.

Conte, J. R. (1985). The effects of sexual abuse on children: A critique and suggestion for future research. *Victimology: An International Journal, 10*(1-4), 110-130.

Finkelhor, D. (1981). The sexual abuse of boys. *Victimology: An International Journal, 6*(1), 76-84.

Finkelhor, D., & Browne, A. (1985). The traumatic impact of child sexual abuse: A conceptualization. *American Journal of Orthopsychiatry, 55,* 530-541.

Garmezy, N., & Rutter, M. (Eds.). (1983). *Stress, coping, and development in children.* New York: McGraw-Hill.

Goodman, G. S. (1984). The child witness: Conclusions and future directions for research and legal practice. *Journal of Social Issues, 40*(2), 157-176.

Goodwin, J. (1985). Post-traumatic symptoms in incest. In R. Pynoos & S. Eth (Eds.), *Post-traumatic stress disorder in children* (pp. 157-186). Washington, DC: American Psychiatric Press.

Greene, A. (1987, October 21-25). *Grey areas and spectrum of child sexual abuse.* Paper presented at the 34th Annual Meeting of the American Academy of Child and Adolescent Psychiatry, Washington, DC.

Joint Commission of the Mental Health of Children. (1970). *Crises in child mental health: Challenge for the 1970's.* New York: Harper & Row.

Lindholm, J. J., & Willey, P. (1983). Child abuse and ethnicity: Patterns of similarities and differences. *Spanish Speaking Mental Health Research Center Occasional Paper, 18.*

Powell, G. J. (1987a, October). *The victim/perpetrator metamorphosis process: Phase I of a follow-up study.* Paper presented at the annual meeting of Child and Adolescent Psychiatry, Washington, DC.

Powell, G. J. (1987b, December 5). *Child abuse and AIDS: Is there a connection?* Paper presented at the First Annual Meeting of California Professional Society on the Abuse of Children, Costa Mesa, CA.

Powell, G. J. (in press). *The last closet: The lives of sexually abused children.* New York: W. W. Norton.

President's Commission on the Mental Health of Children. (1970). *Crisis in child mental health: Challenge for the 1970's.* New York: Harper & Row.

Runyan, D., Coulter, M. L., Edelsohn, G. A., Estroff, S. E., Everson, M. D., Harris, E., Hunter, W. A., King, N.M.P., & Porter, C. S. (1986). *The impact of legal intervention on sexually abused children.* Final Report NCAN #90 CA 921.

Seidner, A. L., & Calhoun, L. S. (1984, August). *Childhood sexual abuse: Factors related to differential adult adjustment.* Paper presented at Second Annual National Family Violence Research Conference.

Saxe, L. (1987). *Children's mental health needs: Problems and services.* Washington, DC: Government Printing Office.

Thomas, A., & Chess, S. (1977). *Temperament and development.* New York: Brunner/Mazel.

Werner, E. E., & Smith, R. S. (1982). *Vulnerable but invincible: A longitudinal study of resilient children and youth.* New York: McGraw-Hill.

Wyatt, G. E. (1986). The relationship between the cumulative impact of a range of child sexual abuse experiences and women's psychological well-being. *Victimology: An International Journal.*

Wyatt, G. E. (1987, August 27-31). *Consideration in the treatment of Afro-American victims of sexual abuse.* Paper presented at the annual meeting of the American Psychological Association, New York.

About the Authors

JUDITH V. BECKER, Ph.D., is an Associate of Clinical Psychology in Psychiatry at the College of Physicians and Surgeons, Columbia University. She is also Director of the Sexual Behavior Clinic at the New York State Psychiatric Institute. She has published more than 50 publications. Dr. Becker has been the recipient of grants from the National Institute of Mental Health.

LUCY BERLINER, MSW, is a Clinician and Researcher and Advocate on the staff of the Sexual Assault Center at Harborview Medical Center since 1973. She is a Clinical Faculty Member of the University of Washington School of Social Work and frequent lecturer. She is actively involved in developing public policy to promote the interests of sexual assault victims.

JOHN BRIERE, Ph.D., is Assistant Professor of Psychiatry at the University of Southern California School of Medicine, and Clinical Psychologist II in the Psychiatric Emergency Services Department of LAC-USC Medical Center. Previous appointments have included a Postdoctoral Fellowship in Crisis Resolution at UCLA School of Medicine (Harbor-UCLA Medical Center), and a five-year term as Clinical Director of crisis and psychotherapy programs at a Canadian community health center. His major research areas are the long-term effects of child abuse, the social psychology of sexual violence, and the use of multivariate analytic procedures in applied research. Author of the upcoming book *Therapy for the Sexual Abuse Survivor*, Dr. Briere is also an Associate Editor of the *Journal of Interpersonal Violence*.

M. AUDREY BURNAM, Ph.D., is a Social Psychologist. She is currently an Associate Researcher with the RAND Corporation in Santa Monica, where she has published many articles on the mental health status of special populations and on methodologic issues in mental health measurement. She has recently authored several papers describing the prevalence of sexual assault and its relationship to mental disorder in a household population.

JON R. CONTE, Ph.D., is currently an Associate Professor at the School of Social Service Administration at the University of Chicago and Founding Editor of the *Journal of Interpersonal Violence*. Dr. Conte is a frequent lecturer at national and international meetings. He has appeared on local and national television programs. His current research interests include the impact of sexual abuse of children, the etiology of sexual violence, and the effects of programs to prevent the sexual victimization of young children. He currently serves on over ten local and national committees and boards.

DAVID L. CORWIN, M.D., is a child, adolescent, and adult Psychiatrist. While completing his fellowship in child psychiatry at UCLA, Dr. Corwin served as Codirector of UCLA's Family Support Program and founded the Los Angeles Task Force on Interviewing Sexually Abused Children. In 1985, he conceived and chaired the National Summit Conference on Diagnosing Child Sexual Abuse. He has lectured nationally and internationally and coauthored the article "Allegations of Child Sexual Abuse in Custody Disputes—No Easy Answers." Dr. Corwin is a founder of both the California Professional Society on the Abuse of Children (CAPSAC) and the American Professional Society on the Abuse of Children (APSAC). One of Dr. Corwin's major interests is the refinement of evaluation procedures and decision making in assessing alleged sexual abuse of young children.

DAVID FINKELHOR, Ph.D., is the Associate Director of the Family Research Laboratory and the Family Violence Research Program at the University of New Hampshire. He has been studying the problem of child sexual abuse since 1977, and has published three books, *Sexually Victimized Children* (Free Press), *Child Sexual Abuse: New Theory and Research* (Free Press), and *Sourcebook on Child Sexual Abuse* (Sage), and over two dozen articles on the subject. He has been the recipient of grants from the National Institute of Mental Health, and the National Center on Child Abuse and Neglect. His other research interests include elder abuse and sexual assault in marriage.

WILLIAM N. FRIEDRICH, Ph.D., is on the faculty of the Mayo Medical School and a Consultant in the Department of Psychiatry and Psychology. He was on the faculty in the Department of Psychology at the University of Washington from 1980 through 1985. His clinical and research interests are in childhood coping with trauma, family inter-action, and family therapy.

JACQUELINE M. GOLDING, Ph.D., is an Assistant Research Psychologist at the UCLA School of Public Health. Her research interests involve the epidemiology of psychiatric disorder, the relation-ship of stress to psychological states, health and illness behavior, and women's issues. She is a coauthor of several journal articles on the epidemiology and correlates of sexual assault.

JEAN M. GOODWIN, M.D., M.P.H., is Professor of Psychiatry and Mental Health Sciences at the Medical College of Wisconsin and directs the Joint Educational Program at Milwaukee County Mental Health Complex. She graduated from Radcliffe College with a major in Anthropology, received her M.D. from Harvard Medical School, and has published over 25 articles and book chapters on child abuse as well as a book, *Sexual Abuse: Incest Victims and Their Families*.

M. RAY MICKEY, Ph.D., is a Research Statistician in the UCLA Department of Biomathematics. His collaborative contributions are reflected in coauthorship, over a period of many years, of numerous publications in medical laboratory and clinical research. He participated as Statistical Advisor on Dr. Gail Wyatt's recent NIMH funded study of sexual experiences of Afro-American and White American women.

STEFANIE DOYLE PETERS, Ph.D., is currently a Clinical Psychol-ogist with the Barrington Psychiatric Center and serves as Research Consultant to the Rape Treatment Center at Santa Monica Hospital. Formerly, a Research Associate in the Department of Psychiatry and Biobehavioral Sciences at UCLA, where she received her degree in Psychology in 1984. Her research has focused on assessing the long-term effects of child sexual abuse on the psychological functioning of adult women. She is the coauthor of several papers examining methodological issues in the study of sexual abuse.

GLORIA JOHNSON POWELL, M.D., coeditor of this volume, is an Associate Professor in the Division of Mental Retardation/Child Psychiatry, Department of Psychiatry at the Neuropsychiatric Institute and Hospital at UCLA. For the past eight years Dr. Powell has been Director of the Family Support Program, an evaluation and treatment program for sexually abused children and their families. Dr. Powell is involved in ongoing research as well as the legal and social policy issues involved in child sexual abuse. She is senior editor of *Psychosocial*

Development of Minority Group Children and author of *Black Monday's Children: The Effects of School Desegregation*, and *The Last Closet: The Lives of Sexually Abused Children* (in press).

MARSHA RUNTZ, M.A., is a doctoral student in Clinical Psychology at the University of Manitoba, Canada. She has worked for the past seven years with survivors of sexual abuse at Klinic Community Health Centre in Winnipeg, Canada, and has coauthored a number of publications on the long-term impact of child sexual victimization. Her most recent works include an examination of the effects of physical and emotional abuse in childhood and a study of the process of revictimization among adult women who were sexually abused as children.

DIANA E. H. RUSSELL, Ph.D., is a Professor of Sociology at Mills College where she has taught since 1969. She is author of *The Politics of Rape* (Stein and Day, 1975), author and coeditor of *Crimes Against Women: The Proceedings of the International Tribunal* (First published by Les Femmes, 1976, republished by Frog in the Wall, 1984), author of *Rape in Marriage* (Macmillan, 1982), *Sexual Exploitation: Rape, Child Sexual Abuse and Workplace Harassment* (Sage Publications, 1984), and *The Secret Trauma: Incest in the Lives of Girls and Women* (Basic Books, 1986). She is the recipient of the 1986 C. Wright Award for *The Secret Trauma* awarded by the American Sociological Association's Society of the Psychological Study of Social Problems for Outstanding Social Science Research.

JOHN R. SCHUERMAN, Ph.D., is Professor at the School of Social Service Administration of the University of Chicago and editor of *The Social Service Review*. His primary areas of interest are statistical and research methods and the use of computers in support of social welfare decisions. He is author of *Research and Evaluation in the Human Services* (Free Press, 1983) and *Multivariate Analysis in the Human Services* (Kluwer-Nijhoff, 1983).

RACHEL A. SCHURMAN, M.A., is a doctoral student in Sociology at the University of Wisconsin, Madison. Prior to returning to graduate school, Ms. Schurman worked for five years at the Center for Health Economics Research in Boston doing applied health economics. Her work to date has focused on a variety of health and mental health issues, ranging from the provision of mental health services by nontraditional providers to the impact of the Reagan budget cuts on health services for the poor. Most recently, Ms. Schurman assisted Dr. Diana Russell with the last stages of her quantitative analysis of incest for *The Secret Trauma*.

JUDITH M. SIEGEL, Ph.D., M.S. Hyg., is an Associate Professor in the UCLA School of Public Health. Her research has focused on various aspects of the relationship between stress and health. She has authored numerous papers on coronary-prone behavior, and has more recently turned her interest to the study of sexual assault. Specifically, she is interested in the epidemiology of sexual assault, the circumstances surrounding assault, and its sequelae.

SUSAN B. SORENSON, Ph.D., is currently an Assistant Research Epidemiologist in the UCLA School of Public Health where she directs a large CDC-funded study of injury in children. Trained as a clinical psychologist, Dr. Sorenson's research and clinical work has focused on violence and victims of violence. She has coauthored a number of papers from the Los Angeles Epidemiologic Catchment Area study, with particular focus on sexual assault. Dr. Sorenson has also been a trainer in a community-based sexual assault prevention program, which was presented to approximately 1,500 school children. This work was under the coordination of the Southern California Rape Prevention Study Center.

JUDITH A. STEIN, M.S., is a doctoral student in Behavioral Sciences and Health Education at the UCLA School of Public Health. Over the past seven years, she was an NIMH Predoctoral Trainee in Psychiatric Epidemiology and a Staff Research Associate for the Los Angeles Epidemiologic Catchment Area (LAECA) Project. Currently, she is a Community Support Specialist for Island Mental Health Center in Coupeville, Washington. A coauthor of several recent publications on sexual assault prevalence and related topics, she is currently developing a multifactorial model based on LAECA data to examine differential vulnerability to affective disorder following sexual assault.

ROLAND C. SUMMIT, M.D., has been a Community Psychiatrist at Harbor-UCLA Medical Center for 22 years, specializing in child abuse and child sexual abuse. His overview as a consultant to agencies and self-help programs has resulted in several papers that define typical patterns of victimization. His Child Sexual Abuse Accommodation Syndrome has provided for professionals and survivors alike an acceptance of normal victim behaviors. His continuing interest is in developing broader and less stigmatizing recognition of sexually abused children and survivors.

KAREN TROCKI, Ph.D., received her doctorate in social psychology from the University of Pittsburgh in 1977. She is currently a postdoctoral scholar at the University of California at Berkeley, School of Public

Health, Alcohol Research Group. She is studying situational norms and situational drinking behavior. She was formerly a Principal Analyst with Berkeley Planning Associates in Berkeley where she was involved in an evaluation of long-term health care demonstration projects. She also worked with Dr. Diana Russell on the analysis of data from the study of Sexual Assault project for the last seven years. Dr. Trocki's areas of specialization also include occupational stress and changes in social norms. She has been an NIMH grantee while studying peer influence processes and normative change.

J. ROBERT WHEELER, Ph.D., received his Ph.D. in counseling psychology from the University of Washington and is a Clinical Director at Luther Child Center, a community mental health center in Everett, Washington. His clinical interests currently are in the area of forensic psychology, especially the assessment and treatment of and perpetrators and victims of sexual abuse. He has conducted studies of personality differences among juvenile sexual versus nonsexual offenders and of the etiology of sexual coercion in young adult males. As a consult, he has worked with court and child protective agencies in applying formal decision-making theories in the assessment of risk among juvenile sex offenders and parents alleged to have committed child abuse or neglect.

GAIL ELIZABETH WYATT, Ph.D., coeditor of this volume, is a licensed Clinical Psychologist and an Associate Professor of Medical Psychology in the Department of Psychiatry and Biobehavioral Science at the University of California at Los Angeles. She is a Research Scientist Career Development Level II Awardee and has examined the relationship of a range of sexual experiences and women's psychological well-being in a 8-year federally funded project. She has coedited a book with Gloria Powell, MD, and Barbara Bass, MSW, entitled, *The Afro-American Family: Assessment, Treatment and Research Issues.* In addition to lecturing and offering workshops on sex-related topics both on a national and international level, Dr. Wyatt has taught and developed sex education programs for children and parents, served as a consultant to researchers designing studies that include multiethnic populations, and is a sex therapist, specializing in human sexuality within a sociocultural perspective.